LEARNING FROM BIRMINGHAM

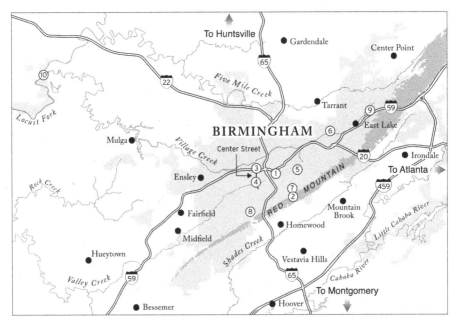

1) Civil Rights Movement Memorial Complex, Sixteenth Street and Sixth Avenue North;
2) Vulcan Statue; 3) Dynamite Hill; 4) Elyton Village Housing Project; 5) Sloss Furnaces
National Historic Landmark; 6) Birmingham-Shuttlesworth International Airport/
Former Location of Lonnie Holley Sculpture Garden; 7) Five Points South/Southside
Neighborhood; 8) Grace Hill Cemetery/Location of Joe Minter's African Village in
America; 9) Roebuck Springs/Village Creek Headwaters; 10) Miller Steam Plant/Village
Creek Terminus. Map by Brad Sanders.

LEARNING FROM BIRMINGHAM

A JOURNEY INTO HISTORY AND HOME

JULIE BUCKNER ARMSTRONG

THE UNIVERSITY OF ALABAMA PRESS • *Tuscaloosa*

The University of Alabama Press
Tuscaloosa, Alabama 35487-0380
uapress.ua.edu

Inquiries about reproducing material from this work should
be addressed to the University of Alabama Press.

Typeface: Arno Pro

Cover images: *Above*, Magic City sign in front of Birmingham's Terminal Station,
photograph by Oscar V. Hunt, Birmingham, Ala., Public Library Archives; *below*,
CORE March in memory of the four little girls, 1963, photograph by Thomas
J. O'Halloran, Library of Congress, Prints and Photographs Division
Cover design: Lori Lynch

Cataloging-in-Publication data is available from the Library of Congress.
ISBN: 978-0-8173-6106-8
E-ISBN: 978-0-8173-9447-9

FOR TOM AND ZACK

I came to explore the wreck.
The words are purposes.
The words are maps.
I came to see the damage that was done
and the treasures that prevail.

Adrienne Rich, "Diving into the Wreck"

White people are astounded by Birmingham.
Black people aren't.
White people are endlessly demanding to be reassured that
    Birmingham is really on Mars.
They don't want to believe,
still less to act on the belief,
that what is happening in Birmingham
is happening all over the country.
They don't want to realize that there is not one step,
morally or actually, between
Birmingham and Los Angeles.

James Baldwin, *I Am Not Your Negro*

CONTENTS

ILLUSTRATIONS

PROLOGUE

Leaving Birmingham, Coming Home

It's 1985. I'm leaving Birmingham for Memphis. My red Honda Civic hatchback is crammed from floorboard to roof. Clothes, books, a stereo, a four-foot stack of vinyl records, and the quilt that I made with my grandmother: a Dutch Girl pattern in polyester floral prints, scraps from her 1960s dresses. My cousin Vicki rides shotgun. We're moving in with her parents to plan our new lives. Vicki—red-haired, twenty-six, and recently divorced—wants to be a flight attendant and see the world. I'm blond, twenty-three, and starting a master's degree in English. It's the only escape route that I can envision.

But getting out of Birmingham means, first, diving in.

Our path, Interstate 59/20, takes us into and across the city, from an aunt's house in the eastern suburbs to just west of downtown, where we pick up I-65 northbound. Locals call the complex interchange where the two highways meet "Malfunction Junction." The term captures the off-kilter geography that makes navigating Birmingham so difficult. The city, nestled between a mountain range and a ridge, follows an Appalachian foothill topography—making it look, on a map, like a rectangle turned forty-five degrees. Malfunction Junction forms a snaky-armed axis that quarters Birmingham at its center. Instead of moving bodies forward in time and space along a city grid, streets below the interstate sometimes coil travelers back to where they started—or they simply dead-end.

As we follow the x-axis of 59/20, Vicki points out that East Lake, the neighborhood where my grandmother lived and I grew up, has started to decline since the interstate went in. Replacing the mom-and-pop businesses, working-class cottages, and gardens of azaleas and rose bushes are empty storefronts, broken windows, and weedy lots. The highway's concrete supports form headstones among these heaps of dry bones. Not far past East Lake, we pass the rusted smokestacks of Sloss Furnaces, a former centerpiece of the city's iron and steel industry, now a ghost of itself.

By the time we hit downtown, about fifteen minutes into a five-hour road trip, Vicki and I are melting, despite our summertime spaghetti straps and Daisy Dukes. My full car keeps the air from circulating. We have the windows down, but a Deep South August morning feels like a fever. Like all self-respecting southern females, we "put on our face" before leaving the house. Already, our blown-big, feathered hair sticks flat to our heads, and sweat runs rivulets through our makeup's pinks and blues. We press McDonald's Cokes—extra large, extra ice—to our cheeks and chests. I bought the Honda new at nineteen, after starting my first job three years before, saving through high school and working full-time in college. Air-conditioning was an unaffordable luxury. The JVC car stereo: a necessity that I installed myself. Driving gives freedom, rock and roll gives voice.

I scream along with Springsteen, "It's a town full of losers / I'm pulling out of here to wiii-in."

"Aren't you sad to leave?" Vicki asks as we wind around Malfunction Junction heading north.

"No way in Hell," I tell her. "I'm never coming back here as long as I live."

I take a last glance in my rearview mirror. Behind me, Birmingham's Red Mountain, the city's southern border and de facto divide between haves and have-nots, looms like a tidal wave, ready to swallow, ready to drown.

Invisible to me then: another divide thunderclouds my hometown's history. Vicki and I drive just east of Dynamite Hill. The neighborhood, technically part of Smithfield, got its nickname from the dozens of racial terror attacks that took place from the 1940s through the 1960s, when African Americans began integrating areas designated, by law, for white people only. "Bombingham," folks called the city, "America's Johannesburg." White girls like me didn't learn such history, even in our integrated schools. We kept mostly to our own neighborhoods, too, cordoned off by railroad tracks, interstates, creeks—and iron-red mountains filled with misconceptions.

What I knew for certain: if I didn't get out of Birmingham, I would explode. Like boiling lava inside of me were the curses and the fists and the guns of the memories that would lead my hands to shake for the rest of my life. After fifteen years spent watching the revolving door of my mother's abusive boyfriends, my Uncle Walter (Mom's brother and Vicki's dad) offered me a free place to live as long as I stayed in school. "You're going to wind up with a PhD," Walter's wife Janis told me. I laughed, unable to imagine such an alien thing.

Aunt Janis was correct. Almost four decades later, I'm a tenured college professor who teaches civil rights movement literature.

Breaking my vow to Vicki, I come back to Birmingham all the time now—never to stay, just to look. I'm writing about that journey from steel-town daughter to civil-rights scholar. The book, *Learning from Birmingham*, feels like its own malfunction junction. Every story about the past leads me to the present, to a movement that didn't stop moving when the news cameras went away. Every story about the present leads me to the past, to the civil rights legacies that surround us all, too often unacknowledged, like air.

Chapters follow a somewhat linear narrative, a route forward in time and space. I grew up in Birmingham during the 1960s and 1970s, as ignorant of historical matters as any white girl in America. Along the way I asked the usual coming-of-age questions about why things are the way they are, but for some reason the conventional-wisdom answers—first about gender and class, later about race—didn't satisfy. Why was that true for me but not so many others? Who knows. Maybe it was nature, maybe nurture, or maybe being smacked upside the head by adults around me doing something egregiously wrong. Church members blaming a school friend for her own molestation. The principal paddling a Black boy, but not punishing me, when the teacher caught us dancing in a hallway. A guidance counselor questioning my desire to go to college after seeing me buy groceries with food stamps. Finally, I got fed up. I left Birmingham for Memphis, then New York, and ultimately Florida, where I live and work today. I kept the Dutch Girl quilt but traded in the Daisy Dukes for J. Jill. I got married, adopted and raised a son, and traveled the world. My feathered locks became a graying pixie. I no longer wear blue eye shadow, but I do sport blue, rhinestone-studded glasses for focusing on the fine print. It's the big picture I keep coming home to figure out. What has changed in Birmingham, what hasn't. How this city—a symbol of hatred, oppression, and violence—seems utterly singular but at the same time no different from Anytown, USA.

One spring morning in 2016, I walk up Center Street, the main thoroughfare through Dynamite Hill. I'm on a pilgrimage through hometown history, trying to understand how the puzzle pieces fit. A string of markers bears witness to a time that this neighborhood of ranch houses and bungalows was not, as it is today, quiet—except for the nearby interstate's whizzing cars. Midway through my walk, I come upon a bridge with a rusty chain-link fence that crosses I-59/20, my original path out. Atop the bridge, a marker's caption quotes a Dynamite Hill resident: "Bull Connor ran the highway right through my house." The same interstate that cut through the heart of this neighborhood devastated my own. My family's Birmingham journey begins here, too: in the Bombingham days when my grandmother escaped Appalachian hill country poverty for a whites-only housing project down the street. Later, my aunt helped to put away the man, Robert "Dynamite Bob" Chambliss, responsible for many of those bombs. When I left home, I didn't think of myself as connected to this place, this past. Coming back, I recognize how many routes loop me around to a history that I am just now learning to see.

SELECTED CHRONOLOGY OF BIRMINGHAM HISTORY

1814   Treaty of Fort Jackson ends the Creek War of 1813–14, forcing Native groups to cede over 21 million acres of their holdings, including the hunting grounds in north-central Alabama that will become Jefferson County/Birmingham.

1817   The eastern half of the Mississippi Territory is designated as a separate, Alabama Territory. Alabama enters the Union as the twenty-second state in 1819.

1821   Jefferson County (named after Thomas Jefferson) founded, with Elyton (or Ely's Town) as the county seat.

1859   Surveyor and engineer John Milner reports to the state on the suitability of running rail lines through Jefferson County; Milner notes the presence of coal and iron ore, key ingredients for making steel.

1871   Birmingham founded by the Elyton Land Company near the crossroads of the Alabama-Chattanooga and South-North (later, Louisville-Nashville) rail lines, and named after the British industrial city.

1880s   Iron and steel production begins in the area, including the Sloss Iron and Steel Company and the Tennessee Coal and Iron Company (later U.S. Steel). Many coal mines, blast furnaces, and steel mills rely on child and convict labor.

1892   A report by the Elyton Land Company president H. M. Caldwell celebrates its original investors' exponential earnings (yielding an annual dividend of more than 2,300%) and the city's increasing growth (between the 1890s and the 1950s, the population would go from 25,000 to more than 300,000 residents). Caldwell refers to Birmingham using a nickname already in popular circulation, the "Magic City."

1904   Giuseppe Moretti's statue of Vulcan (the god of the forge), the world's largest cast-iron sculpture, goes on display at the

St. Louis World's Fair. During the 1930s, the city of Birmingham relocates the statue to the top of Red Mountain.

1926   The Birmingham Zoning Ordinance establishes physical separation of races by neighborhood, confining most local African Americans to areas in and around industrial zones. Ex-
clusionary zoning practices were common across the US after
the 1922 US Standard State Zoning Enabling Act.

1930   The City of Birmingham adopts its General Code, further reinforcing racial segregation. The code is revised in 1944 and
1950 to include more specific segregation policies, making
the laws among the strictest in the country.

1938   First Lady Eleanor Roosevelt violates Birmingham's segregation laws at the Southern Conference for Human Welfare by
sitting in a section designated for African Americans.

1947   A dynamite attack targets the home of Samuel Matthews in
Smithfield. Between 1947 and 1965, dozens of similar attacks
take place against African Americans buying homes in neighborhoods formerly designated as "whites only." During this
time the city earns the nickname "Bombingham," and an area
of north Smithfield becomes known as "Dynamite Hill."

1956   The Rev. Fred Shuttlesworth founds the Alabama Christian
Movement for Human Rights (ACMHR) after Alabama outlaws the National Association for the Advancement of Colored People (NAACP). The ACMHR begins its series of
"Mass Meeting Mondays" to support civil rights initiatives,
including boycotts of segregated buses, attempts to desegregate local public schools, and training in nonviolent direct
action. Also this year the US Congress passes the Highway
Act of 1956, leading to construction, during the 1960s, of Interstates 59, 20, and 65. Across the city the highways follow
lines established in the 1926 zoning map to operate as racial
boundaries.

1961   In May, Freedom Riders (attempting to desegregate bus-
transportation facilities) arrive in Birmingham and endure a
vicious attack by Ku Klux Klan members. Days later the controversial documentary "Who Speaks for Birmingham?" airs
on CBS. Narrator Howard K. Smith draws attention to the
city's violence and nearly intractable racism.

1963   In April organizers from the Southern Christian Leadership Conference (SCLC)—including Shuttlesworth, James Bevel, Wyatt Tee Walker, and Martin Luther King Jr.—initiate the five-week Birmingham Campaign to fight local desegregation laws, using nonviolent direct action strategies that include marches, sit-ins, boycotts, and voter registration attempts. King's arrest on Good Friday leads to the publication of "Letter from Birmingham Jail." In May, as adult participation numbers dwindle, organizers bring in students. Over a thousand participants of the "Children's Campaign" are arrested. Commissioner of Public Safety Eugene "Bull" Connor orders police dogs and fire hoses turned on students and other protesters in Kelly Ingram Park, drawing negative attention on the city from across the world. A truce between SCLC and civic leaders leads to the removal of segregation laws from the city code and desegregation of local stores, businesses, schools, and other public facilities. In September a white backlash against school desegregation leads to the bombing of the Sixteenth Street Baptist Church, killing four girls and wounding more than twenty parishioners. After the bombing widespread violence results in the deaths of two boys.

1964   King wins the Nobel Peace Prize in honor of his civil rights work, including his leadership in Birmingham. The United States passes the 1964 Civil Rights Act (barring race-based discrimination in hiring and public facilities). When proposing the act in 1963, President John F. Kennedy cites "events in Birmingham" as a contributing factor.

1966   After five Black demonstrators are shot at a local supermarket, Rev. Calvin Woods leads a protest against police brutality, one of many to take place in Birmingham during the 1960s and 1970s. In 2021 a Kelly Ingram Park historical marker dedicated to Woods's civil rights activism will be nearly destroyed.

1969   A US district court rules that Birmingham's current ("freedom of choice") plan for desegregating public schools is inadequate, telling the city to establish a new plan, effective for the 1970–71 school year.

1970   A group modeling itself on the Black Panthers, the Alabama Black Liberation Front (ABLF), is founded in response to local police violence against African Americans. The ABLF disbands within a year after organizers are targeted for law enforcement surveillance, found guilty of assault, and sentenced to prison. Also this year, U.S. Pipe and Foundry closes its operations on the former Sloss Furnaces site. Over the next decade, many other iron and steel operations shut down as the city begins its shift from an industrial to a service economy.

1971   In November, as smoke and soot levels become toxic, a US district court invokes the emergency powers of the 1970 Clean Air Act to rule that Birmingham's major industrial polluters, including U.S. Steel, must shut down until the crisis has passed.

1977   In September, Vestavia hotel owner Larry Maddox is found not guilty in the April shooting death of popular transgender salon owner Jody "Ms. Sid" Ford. In November a jury convicts Robert E. Chambliss of murder for his role in the 1963 Sixteenth Street church bombing. Two of Chambliss's coconspirators are convicted years later (Thomas Blanton Jr., 2001; and Bobby Frank Cherry, 2002).

1979   In June white police officers kill an unarmed Black woman named Bonita Carter outside a North Birmingham convenience store. The resulting protests help to propel city councilor Richard Arrington Jr. into the mayor's office. Arrington serves twenty years as the city's first Black mayor.

1982   Jefferson County enters a consent decree agreement (resulting from several lawsuits) to address discriminatory hiring practices in multiple city and county agencies. The decree remains in effect for almost forty years.

1990   Rev. Abraham Woods Jr. (then president of Birmingham's SCLC chapter) stages protests at the PGA Championship, held at the Shoal Creek Golf and Country Club, south of the city. Like many such clubs across the country during this time, Shoal Creek did not allow Black, Jewish, or female members.

1992   The Birmingham Civil Rights Institute, dedicated to the city's movement history, opens at the corner of Sixteenth Street and Sixth Avenue North, across the street from the Sixteenth Street Baptist Church and Kelly Ingram Park. The park is rededicated as "A Place of Revolution and Reconciliation."

1997   A fire in central Birmingham leads to a spill of the chemical

Dursban into Village Creek, resulting in one of the largest fish kills and environmental cleanups in city history. Another fish kill, of the endangered watercress darter, occurs in 2008 at the Village Creek headwaters in Roebuck Springs.

2012   The EPA designates a predominantly African American area of north Birmingham, including homes and schools, as a Superfund site because of high levels of toxic chemicals in the soil.

2013   The town of Gardendale, just north of Birmingham, votes to secede from Jefferson County Schools in order to create its own, mostly white, district. (A US court of appeals decision rules against Gardendale in 2018.) During the summer the US Supreme Court's *Shelby County v. Holder* decision supports the claims of the county just south of Jefferson that federal election monitors are no longer necessary. Critics maintain that the decision negatively impacts poor, Black, and Latinx voters. In September, Birmingham unveils a statue in Kelly Ingram Park, *Four Spirits*, to memorialize the girls who died in the 1963 church bombing. The event culminates the city's year-long commemoration, "Fifty Years Forward."

LEARNING FROM BIRMINGHAM

1 / CENTER STREET

A Snapshot of a Family and a City

In 1947 Hettie Buckner Armstrong left Southern Road in search of a miracle.

Recently widowed, Hettie and her four children were starving in Oneonta, a small farming community in Alabama's Appalachian foothills. Birmingham, forty miles to the southwest, had grown so fast since its 1871 founding that local leaders called it the "Magic City." Perhaps Hettie and her kids could grab some of that magic for themselves.

I've heard the story of my grandmother's move so many times I can see it. Hettie's brother Harley made a dust cloud as he turned his black Ford pickup from the farm's red dirt road onto the paved two-lane that runs from mountains to valley and then to the city. The kids, piled in back, held on tight to the family's meager possessions: cardboard suitcases, a washboard and galvanized tub, mattresses that Hettie made from chicken feathers and pine straw, and a tumble of rickety tables and chairs that my grandfather built while his body was still whole. As a child, I imagined them looking like the Clampett family from the popular 1960s-era television show *The Beverly Hillbillies*, with Granny riding atop the family flivver next to the hound dog. The only difference was that my granny, Hettie, would never sit next to a hound. ("You lie down with dogs, you get up with fleas," she used to say.) Instead, she kept close to her older brother in the truck's bench seat, carefully clutching the pink-and-blue-striped, clay-fired mixing bowl that she eventually passed down to me—along with her thin, silver wedding band that I now wear as my own.

When I set out over half a century later to understand my heritage as a Birmingham daughter, I began with Hettie's journey from Southern Road. One of the family's earliest stops was Elyton Village, the city's first housing project for whites. Elyton Village is located on Center Street, a four-mile, north-south road just west of downtown. Looking at a map, or even driving past, one might not realize Center Street's importance. But here, where my family's Birmingham story begins, lies city history in microcosm.

Center Street, today an unassuming two-lane, was part of the city's original crossroads. Bracketing the street are the interstates and railroads that transport iron and steel to the rest of the country. To the north, Center Street crests on Enon Ridge, overlooking Village Creek, the city's first drinking-water source and later its industrial-waste dumping ground. Moving south along Center Street, one enters the section of north Smithfield called "Dynamite Hill" for the large number of racist bombing attacks during the mid-twentieth century. Below Dynamite Hill sit two housing projects, relics of the city's Jim Crow zoning laws and its antebellum past. On the east side, Smithfield Court, a project once reserved for African Americans, occupies part of a former cotton plantation owned by Joseph Riley Smith, whose parents John and Sallie were among the area's earliest white settlers. To the west the formerly "whites only" Elyton Village project sits on the site of another plantation, Earle-Green. Flowing just south of these projects is Valley Creek, part of Birmingham's first sewer system. Below that lies a third plantation, Arlington Antebellum Home and Gardens, still active as a tourist site (minus, as of 2020, its hoop-skirted southern belles). From there the street jogs toward Titusville—a middle-class neighborhood that, like Dynamite Hill, gave birth to some of Birmingham's most important civil rights movement activists and formed the setting of Anthony Grooms's 2001 novel, *Bombingham*. Center Street ends where the local terrain rises to meet the city's exclusive "Over the Mountain" suburbs. A few blocks away from the street's southern terminus sits the Birmingham city jail, first made famous in the 1920s by country duo Tom Darby and Jimmie Tarlton's "Down in the Valley (the Birmingham Jail Song)" and, later, in a 1963 letter by Martin Luther King Jr.

*

Long before King wrote or Darby and Tarlton sang, Birmingham was Frog Level. This small, swampy trading-post, horse-track settlement emerged during the early 1800s, as Andrew Jackson's troops cleared the South of Creeks, Cherokees, Choctaws, and Chickasaws to make room for slavery. Soon after Alabama became a state in 1819, the Connecticut Asylum for the Instruction and Education of the Deaf and Dumb in Hartford purchased a 2,560-acre plot near Frog Level and sent its agent, William Ely, down to inspect. He reported the spot to be "broken, poor, and barren" and advised the asylum to sell. The resulting bidding war between settlers and speculators grew so heated that Ely hired bodyguards for protection. He ultimately brokered a deal, asking in return that a town be named after him. Surrounding a crossroads at Broad (now Center) Street and Cotton Avenue, Ely's Town, also called "Elyton," plotted in 1821 the houses, businesses, and churches that became fodder for the fires of Wilson's Raiders, who swept through Alabama near the Civil War's end.

In 1870, despite the postwar wreckage, a group of investors saw Elyton's potential to make them rich. The location anchored Jones Valley, running northeast to southwest through the Appalachian Mountains' southern foothills, and offered railroad crossings, the abundant waters of Village and Valley Creeks, and, most important, vast stores of iron ore and coal—key ingredients for making steel. The town they founded in 1871, Birmingham, named after the British industrial city, grew so quickly that the men could not believe their good fortune. Elyton's population had ranged between 300 and 1,000 inhabitants. The first Birmingham census, in 1880, counted roughly 3,000. By 1900, that number increased to more than 38,000. By World War II, Birmingham's population had grown to well over 250,000. In an 1892 report, Elyton Land Company president H. M. Caldwell barely contained his pride in "the Magic City." The ten original stockholders had reason to be happy. A cholera epidemic in 1873 and the six-year national depression that followed almost wiped them out, but they swiftly rebounded. By the time of Caldwell's report, they saw an annual dividend of more than 2,300 percent on their original investment of roughly $1,000 each. During the early 1900s, downtown Birmingham was booming, with the intersection of Twentieth Street and First Avenue North, known as "The Heaviest Corner on Earth," featuring the South's four tallest buildings in the new commercial architectural style that Chicago's Louis Sullivan made famous. By the mid-1920s another modern wonder, a giant electric sign outside the city's rail station, celebrated its founders' vision by welcoming travelers to "Birmingham: The Magic City." By then, the investors' families—known, along with Alabama's other business and agricultural powerhouses, as the "Big Mules"—had removed themselves from skyscrapers and smoke-belching steel mills to tree-lined roads and clearer air atop and over the city's southern border, Red Mountain.

Not everything was magic in Birmingham. Mill and mine owners got rich because labor was cheap. Some, like Tennessee Coal, Iron, and Railroad (TCI, later U.S. Steel), which relocated to Birmingham during the boom years, relied on a largely African American workforce of coerced labor through the convict-lease system. In use throughout Alabama until 1928, the system took advantage of Thirteenth Amendment wording that outlawed slavery but permitted involuntary servitude as punishment for crime. Jails hired out their prisoners to work, with the employers providing food, clothing, and shelter—but no pay. The arrangement was lucrative for everyone but the workers. In 1898 Alabama's convict labor, concentrated primarily in Birmingham-area coal mines, generated more than 70 percent of the state's revenue. When convicts were not available, companies could rely on the large numbers of poor white and Black laborers—and their children—who fled rural poverty after the Civil War. Mill and mine jobs were dangerous, and housing consisted of little more than small, overcrowded, unsanitary wooden shacks without electricity or plumbing. But industrial jobs offered a steady pay that was better than starving under sharecropping or tenant farming. By the Great Depression, Birmingham's population, and its number of urban poor, continued to expand. Finding a decent, affordable place to live was a serious issue for many workers. The US Housing Act of 1937 provided the means for Birmingham to build multiple housing projects. The first, Smithfield Court, opened in 1938 on Center Street's east side, with Elyton Village, across the street and a few blocks south, following in 1940. Not surprisingly, the two complexes, built on sites of former plantations in a southern city founded during Reconstruction, embodied the Birmingham racial divides that would soon explode.

*

While Birmingham boomed, my grandparents met, married, made babies, and farmed a small plot near Oneonta. Hettie Buckner (1904–92) and Hubert Armstrong (1902–44) were introduced by friends at a high school football game. My dark-haired grandmother said that she fell hard for the strawberry-blond Hubert, whom she called "Bud," though she made him wait to marry. After her father, Walter, died in 1919 (followed by her mother, Mary Ann, in 1935), the property was divided among Hettie's four brothers, with the understanding that the five sisters would find husbands to support them. Hettie, a rebel who bobbed her hair and voted before Oneonta accepted such modern notions for women, made a backup plan: nursing school. If Bud truly loved her, she said, he would let her finish out the two-year program. When Bud proposed, he gave Hettie a small silver band that she wore on her right hand. She gave him a kiss on the cheek and nothing more (she claimed) until they wed on September 25, 1926. With her silver band now on her left ring finger, Hettie convinced her older brother Lonzo to lease Bud forty acres out of the Buckner holdings, where the newlyweds could start their lives together.

The couple grew cotton and, for their expanding family, wheat, corn, beans,

1. Hettie Buckner Armstrong and Hubert "Bud" Armstrong, 1926. Image courtesy of the author.

greens, and tomatoes. Their eldest son, Walter, was born in 1929, a month before the stock market crashed, spiraling the country into a decade-long Depression. Talmadge followed in 1933. After that came my mother, Mary Ann, in 1938. Finally, in 1940, Hettie and Bud had another girl, Martha Wynell. Aunt Nell, as I call her, remembers their life in Oneonta as poor but happy. She and her three siblings created fun with what they had on hand. In winter they transformed the tin sheets that fell off the roof of the family's dogtrot cabin into sleds for careening down snowy rises. In summers they ran from the dirt path by their farm to the county road's pavement to play "purse": tying fishing line to one of their mother's used pocketbooks, placing it on the asphalt, and hiding in the kudzu waiting for a car. When unsuspecting Good Samaritans stopped to retrieve the purse, the kids jerked it back into the weeds, rolling about like puppies in their laughter.

Then everything changed.

In 1944 my grandfather Bud died from a malignant melanoma, leaving my grandmother Hettie with four children between the ages of four and fifteen and no steady income. They had always struggled to support themselves through farming. On two separate occasions, Bud went into Birmingham for paying jobs at TCI and Continental Gin. When a mysterious mole appeared on the fair-skinned Bud's back, he had worked just short of the time needed to qualify for the new Depression era program called "Social Security." As the cancer metastasized throughout Bud's body, Hettie's brothers sold the forty-acre farm to her on a five-dollar quit-claim. After the Birmingham welfare hospital told the family there was no hope and turned Bud out, he went for a time to his brother Frank's in the steelworker suburb of Fairfield. He later died at home. Hettie buried Bud at Oneonta's Antioch Cemetery and started selling trees to a paper mill in order to support her children. They survived on kindness. Walter went to Birmingham to look for work, moving in with Hettie's sister Cora and her husband. Talmadge stayed on to help his mother. The two girls went to live with neighbors. My mom, Mary Ann, remembered chopping (weeding) cotton until her fingers bled and celebrating Christmas with one piece of peppermint candy for each kid. After three years of living hand-to-mouth, Mom said, Hettie decided to leave the farm and put her education to work.

The story of the family's move from homespun riches to scattered rags, then a steady climb toward middle-class respectability, became the legend that defined us all. My mom, aunts and uncles, their children, and their children's children are the fruit of Hettie Buckner and Bud Armstrong's tree. From rural poverty Hettie and Bud's sons and daughters grew up to be a corporate executive, a career soldier, a legal secretary, and a homemaker. The legacy they passed on to me was that Armstrong means work hard, rise above, and stand proud. When I became the first of my cousins to finish college and, later, the only one to get a PhD, each of my aunts and uncles, along with their spouses and my mom, flew to New York to clap and roar me across the graduate stage at Carnegie Hall. We'd come a long way from an Oneonta homestead on the aptly named Southern Road.

The Armstrongs left Oneonta in 1947. Hettie rented out the farm to a tenant, then moved the silver band back to her right hand and her kids to Center Point, an unincorporated area just northeast of Birmingham's city limits. In Center Point, her brother Harley had transformed his Buckner inheritance into a shoe store with living space behind it and, down the road, a Baptist church. Hettie and the children rented rooms in a small bungalow made of fieldstone, owned by a woman whose icebox and toilet they shared. The plan was for my grandmother to wake at 4:30 a.m. and ride the Greyhound bus an hour to her new job as a licensed practical nurse at Hillman (now University) Hospital south of downtown. Mary Ann and Wynell would attend school, also made of fieldstone, and keep their side of the rock house "country-style": cook from a wood stove, do laundry with a washboard, and chase their brother Talmadge, hoping to force the house's reigning male into the back porch's galvanized tub for a bath. The routine quickly got old. Hettie set her sights closer to her hospital job.

When Elyton Village opened in 1940, the *Birmingham Post* described it as a "fairyland." "Somewhere in Birmingham," the article explained, "living in dingy flats, drab drafty little frame houses or the crowded semi-privacy of housekeeping rooms are 860 white families of modest means who will move into a virtual fairyland of comfortable living." The projects were definitely a step up from Hettie and her children's Center Point house share. In Elyton Village, where they lived from 1950 to 1953, they had two bedrooms, living and dining rooms, and a kitchen with a real oven and a real sink. In back they had a fenced yard and a community playground. In front they had an oak tree, still standing today.

2. Children in a wading pool in Elyton Village, a federal housing project in Birmingham, Alabama. Image courtesy of the Alabama Department of Archives.

Hettie had high hopes. She didn't know her fairyland sat smack in the middle of a civil rights showdown, metastasizing as sure as the mole on Bud's back.

Center Street was not only the divide between Birmingham's west side and the city proper; portions of it also formed a line between Black and white. The city's first zoning laws, established in 1926 (the same year Hettie and Bud married), codified residential segregation. The rules for A-1 (single family) and B-1 (multifamily) residence districts stated that "no building or part thereof shall be occupied or used by a person or persons of the negro race." Likewise, whites could not live in areas A-2 or B-2, zoned for African Americans. In effect, the zoning ordinance confined African Americans, rich or poor, to areas where most available housing was substandard: rented shotgun shacks with no indoor plumbing located in or near the city's highly polluted industrial areas.

The 1926 zoning ordinance was part of a much larger system of separating races and fostering inequality that permeated much of the United States, especially the South. Birmingham's laws were among the nation's most extreme. The city's General Code, passed in 1944, prevented Black and white people from using the same toilet, drinking from the same water fountain, using the same parks and pools, attending the same schools, or occupying the same theater, restaurant, or streetcar—unless separated by a partition. African Americans could shop in the same stores as whites but could not try on the clothes. Interracial marriage was illegal. So were mixed-race "cards, dice, dominoes, checkers, baseball, softball, football, [and] basketball." In Birmingham, however, segregation was hardly a game. After World War II, when African American families began testing zoning laws by moving to more desirable housing across the Center Street dividing line, those families found themselves targets of a racist bombing backlash.

*

From the late 1940s through the early 1960s, nearly fifty dynamite attacks occurred in Birmingham. My family members said they did not hear or know about the bombings that took place primarily along north Center Street—about seven blocks away—but that is hard for me to believe. I distinctly remember being at our East Lake home during an early-1970s mine explosion on Birmingham's Ruffner Mountain (about a mile away) that rattled our windows and jolted me off the bed.

"Hang your head over, hear the wind blow," Darby and Tarlton sang in

"Down in the Valley." The wind carries some sounds, like train whistles and dynamite, for miles across that forlorn valley.

Perhaps my family didn't remember the explosions because, like train whistles and wind, they were ordinary. If my grandmother registered the noise, she would have said, in her hill country accent, "Danny-maht from the co' mahners."

Perhaps, too, she preferred to think "coal miners" rather than "Ku Kluxers" because the dynamite did not target her home or her belief in a "Magic City."

The first home to fall belonged to Samuel Matthews, a forty-three-year-old employee at Ishkooda Ore Mines. In 1946 Matthews purchased a lot just off of Center Street on 11th Court North slated to be rezoned from "white" to "Black." After building a house there, he sought, but was denied, an occupancy permit. With the help of prominent civil rights attorney Arthur Shores, Matthews filed suit against the city for its zoning ordinance. In the summer of 1947, a US district court judge ruled the ordinance unconstitutional. Before Matthews moved in, someone painted a skull and crossbones on the house and, on August 18, set off six sticks of dynamite in the living room. Matthews lost all of his $3,700 investment (the equivalent of $50,000 today).

Dynamite attacks continued through the mid-1960s. On December 21, 1950, not long after Hettie and her children moved into Elyton Village, the brick bungalow of schoolteacher Mary Means Monk, at 950 North Center Street, was destroyed. Monk, like Matthews, had challenged Birmingham's segregated zoning laws, which remained in effect for another four years after the 1947 court ruling. Arthur Shores, who represented Matthews and local NAACP interests, lived just up the street from the Monks in a large ranch-style home that was targeted three times. An August 1963 attack killed the family dog; a month later a blast injured Shores's wife, Theodora. On a third occasion, Theodora found case of dynamite in her garden but escaped before it went off. Another prominent civil rights activist, Fred Shuttlesworth, founder of the Alabama Christian Movement for Human Rights, was also targeted. A Christmas 1956 bombing shattered windows at Bethel Baptist Church, where Shuttlesworth was a pastor, and collapsed his parsonage. In 1958 and 1962, the church was bombed again. Decades later, men like Robert Chambliss and J. B. Stoner would go to jail for civil-rights-era crimes like these. But during the Bombingham days, investigations typically followed a pattern set with the dynamiting of Samuel Matthews's home. Although Matthews filed a crime report, police detectives stated that their investigation "failed to reveal sufficient evidence to make an arrest."

Responsibility for the bombings was an open secret. "Dynamite Bob" Chambliss, sallow-faced and mean-eyed, often prowled around Center Street. In 1949 William German, a Black insurance salesman from Florida, was inspecting property he had recently purchased at 1100 North Center Street, near the site of a recent bombing: two houses belonging to Bishop S. L. Green, chancellor of Daniel Payne College. Chambliss walked up to German, pointed at the wreckage, and said, "If you move in, that is liable to happen to you." Chambliss, who planted the dynamite that destroyed Samuel Matthews's house, belonged to a local Ku Klux Klan klavern and was frequently arrested for violent acts against African Americans—including his participation in the mob that, in 1956, rioted when Autherine Lucy tried to integrate the University of Alabama.

Chambliss did not operate in isolation. His official job was working in the Birmingham city garage cleaning police cars, but, unofficially, he worked as commissioner of public safety Eugene "Bull" Connor's Klan insider. Chambliss also had an inroad with Sidney Smyer, a local attorney who would, in 1963, help broker a truce between the city and civil rights protestors. Before that change of mind, Smyer was a state legislator, Big Mule lobbyist, White Citizens' Council member, and cofounder of the American States' Rights Association—an Alabama group that differed from J. B. Stoner's Georgia-based National States' Rights Party in location only. Chambliss once bragged about being "the first one in Jefferson County to join the White Citizens' Council," founded in 1954 as a white response to the US Supreme Court's *Brown v. Board of Education* decision. Citizens' Councils and states' rights organizations, whose members included the affluent Smyers of the world, were upscale versions of the KKK, populated by poor and working-class men like Chambliss—but memberships often overlapped and they had similar agendas. The Selma lawyer who set up the first Alabama White Citizens' Council summed up the group's mission, stating, "We intend to make it impossible for any Negro who advocates desegregation to find and hold a job, get credit, or renew a mortgage." The world's Chamblisses did the dirty work for those who wrote the laws and signed the paychecks: threatening, dynamiting, and terrorizing anyone pushing against Jim Crow's boundaries.

When Center Street's houses blew, residents were well aware of who lit the dynamite and how far the fuse extended. Jeff Drew, whose family sometimes sheltered a visiting Martin Luther King in their bunkerlike midcentury modern home, recalled that residents knew a blast was coming when decommissioned police cruisers began charging up Center Street. "Flying up the hill," Drew told National Public Radio's Debbie Elliott. "They'd throw that bomb, and we used to marvel at how fast those guys could drive." Angela Davis, whose family moved in 1948 from the Smithfield projects up the hill to a large Queen Anne, recalled Bull Connor laying the groundwork. He would "announce on the radio that a 'nigger family' had moved on the white side of the street. His prediction, 'There will be bloodshed tonight,' would be followed by a bombing."

Men like Connor justified violence as a reaction to threats against "their way of life": the segregation that kept white people atop African Americans in a carefully designed hierarchy. When those lines were threatened by activities as commonplace as moving from one side of the street to another, white supremacists went to war, using all the weapons in their arsenal. After the 1926 zoning ordinance was declared unconstitutional, Connor designed a new law making it a misdemeanor for a Black person to move into a white neighborhood, and vice versa. The brains behind the law was James A. Simpson, a TCI lawyer and a former state senator. In a letter to Birmingham's city attorney, Simpson explained that the point was less about zoning and more about maintaining segregation: "If you let . . . negroes continue to infiltrate white areas and whites infiltrate negro areas so that your lines of demarcation become broken down, you are in for disorders and bloodshed and our ancient and excellent plan of life here in Alabama is gone." Connor backed up the words of his mentor Simpson with the dynamite of his lackey Chambliss.

Still, nothing stopped African Americans from challenging Jim Crow in ways large and small. If a Black family moved onto the white side of Center Street, Arthur Shores defended them in court. When thugs roamed the neighborhood, local residents defended themselves. In a 1974 interview, Shores stated that he was prepared to fight back: "I wasn't of the nonviolent type. I had a sufficient arsenal there at my house that if I had gotten a chance I would have retaliated in kind." In other parts of town, like Collegeville and Titusville, Black men with shotguns organized watch parties. American Cast Iron and Pipe employee Lloyd Harper described himself as the Saturday man: "Well, it [guard night] was organized. . . . Every night they were there. My night was Saturday night from twelve to seven in the morning, and that's where we stayed." Even the kids fought back, long before the 1963 Children's Campaign ultimately brought down Birmingham's long-standing Jim Crow laws. In her autobiography Angela Davis writes of running with her friends up to white people's porches to ring the doorbell and dash away, or sitting on her own porch waiting for a carload of whites to pass, then yelling the worst epithets she knew: "cracker" and "redneck."

*

Against this backdrop my mom fought her own Center Street battle. The way she told me the story, again and again throughout my life, was that before school one morning a girl hollered that she was "poor." After school, Mom said, she hid in the bushes waiting for the girl to roller-skate around the corner. Then she leaped out and beat the girl into a pulp on the concrete sidewalk. Mom was proud of her actions. "Don't let anyone take you down to their level," she said every time she told the story. Her words echoed the Armstrong code (work hard, rise up, stand proud) that supported me through life—especially the move from working-class Birmingham girl to New York University PhD—taken to a violent extreme.

Whenever Mom told the story, she didn't mention the racial dynamics, and I no more thought to ask than my grandmother did to question the sounds of explosions. Instead, I pictured the girl looking like my mom— white, with dirty blond hair and a "don't mess with me" glare—not like a preteen Angela Davis.

"Of course the girl was Black," my Aunt Nell told me in my fifties, as if this PhD was the dumbest kid in class. "Why else was your mother so angry?"

After the beating Mom got a spanking from Uncle Talmadge, but that was the only consequence. My grandmother, distraught over her wild daughter, began looking for housing elsewhere. "Elyton Village weren't no place to raise kids," she told me in my twenties. The family wound up renting a bungalow in East Lake, a small community about five miles east of downtown. Shortly after that an aunt with property died: a sale that left Hettie enough money for a down payment on a house just around the corner from the rented bungalow, where she lived out the rest of her life—and where I grew up.

My mom's version of the attack had her hiding in the bushes waiting for her victim to roller-skate around the corner. No pictures of bushes exist in the early photos of Elyton Village, and no bushes exist today. Every so often on trips to Birmingham, I park at the gas station/deli across from the projects, now predominantly African American, so I can walk up Center Street. Surveying the scene of my mother's, and my city's, crimes helps ground me as a civil rights movement educator.

This road exposes the tangled roots of my Birmingham history.

The oak tree still stands across from Hettie's apartment. A few yards west of the Center Street-Graymont Avenue intersection, it could have been in the early 1950s wide enough to conceal a lurking tween.

"Poor," Mom said the girl called her.

And they were. In order to qualify for Elyton Village's $26 monthly rent, Hettie's income could not exceed $1,500 annually, equivalent to about $16,500 in 2021. Even today, LPNs make far less than RNs. "Low-Paid Nurse," a Jamaican woman who cared for my dying mother described herself, "not Real Nurse." Hettie's job wasn't much different back then, tending to the bedside, and the bedpan, of a cancerous Birmingham socialite.

While my grandmother focused on the "work hard" part of the Armstrong family code, my mother geared straight for "rise above." Mom chafed against peppermint-candy Christmases. She wanted to distinguish herself from the girls who lived up Center Street in the Smithfield Housing Projects, set aside for African Americans. So she took her anger over a father's untimely death, chopping cotton until her fingers bled, and too many frigid mornings spent hunched over a grating washboard, and balled it up into a white fist.

I know that violence. The diagnoses Mom got in her early seventies were "bipolar" and "borderline personality disorder." Those words clarified so much family history. The bloody beating of a Black girl. My youthful tiptoeing to avoid the pinch, the spanking, the slap. A Christmas memory of my own to carry around as burden: during the late 1970s, when Mom picked up a fully decorated tree and hurled it at me, angel-first. She had been simmering all day over a slight, real or perceived, at work. Her volcanic temper boiled over when I made the mistake of remarking that we had both bought my grandmother the same present.

Yet Mom's actions in Elyton Village were the product of something more than mental illness, more than a manifestation of her childhood trauma, although both were contributing factors. Also at work was another explanation for her actions: "white rage." White rage, as scholar Carol Anderson describes it, permeated the Birmingham of my mother's youth. "The trigger," Anderson states, "is black advancement . . . blackness with ambition, with drive, with purpose, with aspirations, and with demands for full and equal citizenship." During the late 1940s through the early 1960s, Birmingham's African Americans broke down boundaries that had been in place long before the city's founding: from plantation slavery to convict leasing to codes controlling almost every aspect of Black public, and private, space. All over the city, and especially along north Center Street, African Americans crossed into territory that the law decreed "whites only." Their actions prompted a backlash—the dynamite, the fist—but as Anderson explains, such visible violence is only part of the picture: "White rage doesn't have to wear sheets, burn crosses, or take to the streets. Working the halls of power, it can achieve its ends far more effectively, far more destructively." The Big Mules channeled their rage for power into zoning laws. Dynamite Bob used his to light fuses. Mary Ann, my mom, directed hers at a girl that she perceived, because of race, to be beneath her "level" and who dared to upset that hierarchy by calling her "poor."

Visiting Center Street today, I feel the family pride, and its shame. Hettie and her children did find magic in this city. They made a lot from next to nothing. They passed down to me—along with Hettie's wedding ring and mixing bowl—a hearty slice of American Dream pie. But what, in turn, will be my legacy? The Armstrong family code, my mother's white rage, or some combination that I can no more disentangle than the Birmingham in my blood?

2 / HETTIE AND CEOLA

"The History That's Buried and Forgot"

In 1964 my grandmother Hettie fired the help. Her name was Ceola, and she was my babysitter for about a year. I don't remember the incident; I barely remember Ceola.

She was African American, middle-aged, big, and nice. She read the Bible to me and let me hop around like a bunny to look for hidden treats like carrots and tangerines. Ceola was strict about one thing only. All hopping stopped after lunch when I napped and she turned on her "stories": soap operas like *The Guiding Light* and *As the World Turns*. We spent most of our time in what Hettie called the "den," which doubled as my bedroom and a family room. It was sparsely furnished, with a pull-out sofa where I slept, a small black-and-white television, and a tan, ratty wingback chair where my grandmother sat to watch the 5:00 news and where Ceola sat to watch her stories.

One afternoon that I don't recall, I must have woken up from my nap to find Ceola gone and Hettie making our usual meat-and-two-vegetables dinner—only Ceola never came back.

Many years later, when I was in college, her name came up randomly in conversation. Hettie was in her eighties: declining, but living in the home where I grew up, quite mobile, and very much in control of her memory— but not so much her filters. A silver-haired, blue-eyed piece of Birmingham steel who never quite got the magnolia part right.

"I loooooved Ceola," I squealed. "Whatever happened to her?"

"I fired her," Hettie snapped. "She shit in the closet."

Little did I know at the time that I had stumbled onto one of the southern imagination's biggest clichés: the Black female domestic worker whose presence pollutes the otherwise "pure" white home. My conversation with Hettie took place at least two decades before author Kathryn Stockett turned white women's obsessions with Black women's bathroom habits into a bestselling novel and popular film. *The Help* (book, 2009; film, 2011) focuses on a white character, Skeeter, who collects and publishes stories of Black female domestic workers during early 1960s Mississippi. In one plot line, a maid named Minny gets revenge on her racist employer Hilly, who is terrified by the idea of integrated bathrooms, by telling her to "eat my shit!" and then, literally, baking it into a chocolate pie. Under the ruse of making amends, Minny brings the pie to Hilly, who enjoys it so much that she eats two slices—thus getting her "just desserts."

If Hettie had mentioned the Ceola incident after *The Help*, I might have thought she conflated imagination and reality—as I watched her do in her nineties when she told me about food items on her hospital tray table talking in her late sisters' voices. But Hettie had many years to go before experiencing deathbed delusions. Back then I knew her only as the formidable, compassionate grandmother who lifted her children out of poverty and (I thought) made a place for anyone, no matter how down or out, at her kitchen table. Her statement about Ceola seemed beyond my perception, like a random, foreign object quickly entering and exiting my sight line. Most of the time I pretended that the strange object, because it didn't fit what I knew, simply did not exist.

I did ask a few questions in the years before Hettie's 1992 death. My mother corroborated my grandmother's story to a point. Hettie told Mom that she dismissed Ceola after coming home from her nursing job to find poop in the bedroom closet. Mom, who got home from work about an hour later, never saw the "evidence."

Mom's sister heard a different version of events. Hettie told Aunt Nell, who lived in her own home at the time, that she fired Ceola "for getting mixed up in all that Martin Luther King business."

Logic dictates that if anyone actually pooped in the closet, the not-fully-potty-trained toddler who fancied herself a bunny rabbit living in a den was the most likely culprit.

This story, however, never followed logic. Instead, it tangled like a dirty string through the warp and woof of Birmingham's civil rights movement.

*

Ceola came to work for us, Mom said, when I was a toddler. I needed a babysitter, but, perhaps more important, affording help was a sign that, financially, we had "arrived."

The family's new life in East Lake was beginning to look up. After leaving Elyton Village, Hettie got a better-paying nursing job at St. Vincent, the Catholic hospital that she pronounced "Saint Venison," like the deer meat she often ate back on the Oneonta farm. Indeed, at $4,500 a year (in the early

1960s) compared to the $1,500 she made when living in the projects ten years earlier, the job put sustenance on the table and also paid for the furniture. The boys joined the military, the army for Walter, the air force for Talmadge. The girls graduated from Woodlawn High School; then Mary Ann started an office job, and Wynell got married. In the spring of 1961, Hettie took her first vacation, to a nursing seminar in Washington, D.C., unaware of the storm clouds gathering at home. She came back to learn that Mary Ann was pregnant, had married the young man but refused to live with him. (They would divorce shortly after my birth, and I would never meet him.) Mother and daughter, both difficult women, fought over the new mouth to feed—mine—arriving in September. Hettie told Mary Ann that she was a working nurse, not a free babysitter. Mom remembered retreating to the front porch swing to smoke, a habit she told me that started when she learned she would have a baby. Meanwhile, Hettie created order from chaos by cleaning the kitchen and singing Baptist church hymns in her reedy, off-key voice. "Just as I Am" let those around know that she was ready for some Old Testament–style smiting.

Babysitting was a real problem in the years before widespread day care. The early 1960s formed the tail end of the *Leave It to Beaver* years, when families supposedly looked like the ones in this and other popular sitcoms. Dad Cleaver went off to work while Mom Cleaver stayed home, keeping the house tidy and the kids in line, while dressed in heels and pearls. That was not our life. Instead, my mom wore her low-heel pumps—but not pearls, because she couldn't afford them—to work downtown from 8:00 to 4:30. Hettie worked the 7:00–3:00 shift on Birmingham's Southside. Someone needed to watch me during those times. For a while, neighbors pitched in. Mr. and Mrs. Hinds, next door, were retired, like Mr. and Mrs. Sewell across the street. They enjoyed having a cooing baby around, but a toddler, into everything and sending out high-pitched wails when thwarted, was different. By the time I hit two, in 1963, Hettie and Mary Ann needed a different solution. A work friend of Mom's recommended a woman that she knew, Ceola. They hired her, probably paying about four dollars a day, the going rate for Birmingham's Black female domestic workers.

But Ceola didn't just start a job. She walked directly into my family's racist paranoia.

The civil rights battles going on at the time terrified my mother and grandmother. Although they claimed not to hear the bombings when they lived in the Elyton Village projects, Hettie and Mary Ann clearly inhabited the tensions of a 1950s-era Dynamite Hill. Movement activity in Birmingham began reaching a fever pitch the year I was born. In 1961 the Freedom Riders, a racially mixed group attempting to integrate buses and terminals across the South, met extreme violence in my hometown. After a mob burned one of their buses in Anniston, the group traveled to Birmingham on Mother's Day, when the police stood by to let a group of white thugs beat them with iron pipes and baseball bats. About the same time that Hettie and Mary Ann fought over an unintended pregnancy, they agreed that people like the Freedom Riders, whom they called "communists" and "outside agitators," were threats. For my Southern Baptist grandmother, "communists" had less to do with any economic theory than with the Devil himself, set on destroying "American Christian values" and our "southern way of life." For my mother, "outside agitators" were not evil personified as much as chaos embodied. When Martin Luther King joined local activists to desegregate downtown restaurants and businesses in spring 1963, she described their nonviolent protests as "running through the streets like wild animals." Later that year, after a Ku Klux Klan faction bombed the Sixteenth Street Baptist Church, my grandmother sheltered me in our house's central hallway, as if white girls rather than Black ones were in danger. She hid me there again years later, after King's 1968 assassination. "It's the end of the world," she said. "And they're coming to get us."

For Hettie to think differently about race back then would have been extraordinary. For every white female civil rights proponent—a Virginia Foster Durr, an Anne Braden, a Lillian Smith—were thousands, if not millions, supporting a racist status quo. My grandmother was born in 1904, amid the turn-of-the-century decades that historians call US race relations' "nadir," or lowest point. During this time states codified Jim Crow segregation laws, which were validated by the US Supreme Court's 1896 *Plessy v. Ferguson* "separate but equal" ruling. Violence peaked, with nearly 4,500 racial terror lynchings documented between 1877 and 1950 across the country, but mainly in the South. Oneonta, Alabama, where our family lived before moving to Birmingham in the 1940s, was very likely a "sundown town." Such places, explains James Loewen, used laws, intimidation, and often violence to keep out nonwhite people, especially after dark. Blount County, where Oneonta was located, had a large, popular Ku Klux Klan presence that recruited new members through the newspaper and committed multiple acts of violence, including the April 1926 lynching of a Black woman named Lillie Cobb. East Lake, where our family lived during the mid-1950s through the 1980s, had its own Klan history. In 1923 East Lake Park, three blocks from our house, was the site of the largest Klan initiation in the Southeast, inducting over 4,100 members in front of an estimated 50,000 spectators.

Underlying such performances of white supremacy was the culturally ingrained belief that African Americans were put on the planet to do our dirtiest work—and those who didn't were dangerous.

Consider the most well-known books and movies about race relations in the South. A widely popular film from my grandmother's school days was D. W. Griffith's *Birth of a Nation*. This 1915 silent feature celebrates the Klan as avengers that kill a Black man who tries to rape a white woman and that rescue the populace from a Reconstruction-era Black rule depicted as bumbling and incompetent. In *Gone with the Wind* and *To Kill a Mockingbird*, which my family members repeatedly read in book form and watched as movies, domestic workers like Mammy and Calpurnia labor around the clock to put food on the table and clean up after everyone is done. They're "just like family," as the saying goes, except that they can't eat in the same room as everyone else. If I did poop in the closet, the white southern mind believed that Ceola should have cheerfully cleaned up her little bunny's mess, for, as William Faulkner says of *The Sound and the Fury*'s Dilsey, "they endured." Perhaps, if Ceola had not been fired, we could have teamed up to defeat a villain, like Idgie and Sipsey in my mother's favorite, *Fried Green Tomatoes*. Or I could trace my long career as a civil rights educator back to that little bunny den, with Ceola as *The Help*'s Aibileen and me as Mae Mobley: the two of us snuggling in the wingback chair while, instead of watching her stories, Ceola devoted herself to reminding me, "You is kind. You is smart. You is important."

Popular culture going back to the nineteenth century casts white girls like Mae Mobley as key figures in the development of what historian Robin Bernstein calls "racial innocence." Racial innocence allows white people to feign ignorance about the ways that race and racism structure society and, while doing so, to feel as guileless as children. The "use of childhood to make political projects appear innocuous, natural, and therefore justified," Bernstein explains, scaffolds the belief that white people of all ages inhabit the top tier of a God-given, not human-invented, racial hierarchy. Atop the pinnacle are angelic white girls like the ethereal Eva, from Harriett Beecher Stowe's 1852 novel *Uncle Tom's Cabin*, and Shirley Temple, the precocious, ringlet-haloed star of more than two dozen movies during the 1930s and 1940s. For well over a century, books, films, dolls, cartoons, advertisements and more depicted the world's Evas and Shirleys as embodiments of purity and virtue.

Their counterparts were, at best, an Uncle Tom or a Mr. Bojangles, ready to serve and happy to entertain. At the worst were dark strangers like *Birth of a Nation*'s Gus, hell-bent on doing those white girls harm, or *The Help*'s Minny, whose idea of service entailed dishing up shit.

Equally pervasive as the concept of racial innocence was the belief that Black female domestics, while necessary, brought filth and disease into their white employers' houses. Historian Tera W. Hunter describes how white southerners perceived Black domestics as "pathological agents" and "perpetrators" of contamination during the Jim Crow era. In her book *To 'Joy My Freedom: Southern Black Women's Lives and Labors after the Civil War*, Hunter reproduces a 1914 cartoon published in the *Atlanta Constitution* that features a woman looking like a stereotypical mammy, surrounded by flies and leaving a shack near the city dump to enter a "sanitary," "average white home." Such an image informed what my average white grandmother and mother thought

3. Julie Buckner Armstrong, ca. 1965. Image courtesy of the author.

about a woman like Ceola before she ever "darkened their door" to care for the little girl they liked to dress up as a princess.'

Outfitted in her tiara and white lacy dress, their princess looked the perfect picture of innocence. Not at all someone who would squat on a closet floor to do her business like an animal, even if she did consider herself to be a tiny hopping bunny.

*

A search for the actual, rather than a white-imagined, Ceola yielded limited information. I combed through the Birmingham Public Library's city directories, real estate tax records, microfilm newspapers, and census data. Ceola was born in 1910, lived in Smithfield, belonged to St. Joseph's Baptist Church, died in 1995, and was buried at Grace Hill Cemetery. Her husband worked for a moving company. They had one son, with a name so common that city and suburban directories had rows of listings. Beyond these basics were no more records. If I wanted to move beyond the archive's relative silence, I needed to dig more creatively.

I started with her Smithfield home. The location, deeply rooted in local history, provides clues to Ceola's story even though the house itself no longer exists.

In the early 1800s, the land that would become Smithfield was a 2,000-acre cotton plantation owned by Joseph Riley Smith, who enslaved roughly sixty African Americans to work his land. Smith's parents had been among the first white settlers to come in after Andrew Jackson's troops cleared the area of its Native inhabitants. During the late 1800s, Smith turned his former plantation into a small community that he named after himself. Unlike other developers, he sold lots to families from a mix of racial, ethnic, and class backgrounds: Irish day laborers, Italian shopkeepers, African American lawyers. Some of these families lived in shotgun houses, others—like Ceola's family—in small wood-frame single-family or duplex homes, still others in the gambrel-roofed cottages that the nationally known Black architect Wallace Rayfield designed. (Rayfield's most famous local project was the Sixteenth Street Baptist Church, built in 1911.) Birmingham's 1926 Zoning Ordinance tried to solidify the city's racial divisions, but the permeability that existed in Smithfield's early decades led it to become, after World War II, the testing ground for housing desegregation. During the 1950s and 1960s, Ceola's family lived about six blocks from the Dynamite Hill epicenter. They kept the same address from the 1970s through the early 1990s, which means they survived the April 4, 1977, tornado that destroyed large parts of Smith-field and was so severe it has its own Wikipedia page. Eventually the family moved, but where is unclear: neither Ceola, nor her husband, nor her son appears again in local records until her 1995 obituary. The spot that used to be their Smithfield house now sits under the rebuilt (in 2011) A. H. Parker High School.

Growing up, I knew Parker only as a high school that mine, Banks, played in football. Earlier known as Industrial High, Parker formed in 1900 as the city's first secondary school for African Americans. Its alumni base includes a who's who of Birmingham celebrities and dignitaries: musicians Sun Ra and Erskine Hawkins, singer Nell Carter, former mayor Larry Lankford. My white peers and I would not have talked about Parker's pride, but we would have absorbed our parents' perceptions that Smithfield was "poor" and "dangerous." Occasionally, we attended high school or University of Alabama football games at Legion Field, a few blocks south of Parker. Game day meant passing quickly through Smithfield, staying only to park if no spaces were open closer to the stadium. "Over by Legion Field" ultimately became Birmingham code for a Black neighborhood that whites avoided except on game day.

The area got this reputation from Smithfield's time as a border zone between Birmingham's Black and white populations, when it was officially marked "undesirable." Records from the Home Owners Loan Corporation (HOLC), which valued real estate for lending purposes during the 1930s and 1940s, show Smithfield, like all Birmingham's Black or mixed neighbor-hoods, described as "fourth grade" or "hazardous." A white pocket between Smithfield and Birmingham Southern College, by comparison, achieved a "second grade"/"still desirable" ranking. Our East Lake neighborhood had similar designations, with the African American neighborhoods closer to the Birmingham Airport labeled "hazardous," and our white section marked "third grade"/"definitely declining." (As a point of contrast, the only place to receive a "first grade" rating was Mountain Brook, the suburb south of Red Mountain that was home to the city's elites.) These HOLC maps were in-strumental in determining property values and, thus, relative wealth. Such was clearly the case for Ceola. Tax records from the 1960s show her house following the same basic composition and floorplan as my grandmother's but appraised at one-tenth ($2,000 versus $20,000) the value of our own.

From the readily available documents, I learned that Ceola came from a proud, working-class community that differed from ours only in the ways that white people perceived and therefore dictated. But what about the "Martin Luther King business"?

My grandmother might have suspected (at the time or in retrospect) that Ceola was involved in local movement activities because she belonged to St. Joseph's Baptist Church, a few blocks from her house. St. Joseph's minister during the late 1960s, Abraham Woods Jr., was second-in-command, under Fred Shuttlesworth, of the Alabama Christian Movement for Human Rights (ACMHR), a movement organization founded in 1956 after the state of Alabama banned the National Association for the Advancement of Colored People (NAACP). The ACMHR helped to coordinate local civil rights activities during the 1950s and '60s, including the 1963 Birmingham campaign that brought in King. Proximity does not imply connection, however. Just because Ceola went to a church that, a few years after our family fired her, hired an activist minister does not mean that she belonged to the ACMHR, had anything to do with King being in Birmingham, or participated in local protests. Many working people did not, from fear that doing so might cause them to lose their livelihoods (as Ceola did), or worse, their lives.

I can't even be sure how much Ceola participated in church. A 2005 directory lists her and her husband among its deceased members, but other available church records don't mention them. In 2015 I attended services at St. Joseph's and asked the minister, the church secretary, and a few members about Ceola. A couple of old-timers remembered the name but not much more. By that time Ceola had been dead for twenty-five years. I'm not fully sure what I expected them to tell me. White people have done enough damage in Smithfield for locals not to trust one they don't know coming into their church and asking a lot of questions.

It is also possible that my grandmother suspected Ceola of being involved in the movement because of the increased militancy on the part of Black women during the civil rights era. Many were not afraid to fight back against individuals or authority figures—or to get arrested for acts of resistance.

As historian Robin D. G. Kelley explains, bus lines especially became contested terrain. Kelley calls buses "moving theaters"—using "theater" to mean both "a site of performance and a site of military conflict." Kelley writes specifically about the South East Lake-Ensley line, which Ceola and Hettie both used, although traveling in opposite directions. On that line, Kelley explains, Black female domestics often fought battles over their "deliberate humiliation." They refused to give up their seats to white passengers long before Rosa Parks, they cursed drivers who shortchanged them, and if challenged

4. African Americans clap and sing "I want to be free," as officers urge them to move on during racial demonstrations in Birmingham, 1963. Photograph by Bill Hudson courtesy of the Associated Press.

they were not afraid to get physical. Mary Rutledge, an East Lake domestic worker, describes how she carried "a little something in my pocket [often a transistor radio, for throwing or head-clocking] where I could defend myself if any of them tried to attack me." Such actions, Kelley states, formed a continuum of opposition that included workplace resistance and even workplace sabotage. Breaking household items, tearing the wash, burning the bread, showing up late—behaviors that whites attribute to Black incompetence (the old "trouble getting good help these days")—can be subtle forms of using labor as a weapon.

Still, such history tells me little about my babysitter. Just because many Black female domestics found creative ways of fighting back against Birmingham's daily racism does not mean that Ceola followed their example. She could have been a respectful employee. She could have been oppositional. Who knows? Maybe insisting upon her soap opera "stories" every day was her form of resistance because, as Mississippi activist Fannie Lou Hamer said, she was "sick and tired of being sick and tired."

*

Ceola died in 1995. I don't know what killed her. I cannot pinpoint exactly where she is buried. Her obituary said Grace Hill Cemetery, just south and west of Titusville—like Smithfield, a historic African American community. Back in the Jim Crow days, Birmingham segregated even its dead people. The city's premier white cemetery through the 1970s was Elmwood. Although Grace Hill, a Black burial ground, is not across the railroad tracks from Elmwood, it does border them. The racial divide could not be any more stereotypical.

Not long after I visited St. Joseph's Baptist, I made the trip out to Grace Hill. The office gave me Ceola's plot number and sent me to find a groundskeeper named Charles. We met by the entrance, and I followed his red truck through the winding paths of graves. We wound up near an oak tree at the farthest reaches of Grace Hill's southeast corner.

Charles opened the truck door with a graveyard-appropriate creak. He was an African American man in his sixties, fit, wearing jeans, a blue work shirt, scuffed Timberlands, and a John Deere cap. He surveyed the terrain.

"She have a headstone?" he asked.

The question never occurred to me. Of course it wouldn't: that's how racial innocence operates. I could drive to the cemetery expecting to find Ceola's grave marked with a large, granite headstone just like Hettie's in Oneonta and, instead, find myself shocked that one didn't exist. I could pretend not to see how Birmingham's racist economy valued Ceola's work and her home at a fraction of my grandmother's, how our family's race and class privilege, limited though it was, carried forward into death.

Racial innocence led me to feel virtuous for picking up a $4.99 bouquet of Walmart flowers in order to pay my respects.

I held them awkwardly by my side as Charles telephoned the office to double-check the coordinates. He pulled a pink surveyor's flag from his truck's aluminum storage box, walked over to a marked grave, and then paced out a few steps closer to the road.

"She your family's maid?" he asked matter-of-factly.

"My babysitter," I said.

Charles plunked the flag into the ground.

"Well, this is the spot, as near as I can tell, without digging out my measuring tape. I'm sorry there's nothing more."

I stared at the flag: an odd, fierce flower amid the brick red Birmingham dirt and a few blades of struggling green grass.

Before Charles and I parted, he asked what brought me to Grace Hill. I told him that back in the movement days, my grandmother accused Ceola of doing something wrong and then fired her.

The truth was that I would never know what happened back then and had no idea why I came to the cemetery. What did I want? Information about my babysitter? Confirmation that my grandmother was a product of Jim Crow? Absolution for myself?

"Mm," Charles said, shaking his head.

It turns out that he attends another of Birmingham's important civil rights churches, Bethel Baptist, former home to Fred Shuttlesworth. I told him that I was writing a book, that I wanted to focus on the regular folks like Ceola whose stories need to be told.

Charles said he liked the idea, then turned to go. He had his own work to do—not time to spend helping a white woman he didn't know chase down a racial-healing pipe dream.

Before getting back into the red truck, he said something that stuck with me through every chapter of this book.

"There's the history they write down," Charles told me, "and under that, there's history that's buried and forgot."

3 / GOD OF THE FORGE

A Queer Lesson in Coloring outside the Lines

When Hettie first moved to the East Lake house, in the late 1950s before I was born, family members told her she was crazy for buying such a dump. The neighborhood was pleasant enough. A bus stopped on our corner to carry working people from their small bungalows to their jobs downtown, about five miles west. Hettie, who didn't drive until the early 1960s, could walk to a grocery store, a drugstore, the beauty parlor, and her church. But the only house she could afford had fallen into disrepair. A scrubby yard grew little beyond crabgrass and vines that overtook the outside walls. Inside was a scramble of discarded furniture and peeling paint. Hettie's nephew David, just out of high school and looking for work, helped her redo the place inside and out. A budding artist and future interior decorator, he had the vision—and the skills—to transform chaos into order, ugliness into beauty.

David's most significant transformation involved painting murals on the living-room and kitchen walls. Growing up, my favorite was a red-brick well surrounded by bluebirds above the kitchen table, the center of our large extended family. Evenings, waiting for Mom to come home from work, I sat there watching Hettie fry chicken or knead biscuits. The kitchen window looked west, onto the sunset pinks and oranges behind our pecan tree's green boughs. When the sun came through the window in just the right way to bounce light glimmers and pecan leaf shadows off the wall, the painting came to life. Some birds pecked at the ground for worms. Some busily washed themselves in a bucket. Others fluttered about the sky ready to land or take flight.

David, this fantasy's maker, remained a mystery. He left Birmingham when I was four and died two years later. When I asked about him, family members spoke in hushed tones:

Artist.

Queer.

Suicide.

David didn't leave a note. Searching for reasons, others wrote his life backward, seeing his story from one perspective: its end. Hettie said David's father kicked him out for not being a workingman, for, she said, being "funny." Bull Connor's Birmingham crushed David, as it did most anyone who colored outside of the time's white, patriarchal, heteronormative lines. He moved to Huntsville, trying but not succeeding to cash in on the city's booming military and NASA economy. On December 15, 1967, he took his last breath in a carbon-monoxide-filled car.

When I was a child, Hettie used to tell me that I have the David Armstrong gene. As an adult, seeking to know more about the Birmingham in my blood, I needed to find out what she meant. Did she think that I would die young? That I would grow up "funny"? Or that I, too, could see things about the world that others did not?

Were my grandmother's words omen or guiding light?

*

My research began with family photographs. The class difference between Hettie's family of origin, the Buckners, and David's, the Armstrongs, could not look any more pronounced. In one shot of the Armstrongs, taken around 1920, my grandfather Hubert's parents and siblings (including David's father, Frank) appear respectably middle class. They wear crisp, store-bought outfits and pose for a studio shot in their hometown of Cullman, a small city between Birmingham and Huntsville. In one picture of the Buckners, taken around 1900, my grandmother's family members look like Appalachian hillbillies. They sit outside, in front of their handmade Oneonta homestead, wearing ill-fitting handmade clothes.

After Hettie and Hubert married, they lived in Oneonta surrounded by Buckners, with occasional visits to the Cullman Armstrongs. After Hubert died Hettie's life centered on her children and her siblings, some in Birmingham, some back home. My childhood was full of Buckners and Hettie's Armstrongs, but I didn't know much about Hubert's until I was grown. When I was little, we went to the Oneonta homestead so often that after a twenty-year absence, I was able to find the place on my own without asking for directions. The only times I recall going to Cullman were for funerals. One of them was probably David's.

I didn't find it unusual that I'd never seen his photograph. The only picture Hettie had of her husband's family was the studio shot. So I combed old newspapers to see if anything turned up. One did: in microfilm too grainy to reproduce here. On December 5, 1957, the *Birmingham Post-Herald* profiled David as "Teen of the Week." The paper described him as bitten by the "art bug" and wanting to attend college in Chicago. The story claimed that US senators and even a president had praised David's talent. In addition to painting, he performed comedy routines and played the piano, accordion, and flute. In the picture he stands before a Fairfield High School Tiger. Did he paint it? I notice that the stripes in David's V-neck, faux-vest shirt echo the tiger's. At seventeen he was so much like that high school mascot, crouching, ready to pounce.

Exactly ten years and ten days after this picture, David took his life.

He never went to Chicago. Instead, he tried to make it as an artist without formal training. After high school he worked as sign painter in Fairfield (about five miles west of Birmingham), where his family lived for a brief time during the post–World War II boom years. Fairfield (neither fair nor a field) was named after the Connecticut hometown of a U.S. Steel executive and was built to house workers from the Tennessee Coal, Iron, and Railroad Company. David left Fairfield in the early 1960s for Birmingham's bohemian Southside, where he showed a knack for rehabbing houses. He got work designing interiors. He painted murals like the ones he did for Hettie.

To my knowledge none of those murals survive. At some point Hettie covered hers with wallpaper: orange, green, and gold vertical stripes like multicolored bars of a jail cell. After she sold the house in her late eighties, the new owners ripped down the paper and painted the walls a flat white.

I do have one picture, taken about a year before David's death, where a mural fragment is visible. I'm standing before one of the flowerpots on Hettie's living room wall. Four rows of pots ran from floor to ceiling, with fat clumps of gold and white hydrangeas. My smile, tongue poked into lower lip, is genuine, not like the full-toothed, vacant-eyed southern-girl grin I've been taught to produce any time someone brings out a camera. These pots made our house feel special: my own private wonderland.

People tell me that David and I look alike. Seeing his face for the first time in the newspaper made me gasp. Then I chuckled. He and I share a lot: an off-center smile, impish eyes, a love of quirky shirts.

A favorite story of my mom's confirmed our mutual irreverence. In family lore, she took me to a dinner party at David's Southside home and dressed me, as she often did, like a pageant princess: a ruffled and bowed white dress, white lacy socks, black patent-leather shoes, and a tiara. When I sat down in the dining room, I leaned back in the chair and propped my feet, black shoes and all, on the properly set white linen table. Mom was horrified. She said that David laughed out loud, clapped his hands, and gave his little princess a big hug.

When Mom was in her seventies, I probed her for details. Dementia kept her from remembering anything specific, but she told me that, during the early 1960s, the two of them used to go out drinking and dancing.

"You know David," she said. "He always was funny."

I asked her to clarify: "funny" as in "amusing," "weird," or "queer."

"Funny," she repeated, laughing a gravelly smoker's laugh that told me nothing.

Around the same time, I asked Aunt Nell about David, but all she remembered was that my grandmother thought his dad, Frank, was a bully. Maybe that, rather than the class dynamic, was the reason Hettie had little to with Hubert's Armstrongs after his 1944 death. When Hubert was diagnosed with malignant melanoma and went into Birmingham's welfare hospital, Hettie stayed on the Oneonta farm to care for their four children. My grandparents could not afford a car or phone, so the doctors called Frank to say there was nothing they could do. Frank drove Hubert the five miles back to his house instead of the forty back to Hettie's. David must have been a toddler. When Hettie discovered that her husband had been discharged from the hospital without her knowledge, she was livid. Hettie, a good Christian woman, would never verbally express that anger. But she had a way of furrowing her brow that could bring down fire. I don't know what happened between Hettie and Frank, but Hubert somehow got back to Oneonta, died at home, and was buried in a small cemetery down the road. Not in Birmingham. Not in Cullman.

I sometimes wonder if Hettie opened her home to David because she loved him, and, unlike most Southern Baptist women of her day, she looked past his homosexuality. Or did she try to spite Frank?

Aunt Nell convinced me to reach out to the Armstrongs and call David's sister Susie. Having never met that side of the family, I was afraid. What if they were bullies like Hettie's version of Frank? Susie turned out to be a sweet country lady. She called her baby brother "funny," and she meant "ha-ha." She was twelve years older than David and said that she struggled trying to make him mind as a child. He never did. Once when he was little, he stood on a chair and ran water in the kitchen sink to take a bath. She tried to stop him, but he stripped naked, ran around the house yelling that when he grew up he would beat her kids, and slid from her grasp into the sink. She said David killed himself because it was Christmas, and a lot of people owed him money. She told me he was buried at the Etha Baptist Church—she pronounced it "Ethie"—next to his parents and someone she called "Myrtie, the old maid schoolteacher."

Susie let me know in that roundabout southern way when our conversation was over.

"The coroner called Daddy on the phone, and he like to have had a heart attack," she said. "That's not how you do things in Cullman. You get a family member to go to the house. Have you had rain down there? It's so hot and dry. My goodness."

Was David's the funeral I remember going to with my grandmother when I was a little girl? We drove far away from Birmingham down two-lane roads in her fat, rattling blue-and-white Chevrolet. I recall a bunch of older people that I did not know. A cramped wooden church. A minister ranting about the fiery pits of Hell and lamb's blood washing souls clean. On the way home, I lay down in the front seat with my head in Hettie's lap and looked up at the trees.

"Look, Granny, the trees are nekkid!" I said, describing their bare winter limbs. She told that story until she died, and my mother told it after that: evidence of me being "funny." Ha. Ha.

Old maid schoolteacher—outcast, unwanted: that's what people warned me I would become when I left Birmingham for graduate school in New York.

David dreamed of Chicago. He got no farther north than Huntsville—then, the third-largest city in Alabama.

So much promise in that high school tiger pounce. I think of David's queer artist ghost next to old Myrtie, and I feel cold.

A lone naked limb on a frozen tree.

*

Trying to learn more about David, I requested his State of Alabama Death Certificate. It calls his 1967 death a suicide from carbon monoxide poisoning. On a frigid Friday night, outside his Huntsville, Alabama, apartment, he duct-taped a vacuum cleaner hose to the exhaust pipe of his Volkswagen Beetle, ran the hose through the window, got into the driver's seat, closed the door, closed the window, and started the engine. I asked a colleague who taught forensics how long it took for David to die. Less than half an hour. Whoever found him the next morning would have noticed that his skin had turned a deep, cherry red from carboxyhemoglobin, the compound that results when carbon monoxide replaces the oxygen in someone's blood.

The apartment complex does not look as if it has changed much since he lived there. Parking spaces are covered but not enclosed.

David wanted to be seen.

He left his mark, just not how he expected.

My mom saved an undated newspaper clipping about David's one-man show at Birmingham's The Club, an exclusive, members-only restaurant. Among the works noted were paintings in the "Birmingham Trilogy," featuring famous local landmarks: Arlington Antebellum Home, the Vestavia Hills gazebo, and Vulcan—the city's beloved god-of-the-forge statue.

Those paintings now hang in the home of David's former roommate, Hugh. I tracked him down using the Birmingham Public Library's city directories. When I identified myself, he seemed happy that I called. He insisted that I see David's art. Hugh was kind to me, said I had David's face. He lives in a suburban ranch-style house around the corner from a male friend and traveling companion. Hugh is an old man, like David would be now. He is tall and thin, with thick black glasses and wispy gray hair. Some things haven't changed. He still teaches piano from a baby grand in a formal living room.

The two of them rented the Southside house with a man named Barnie. Hugh talked about the parties they used to have. Halloween bashes. Dress-up dinners. Art shows. I said it sounded like the Brooklyn brownstone where

5. David Armstrong painting during an art show outside his home studio, ca. 1965. Image courtesy of the author.

Carson McCullers, W. H. Auden, and Gypsy Rose Lee lived—full of artists, drinking, and wild times. Herb corrected my impression.

"I had my piano students to think of," he said. "We had to be respectable. Still, we were young and single. We had some fun."

Hugh told me that David loved to cook, was always trying out new meals, that he mixed fancy cocktails and kept a full bar.

Hugh recalled David being a great carpenter, that he did most of the rehab work on the old house himself: the floors, the stair rails, the molding. He was always tinkering, always had a project. While Hugh talked I tried not to see David, kneeling carefully behind his car, one hand twisting on a vacuum hose, the other holding duct tape.

Hugh interrupted my train of thought to tell me that David was in demand as an interior decorator.

"That was the problem," he said. "David could make money as a designer but not as an artist."

Hugh explained that David was fine as long as he worked for someone else, but not when he worked for himself. That's what happened when David moved to Huntsville, Hugh conjectured. He stopped working at the Birmingham interiors job, followed a love interest north, and opened his own studio. The love interest didn't pan out. The paintings didn't sell. David gave up.

Hugh walked me around his home to show me the David Armstrong works he collected, five in all. A landscape in pale grays and snowy whites behind his dining room table. The Birmingham Trilogy in a spare bedroom. My favorite was an abstract mess that hung in Hugh's kitchen, next to a 1960s-vintage wall telephone. David called the painting "Cleaning off the Brushes." On a good day it might pass for a bad Jackson Pollock.

Why did David never go to art school? Money? Self-esteem? Did he lack the talent to move up to the next level? Did he even apply?

I asked Hugh how he came to own the works. He said he found them for $25 apiece not long after David's death in a store called the Trend House, among the fashionable home decor. I told him I would buy them when he was ready to sell. But their value, economic or artistic, is not the issue.

The paintings connect us, tangibly, to memories of David's life.

*

David's more successful art was ephemeral. In addition to the decorating and the one-man shows, he made a local reputation designing stage sets. The Actors Theatre produced Cole Porter's *The Can-Can* during the autumn of

1965. Reviews of the play were mixed, but the *Birmingham News* and the *Post-Herald* both praised David's work. The *Post-Herald* writer said, "The sets in this musical were some of the most tastefully done that I have seen this season." Lily May Caldwell in the *News* went even further: "Right here, let's pause to say that the sets were the 'stars' of the show. Designed by David Armstrong, they gave the show atmosphere and color and were the best we've seen on any local theater stage."

I learned about David's theater work from a man named John, who knew him briefly that year. John contacted me after seeing a 2012 query I posted in Birmingham's former independent weekly *Weld*. I wanted to tell David's story but at that point had little information.

John and I met outside the library on a hot summer day and talked for more than two hours. He was in his sixties, with gray hair and blue eyes. He walked with a cane. We got along like old friends, except that he didn't want to tell me his last name. Both John and Hugh, who requested that I use pseudonyms when referring to them, reminded me of people that I interviewed in Valdosta, Georgia (during the early 2000s), about a notorious local lynching. The elisions and silences sometimes spoke more powerfully than their words about a painful past.

John met David when the former was seventeen. John lived in a housing project with an alcoholic, abusive father. He hung out with other teenage boys in what was then called Woodrow Wilson (now Linn) Park, in the center of downtown. They would idle around the park at night waiting for cars to cruise by and offer them money for sex. John called it "selling meat." The man who ran the Actors Theatre picked him up one night for a platonic drive, John said, and he soon fell into the local arts scene.

John liked the first play he saw, *Moon for the Misbegotten*, so he stuck around. During *Can-Can* rehearsals, he noodled on the piano while David built sets. David helped him get a job at the interior design company. The job afforded him a room around the corner from David and Hugh, where he set up house with a boy who passed as a girl.

John said that David was sad a lot and could not sell his paintings. He couldn't finish one with a basket of flowers, in particular. One day he packed up all his art and moved to Huntsville. That was the last he heard of David until the suicide.

While John spoke he drew me a picture of the Southside house's floor plan, showing where David's room and studio were. The house has been replaced by an office building, but when I looked up the real estate records,

I saw that, almost fifty years after being inside, he rendered the interior perfectly.

John told me that seeing my inquiry in *Weld* brought back memories of an important time that he consigned to a closeted past. He hung out with the arts crowd for a few months in 1965. Then someone painted "queer" on the house where he lived with the drag lover. The lover left. John moved on.

"I just closed that door and never opened it back up again," John told me. He said he has lived as a heterosexual, faithfully married to the same woman, for decades.

After talking to Hugh and John, I contacted Howard Cruse, author of the 1995 graphic narrative *Stuck Rubber Baby*. The book is based on Cruse's experiences coming of age as a gay man in 1960s Birmingham. When I first read it, in the early stages of my research, I emailed Cruse to ask if he had known David. He had not, but the two of them traveled in the same artistic circles. So much of his protagonist Toland's story could be David's and his friends': the steady hum of parties and passing, the interrupting pop of violence. Birmingham, and the rest of the South, Cruse told me in a 2014 interview, "had more nuance than people might expect." But "the danger was palpable."

In *Stuck Rubber Baby*, Toland is attacked, and his friend Sammy is killed, in a hate crime. Cruse cast the story as a flashback, with a present-day Toland unburdening a traumatic history to his partner. While Toland remembers, the partner places a comforting hand on Toland's shoulder.

The gulf between David and me is too wide for my hand to reach.

When I moved to New York in the early 1990s, I lived just a few blocks from what used to be the Stonewall Inn, the bar where, in June 1969, patrons resisting a police raid galvanized a movement for lesbian, gay, bisexual, and transgender (LGBTQ+) civil rights. I passed by the site on my walks to and from class at NYU, wishing that David had lived for just eighteen more months to see the news. Would it have made a difference? I don't know.

Empty hands. Empty wishes. Empty words.

From the former location of David's Southside house, the view of Vulcan is clear. Both Hugh and John said that David could see the statue from his studio window. Vulcan was built to advertise Birmingham's steel industry in the 1904 St. Louis, Missouri, World's Fair. Since the 1930s, this 180-foot icon has stood atop the city's tallest geographical feature, Red Mountain, so named for the iron ore that helped make Birmingham's founders rich.

6. Vulcan Statue, atop Red Mountain. Image courtesy of the Birmingham Public Library Archives.

The god Vulcan is son of Jupiter and Juno. The parents cast out their baby from the family heaven for being ugly. He fell so far and so hard that he permanently injured his foot. Homely and crippled, he married Venus, the goddess of beauty.

Most Birmingham residents don't know the mythology. My working-class hometown loves Vulcan for three reasons. It is the largest cast-iron statue in the world, something our city has—finally!—that rival Atlanta does not. Also, the statue wears a blacksmith's apron but no pants. He is positioned with his naked backside facing a leafy suburb south of town. When I was in college, in the early 1980s, some disc jockeys recorded a novelty song about it: "Moon over Homewood." When I was a child, the spear that Vulcan held aloft was wrapped in a light. Locals called it his "popsicle." If the light glowed red, someone had died in a traffic accident. A green light meant city streets were death-free.

Even without the lights, Vulcan seems to watch over Birmingham like a guardian angel.

My uncle Bobby, Aunt Nell's late husband, once told me that David went to a Halloween party dressed as Vulcan. He said David put on a blacksmith's apron and painted it, along with his whole body, aluminum grey.

I had to ask: "Did David have on anything else?"

"I don't think so, no," Uncle Bobby replied. "I tried not to look. Maybe one of them G-strings."

"What color was his popsicle?" By then, I was in full giggle.

Uncle Bobby deadpanned, "I think it mighta been green."

I'm surprised that Uncle Bobby went to a Southside party. He called David "funny" too; he did not mean "ha-ha."

Uncle Bobby was the kind of man David's father wanted him to be, according to a cousin named Mary Sue. I called her back in 2012, after I called David's sister. She told me the father was disappointed in his son's lifestyle.

Mary Sue said, "Uncle Frank always wanted a he-man. He got that later on with Donald. He's a real man's man."

David's younger brother Donald served in Vietnam, worked a steady job, married a woman, had children. I had to get my nerve up to call him after talking to Mary Sue—afraid of what he might say. I had no need to fear; I couldn't understand half of it. Donald's voice sure sounded country. It also sounded kind. While he spoke, I thought of the novel *Song of Solomon*, where author Toni Morrison writes about ways people communicated before language. I didn't need to sort through Donald's accent to know what he said when he talked about his brother. I felt it, blood to blood. David was older by seven years, like Hubert to Frank. Donald's voice slowed and cracked when he spoke of the death. "Vacuum cleaner hose," I picked up, "forty-five years ago this year." People owed David money, he said, and he could not collect— the same story I got from Susie. Donald didn't say anything about family disapproval. That's a version of David's suicide that came from Hettie, the Christian who forgave everyone but Frank.

Donald invited me to Cullman for an Armstrong family reunion. We ate a feast of southern home cooking: fried chicken, ham, potato salad, baked beans, fried okra, squash casserole, and sweet iced tea. Susie and Mary Sue were there. I met David's niece and nephews, now adults, and a dozen more Armstrongs that looked to me just like Buckners: fair skin, blue eyes, and too many chins. I might as well have been at a family reunion in Oneonta. I'm not sure why Hettie kept her distance.

I learned, however, that Frank could be scary. Susie told me that when she was young she was not allowed to paint her fingernails. She did anyway. When Frank saw what she had done, he scraped off the polish with a hunting knife.

Donald is not Frank. He has a bit of David in him. He took me into his shop, where he was fixing up an old red truck. Like his brother, he's always tinkering. He showed me pictures of the projects he's done over the years. Like David, Donald is an artist—whose medium is automobile restoration.

And he keeps careful watch over his brother's memory. After the shop, Donald brought me into his dining room. On the table were family photographs, printouts of genealogical research, and a scrapbook full of David Armstrong news clippings, drawings, art show brochures, and two unexpected finds. First, pictures of David as Vulcan for Birmingham's 1964 Festival of the Arts. Under the apron, indeed . . . no pants.

Second, a curious letter: from Birmingham's former commissioner of public safety, Bull Connor. Dated May 25, 1962, it's the last item in the scrapbook. He thanked David for the Connor family coat of arms that he commissioned and asked for a name history so that he could hang the two side by side.

Around the time that Connor and David were corresponding, the commissioner was fighting a two-front war that's rarely discussed in city histories.

Connor's attacks on African American civil rights are well documented. In 1961 he held police back for fifteen minutes while the Ku Klux Klan used baseball bats and iron pipes against Freedom Riders passing through the Trailways bus station. In 1963 Connor ordered police dogs and fire hoses turned on nonviolent Civil Rights Movement protestors in Kelly Ingram Park. The photographs made Birmingham infamous.

Less well known are Connor's assaults on LGBTQ+ civil rights. Just three months after Connor penned the letter I found in David's scrapbook, the *Birmingham News* reported the commissioner's "Crackdown on Sex Perverts." Vice squad cops trolled local clubs, restrooms, and parks—looking for men violating sodomy laws to throw into the Birmingham jail. David's friend John did not mince words about what went on in Woodrow Wilson: "I saw a few guys get pistol-whipped."

All those photographers circling Kelly Ingram Park in the early 1960s, and no one took pictures of the violence taking place five blocks away?

Maybe they didn't see the queer history happening around them because it was not the image of Birmingham they already had in their heads.

Can anyone see beyond the stories that color their sight lines?

*

David's story was the genesis of this book, many years ago when it was a very different project. I had planned to write a series of linked essays that used people's obituaries as a jumping-off point for a more in-depth investigation of their lives. The history that's buried and forgot, as Charles from Grace Hill Cemetery articulated the idea.

I have long been fascinated by the ways that multiple perspectives vie for truth. Growing up with a parent who was mentally ill and later developed early-onset dementia, I had no trouble in graduate school grasping a basic premise of poststructuralist literary theory: that reality is not fixed but constructed. To get my PhD, I wrote about how authors Nathaniel Hawthorne, William Faulkner, and Toni Morrison probed what the latter describes in *Song of Solomon* as the "dead lives and fading memories . . . buried in and beneath the names of the places in this country. Under the recorded names were other names. . . . Names that had meaning." It was a crappy dissertation, with tortured syntax that never seemed to spackle over the working-class-imposter syndrome peeking through each chapter like bad drywall seams. Twenty-five years and a full professorship later, trying to write like a straight-up academic makes my hands sweat. But I still dig the history beneath the history.

Remnants of that earlier obituary project, like David and Ceola, remain in these pages. The further I got into the research, however, the more I realized that all my subjects were rooted in Birmingham, and all had some connection, direct or indirect, to the city's midcentury civil rights transformations. They *were* the history beneath the protests and the violence that most people take to be the history. They were the ordinary people muddling, for better or worse, through extraordinary times. Finding a letter from Bull Connor in David's scrapbook made this point hit home.

And gave it nuance.

The violence that made Jim Crow possible—the brutal rejection of anything outside the status quo—touched most everyone in Birmingham, albeit in different ways. Connor's minions terrorized one park by day, another by night. To survive economically, David did business with a man who considered him less than human, a pervert. He shook the hand of someone who would just as soon pistol-whip him or lock him up in jail. What price did they agree upon? What was the cost to David's self-esteem, his soul?

My grandmother told me as a child that I have the David Armstrong gene. I still don't know what she meant. I do know that for most of my adult life, I have thought about my relationship to him not in terms of biology but in terms of guardian angels.

On one hand, I used to see myself as his protector, preserving his dead life and fading memory. But that turned out to be his brother Donald's job, not mine.

On the other hand, I sometimes see David as my protector. Like Vulcan, he was my spiritual god of the forge. When I moved to New York and went to NYU, against the warnings and the name-calling—"you'll wind up an old maid schoolteacher!" (and worse)—I had an inkling that David was somehow responsible for my being there. When I began asking questions about how my family and I fit into the bigger picture of Birmingham's history, I felt David's presence long before seeing that letter from Bull Connor. When I was young and impressionable, David's murals shaped my view of the world; they gave me a lens to see beyond what everyone else believed was obvious, real, or true. David was the first person I knew of who dared to be different, who lived a rich, full life outside the lines of what his time considered "normal."

David held aloft the clear green light of beauty to illuminate my way out of an ugly world.

4 / THE SCHOOLHOUSE DOOR AND THE STEEL FRAME OF RACISM

During the 1960s, when my mother Mary Ann wasn't partying with her cousin David, working at her job for a federal judge, or bowling with her legal-secretary friends, she wrote letters. After reading in the *Birmingham News* about Homewood Junior High School, in a wealthier part of town "over the mountain," getting a makeover, she wrote to columnist Richard Pitner contrasting his description of the gleaming hallways and state-of-the art classrooms with what she saw at our working-class elementary school, Robinson. In her trademark style—underlining, boldface, all caps—she described peeling paint, rotting wooden floors, and rats. Shortly after "Pitner's Patter" printed some of her descriptions, Robinson cleaned up. When I was in second grade (1968–69), another of Mom's enthusiastic, adjective-filled letters earned Robinson's beloved Sarah Ann White the Alabama Teacher of the Year award. Shortly before I began fourth grade, in 1970, Mom launched a less successful writing campaign. Birmingham's city schools were poised to begin court-ordered desegregation to achieve racial equity. Like many other white parents, my mother penned horrified missives to her congressmen, Gov. Albert Brewer, and President Richard M. Nixon, hoping to stop a tide of civil rights progress that was, at the time, still rising.

Here's the backstory.

In 1954 the US Supreme Court ruled in *Brown v. Board of Education* that racial segregation in public schools was unconstitutional. Rather than creating a desegregation plan, however, the court ruled in 1955 (*Brown II*) that states should comply "with all deliberate speed." Like many states, in and beyond the South, Alabama's response to the decision was deliberate but certainly not speedy. Two factors kept Birmingham schools segregated. First were the city's draconian laws that, until 1963, enforced the separation of Black and white people in all facets of life, from housing to transportation to social interactions. Second was a 1956 "freedom of choice" law, written by then-state-senator (and later Birmingham mayor) Albert Boutwell, which circumvented the Supreme Court by providing white parents with funding to send their children to the all-white private schools, known colloquially as "segregation academies," that began cropping up after *Brown*.

Freedom-of-choice laws and all-white, private academies are just two examples of massive resistance, a white backlash against public school desegregation that took place across the country. During the late 1950s and early 1960s, opponents used multiple strategies—legal and illegal, taking to the halls of power and to the streets—to keep segregation in place. Iconic images from the time point to this broader story: a photograph of Elizabeth Eckford, in 1957, wearing dark sunglasses and a stoic expression as she navigates a mob of white women outside Little Rock, Arkansas's, Central High School; a painting by Norman Rockwell, *The Problem We All Live With*, depicting racist epithets and a blood-red tomato hurled at six-year-old Ruby Bridges, integrating in 1960 a New Orleans, Louisiana, elementary school.

Birmingham had its own riots. In 1963 a US appeals court ruled in favor of local barber James Armstrong (no relation), whose class action suit against the Birmingham Board of Education paved the way for Black students to begin classes at all-white schools across the city. The school year's beginning saw local residents parading through different neighborhoods, waving Confederate flags, singing "Dixie," and carrying signs that said:

Boycott!
We Want Private Schools!
Keep Birmingham Schools White!

When Armstrong's sons Floyd (10) and Dwight (11) tried to start classes that fall at Graymont Elementary (in Smithfield), they found the school surrounded by a mob of about 250, and roughly a hundred Alabama state troopers. The commanding officer, Col. Al Lingo, blocked the entrance and waved the Armstrongs away.

Lingo's actions resembled a better-known incident from three months earlier: Gov. George Wallace's "stand in the schoolhouse door" when Vivian Malone and James Hood attempted to integrate the University of Alabama—except that Wallace had a camera crew and a prepared speech. Wallace told those present that it was his "solemn obligation" to defend the rights of his state against what he described as, "the unwelcomed, unwanted, unwarranted and force-induced intrusion upon the campus of the University of Alabama today of the might of the Central Government," which he said "offers a frightful example of the oppression of the rights, privileges, and sovereignty of this

7. White students drag an African American effigy past West End High School, 1963. Image courtesy of the Associated Press.

State." Wallace had been arguing that segregation was a constitutional conundrum, a matter of states' rights versus those of the federal government, since his gubernatorial campaign. His 1963 inaugural address made plain that his idea of "states' rights" was limited to white citizens, rallying his political base around the battle cry of "segregation now . . . segregation tomorrow . . . segregation forever." As Wallace spoke during his inaugural, he called attention to the fact that he stood on the steps of Alabama's state capitol in Montgomery, where Jefferson Davis, just over one hundred years earlier, had been sworn in as president of the Confederate States of America—describing the location as the "Cradle of the Confederacy . . . the Heart of the Great Anglo-Saxon Southland" that refused to bow to the federal government's "tyranny."

What Wallace perceived as tyranny, James Armstrong saw as protection of the rights denied to his family solely on the basis that they were not "Anglo-Saxon." President John F. Kennedy saw Armstrong's perspective too. Among the many sweeping transformations that the president put forward with the 1964 Civil Rights Act were provisions that allowed the federal government to withhold funding from school districts that refused to desegregate.

Birmingham grudgingly complied. That year saw nine Black students enrolled in formerly white city schools. In 1965 there were fifty-seven. In 1966, the year before I started first grade, there were 361. Three years later, a US district court ruled that the earlier freedom of choice plan was not allowing desegregation to move forward quickly enough, and it ordered Birmingham City Schools to submit a better plan, effective for the 1970–71 school year.

So in January 1970, my mother, Mary Ann Gamblin, sat down before a green Smith-Corona typewriter to make her own contribution to the white resistance effort: giving elected officials what she called "a piece of [her] mind."

*

In one of the many scrapbooks that Mom kept of my school days is a partial copy of a letter (three of four pages), dated January 22, 1970, to President Richard M. Nixon. Nixon did not respond or, if he did, we no longer have what he wrote. Other officials to whom she sent copies did write back, including Governor Brewer, US senators James B. Allen and John Sparkman, and US representative John H. Buchanan Jr., who penned three pages. Also with Mom's correspondence is a copy of the Congressional Record from October 16, 1969, discussing public school education. Mom went through the text, circling and numbering different passages, presumably to gather information in support of her points.

Mom's letter to Nixon is typical of those she wrote in other circumstances: passionate, effusive, and filled with uppercase, underlined points of emphasis. She employs the buzzwords common to white backlash against Black advancement ("states' rights," "freedom of choice")—focusing her argument on the detrimental impacts of moving children (specifically, me) from one school to another on what she perceives as the federal government's whim. "Mr. President," she states in paragraph two, "this is unfair, ridiculous, and unconstitutional, and . . . in violation of <u>our rights</u> and the <u>rights of our children</u>." Similarly, her third paragraph notes, "JUST TO TELL HER THAT SHE CANNOT ATTEND THE SCHOOL OF HER CHOICE IN HER OWN NEIGHBORHOOD is absolutely ridiculous." Mom's fonts and word choices—such as repeating, often, the word "ridiculous"—indicate palpable frustration. Despite the anger, the letter also reveals a distinct sense of rhetoric that provides insight into the mind-set of other white southerners hostile to desegregation, who were picking up pens, waving Confederate flags in the streets, and worse.

It's important to examine the connections between words and actions, so let's look closely at how such rhetoric works.

In her letter Mom pleads with the president to explain why the federal government is imposing its will, unduly, upon regular, working-class people "that make up the population of our Country." Short on *logos* (logical argument supported with appropriate evidence), the letter is grounded in *ethos* and *pathos*. In terms of ethos (the characteristics that make a writer credible), Mom presents herself as an upstanding American. "I was raised to obey and respect the laws of our land," she tells Nixon, adding later that she gets tears in her eyes "each time I hear our National Anthem and . . . see our United States of America flag raised." Such a description positions Mom as a model citizen whose rights are being violated by government intrusion. Reinforcing this idea is a great deal of pathos (emotional appeal), to create a sense of empathy that, ideally, should prompt Mom's readers to act on her behalf. Using a string of "even though" clauses, her writing carries readers through a litany of economic difficulties:

> I never demonstrated and broke the laws of our Country, even though I had to eat beans and corn bread many, many times, and even though I never saw a television set until I was in high school . . . and even though I had to pick cotton during the summer to help with my schooling, and even though I had to work after school to help with the expenses at home, and even though I don't have an automobile now.

Mom's point is that if desegregation takes place, regular people like her "cannot afford private schools"—presumably where white students would flee if their public schools integrated. Instead, she comes from a poor, humble background, at the mercy of leaders who, she says, "have the money to do as they please and don't stop to consider our feelings and the future of our children." As a true American, she considers herself the situation's true victim.

Underlying the notion of imperiled citizen is Mom's belief that the African Americans who potentially will attend white schools pose a threat because they are inferior non-Americans. Her impassioned "even though" clauses culminate in negative stereotypes. She grew up poor, she explains, but still never complained "just because the Federal government did not give us money." She implies here that those who protest for civil rights gains, who presumably should be working instead of demonstrating, seek something for nothing. Mom tells the president, "It certainly makes you appreciate things when you have to work for them yourself." Following Mom's logic, African Americans are not only lazy but ignorant. She asks, "Do you think sending a Negro to a white school is going to make him any smarter?" Her implied answer is "no." Mom implies, too, that African Americans do not fully count as citizens.

Her letter does not acknowledge desegregation as a solution to a problem (the Supreme Court ruled in *Brown* that "separate" was not at all "equal"). She does not stop to consider that people like James Armstrong risked their own and their children's lives for educational equity. Instead, she allies herself with her letter's target audience through whiteness. "It seems as if the leaders of our Country are trying to make everybody throughout the world satisfied except their own people," she states—casting African Americans not as the nation's "own people" but as a people apart from "our Country." The idea that they will come into "our schools," a term of ownership that Mom uses throughout the letter, makes this model American citizen feel as if "all of my rights are gradually being taken away from me."

Mom was hardly the only person to feel this way.

The Alabama Department of Archives and Manuscripts houses folders full of similar protest letters from across the country. They begin trickling in during the latter months of 1969 to Governor Brewer, who responded to Mom with a brief note, dated February 11, 1970, expressing his appreciation for her recent letter about "this complex and difficult problem." By 1971, when George Wallace took office for his second gubernatorial term, the volume of letters increased so much that the method of filing them changed. At first mixed in with general correspondence on the topic of education, the post-1970 protests eventually claimed several fat file folders of their own. In an August 31, 1971, letter to Birmingham attorney William McCollough, Wallace complains that he has "a stack of mail" on the subject "that is 10 feet high (and that is no exaggeration)." As the letters kept coming, creating a stack that was closer to six inches, Wallace also changed his way of responding. In general, the governor forwarded correspondence about curriculum, teachers, discipline, and building conditions to Alabama school superintendent LeRoy Brown—but wrote back personally to anyone who complained about federal intervention. For instance, Wallace's June 10, 1971, letter to a Mrs. Eva M. Jackson of Indianapolis, Indiana (who, like Mom, wrote a lengthy letter with many underlined and uppercase passages), agrees that "there is nothing wrong with schools being operated on a freedom of choice basis" and that trying to achieve "something that some social planner thinks is best" violates "basic civil rights." Later in the year, however, Wallace began sending form letters to those who, he states, "are deeply concerned about the bureaucratic meddling of the Federal bureaucracy in local affairs," assuring them that he will not stop his efforts "to speak out against the continuing encroachment by the Federal Government on the neighborhood school system."

Letters that Mom received from her congressional representatives use language similar to Wallace's, focusing on the federal government violating white rights. US senator James B. Allen wrote on January 27, 1970, to thank Mom for her "correspondence concerning the intolerable school situation in the South," noting that the current administration is "more interested in social change than in quality education for *our* children" (emphasis mine; read: white children). US representative John H. Buchanan Jr. expressed similar, albeit lengthier, sentiments in his January 29 response, which explains that he is "particularly sympathetic toward the young [again, read: white] students who are the victims of this tragic disruption." Buchanan gives a nearly three-page history of school desegregation—and efforts to thwart it—from the *Brown* decision to the Nixon administration, expressing "particular regret" that "court-ordered desegregation plans . . . show a total disregard for the rights of our nation's students."

Such letters, including my mother's, represent the southern party line that undergirded massive resistance efforts and helped make possible the violence of white rage. The story went something like this: school desegregation was one more example—along with the Civil War and Reconstruction—of how the federal government overstepped the boundaries of states' rights to force southerners (meaning white ones) to obey its wishes. Civil rights gains, many white southerners believed, were examples of "Negroes" asking for undeserved government handouts. Mom's long diatribe about working hard and obeying the laws rests on the assumption that African Americans would break laws to get what they wanted rather than work hard. Slavery, as the southern party line goes, kept those tendencies in check, while Reconstruction let them loose, allowing lazy, criminally minded Black people to take over and, as Mom said in another context about Civil Rights Movement protestors, run wild. The real losers in this history, Mom's letter suggests, are hardworking, God-fearing whites, who believe they have accepted such situations graciously but now must beg their leaders, in large uppercase letters, to explain why their rights to discriminate and segregate are being taken away.

*

On one hand, I'm not sure why Mom, or her elected officials, worried about school desegregation. If they paid attention to what students like me were learning in school, they would have known that both the southern party line and the edifice of white supremacy behind it remained in place. On the other hand, perhaps they understood the schoolhouse door stand's futility. They could do their best to block the entrance, but eventually the Floyd Armstrongs and the Vivian Malones of the world would work their way inside.

Robinson integrated fully in 1970. In 1967, my first-grade year, no Black students attended the school. A photograph of my fifth-grade class, in 1971, shows thirty-one students: twenty white, ten Black, and one Puerto Rican. By 1974, our last year before starting high school, the racial mix was about the same. As we learned how to become schoolmates, our interactions reflected the rhetoric we picked up at home, from teachers, in textbooks, and from our elected officials. That rhetoric was decidedly racist.

Our lessons started on Day One. They were not always overt. Sometimes they seeped into our consciousness in the same way that the polluted air from local steel mills entered our lungs with each breath. If Birmingham's school children had never seen clean air, how were they to know theirs was dirty?

My fellow first-graders in 1967, all of us white, never thought to question our teacher when she organized our reading instruction alongside subtle messages about race, space, and educational advancement. She told us something like this: "Children, this class has three reading groups. Those of you in the front are advanced readers. You are my Bluebirds. Those of you in the middle of the classroom need a little extra practice. You are my Redbirds. Those of you in the back have to work much harder. You are my Blackbirds." Such language made clear the racial hierarchies informing our classrooms and our lives. On Sundays we might sing in church how Jesus loved all the children of the world—red and yellow, black and white—but Monday through Friday we sat in groups that made a color-coded ranking system seem normal. The top level of bird-learners, blue like most of our eyes, was considered the best. In the afternoons we gathered in a semicircle of chairs at the room's front, under our teacher's smiling gaze, to take turns reading aloud. If we missed a word, then we moved to the line's last seat (on the left), where we'd wait for others to make mistakes so we could inch our way rightward. My failure was "Alice," friend to Dick and Jane in the popular first-grade readers, whom I called "Ah-lick-ee." I regained my first-seat spot, however, as, one by one, my Bluebird classmates stumbled over the silent "w" in "sword." With my metaphorical "sord" in hand, I remained an intellectual fighter, guarding my seat on the right. In my six-year-old opinion, nothing could be worse than sitting on the floor at the back of the room with the Blackbirds. Each time the teacher worked with this set of struggling white students, she sighed, frowned, and sent kids to the principal's office for paddle licks.

As with our first-grade reading lessons, our textbook from fourth-grade history—the year our school integrated—reinforced racial stereotypes and inequalities. A special feature of the book, titled *Know Alabama*, was its second-person writing, with selected chapters addressing readers as "you" and asking them to imagine themselves as children during particular historical moments. The children in these scenes (always white and male) follow an Alabama story that begins with white "pioneer" settlement and ends by explaining the origins of different symbols, such as the state bird (the yellowhammer—not, as one might assume, Harper Lee's mockingbird) and the red St. Andrew's Cross flag that intentionally echoes the familiar Confederate emblem. Along the way, child readers learn that Native Americans were "ignorant savages," African Americans were smiling workers, the Ku Klux Klan was made up of "honest men" who restored "law and order" after the "War Between the States," and "Dixie" is a song that should bring tears to the eyes of "all true Southerners" (in the same way, presumably, that the American flag brought tears to my mother's eyes). Throughout the book, children, even our new Black classmates, were encouraged to take pride in a history that celebrates racist iconography and institutions—in a state that Wallace had called "Cradle of the Confederacy . . . the Heart of the Great Anglo-Saxon Southland."

A good example of *Know Alabama*'s ideology can be found in chapter 8, "Plantation Life," which opens by explaining, "Now we come to one of the happiest ways of life in Alabama before the War Between the States. This is life as it was lived on the Big Plantations. . . . The owners raised thousands of bales of cotton on the big plantations with Negro slaves to help with the work." Here the child-reader imagines himself living in a white-columned antebellum home, being served breakfast by a fat, smiling mammy, and then riding horseback alongside his father to survey the plantation. During their ride they meet enslaved people who like doing what the book calls "help with the work," even though the enslaved are the only ones picking cotton:

> As you ride up beside the Negroes in the field they stop working long enough to look up, tip their hats and say, "Good morning, Master John." You like the friendly way they speak and smile; they show bright rows of white teeth.
>
> "How's it coming, Sam?" your father asks one of the old Negroes.
>
> "Fine, Marse Tom, jes fine. We got 'most more cotton than we can pick."
>
> Then Sam chuckles to himself and goes back to picking just as fast as he can.

The plantation offers opportunities for the child reader beyond watching people work to make him wealthy. This chapter's "you" especially enjoys playing with enslaved children. "You play many games like ball and hide and seek, but the best one is 'Indian,'" the book explains. "One of the little Negro boys is called 'Jig.' He got that name because he dances so well when the Negroes play their banjos. Jig comes up and says, 'Let me play.' And you say, 'All right, but you be the captive Indian.' 'That will be fun,' Jig says, and he goes off gladly to be the Indian, to hide, and to get himself captured." Underneath this chapter's smiles and games is a subtly encoded message not too different from what my fellow students and I received in first grade. Some children are born Bluebirds, in front and in charge. Other birds, the Red and the Black, are born to enjoy enslavement, captivity, and—even though white people like my mom insisted upon their inherent laziness—working much harder.

The only problem, perhaps one Lingo and Wallace believed when they stood in their respective schoolhouse doors and my mother intuited when she wrote protest letters, was that school desegregation made some students realize that the jig was up.

*

Know Alabama was the textbook that our fourth-grade class used in 1970–71, the first year that my elementary school, Robinson, integrated. I don't remember my mother's thoughts on the issue when it was happening; instead, I learned them from looking many years later at the scrapbooks she made for me. What I do remember is being excited that something novel and different would happen at school. Children were IN THE NEWS! When my second-grade teacher Miss White was honored by the state, reporters came to our school to take photographs. I wound up in the paper, pictured with Miss White holding a jump rope that I sailed over, blond hair flying. I was eager, again, to be a celebrity. What could be more praiseworthy than taking it upon myself to make sure Robinson's new children felt welcome?

For my special friendship, I singled out an African American girl named Jane who sat near me in class. I observed her carefully so that I could report on her actions. See, I told the other blond girls, Jane is just like us. She wore shiny loafers, white knee socks, Peter Pan collars, pigtails—only she had four where we had had two. Jane did not stink at all, I said; she smelled like Dial soap and mint toothpaste. She was not ignorant but got all the answers right on tests. (I knew this from peeking at the neat cursive she produced from her row of perfectly sharpened pencils.) She was quiet, I cautioned the white girls, and needed extra help making friends. Jane was so shy, I noticed, that she froze each time I talked to her and looked as if she might cry. To alleviate her fears, I shadowed her in the halls and at recess asking questions to help me get to know her better:

Did you ride a bus here?
Do Negroes get sunburned?
Do Negroes blush?
Can I touch your hair?

It didn't occur to me that Jane might need space from a girl who, in retrospect, followed her around administering daily doses of micro-aggression. Instead, I convinced myself that I was being a good southerner, hospitable and gracious.

If I didn't think then that my own behavior was out of line, I did notice that teachers treated my new classmates differently. One incident from fifth grade, involving a boy named Howard, stands out in particular. I often played with Howard at recess because he was handsome and liked to dance. At home my female cousins and I entertained our parents by pretending to be the Jackson Five. We lined up in front of my grandmother's fireplace to dance and lip-sync to catchy tunes like "I Want You Back" and tender ballads like "I'll Be There." Because my steps were always a beat or two behind those of my more rhythmic cousins, I got stuck on the end, partially hidden behind the corner's decorative plastic plant. I hoped that Howard, who owned a groovy newsboy cap just like Michael's, would be the right person to help me reach the front and center of my cousin band. One day I convinced him to let me wear his hat and play Jacksons in the lunch line. We sang and danced to "ABC":

ABC
Easy as 123
Simple as do re mi
ABC
Baby you and me, girl!

Midway through our routine, our teacher came running up, yelling at us to stop. She snatched Howard's hat off of my head and screamed that I would get head lice. Then she dragged Howard off to the principal's office for paddle licks. I went on through the lunch line, and later Howard's mother moved him to another school.

I didn't question the teacher. Boys, especially Black ones, getting sent to Principal Murphy was a fact of elementary-school life. Once I lay down in the nurse's office with a headache and watched the principal bend three boys over and whack their bottoms multiple times with a two-foot-long wooden paddle. I didn't fear the paddle, myself. Girls typically did not get spanked. Besides, I discovered around the time that if I got caught doing something naughty, all I had to do was open my blue eyes wide and deny it. Once in the school library, a Black teacher named Mrs. Williams asked me to be quiet. Instead of obeying, as I would for a white teacher, I flipped Mrs. Williams my middle finger—the widely understood sign for "fuck you." Mrs. Williams reported me to Mr. Murphy, who called in my mother the next day. "No sir, no ma'am," I told the two of them firmly, shaking my blond hair. "I would never do something like that." And they agreed. Mrs. Williams must have imagined it, they said.

I liked making authority figures believe in my innocence and, after the incident with Mrs. Williams, saw that such power was rooted in blue eyes, blond hair, and white skin. Still, I didn't perceive my actions as part of any larger structure. My power, I believed, was more like a gift, one that came to me, deservedly, by virtue of being a Bluebird. In retrospect, such thinking was less gift than trap. As writer Lillian Smith explains, the mental frameworks that southerners developed to justify white supremacy harmed not only racism's victims but also its perpetrators. Smith states:

> I began to understand slowly at first but more clearly as the years passed, that the warped, distorted frame we have put around every Negro child from birth is around every white child also. Each is on a different side of the frame but each is pinioned there. And I knew that what cruelly shapes and cripples the personality of one is as cruelly shaping and crippling the personality of the other. I began to see that . . . we are stunted and warped and in our lifetime cannot grow straight again any more than can a tree, put in a steel-like twisting frame when young, grow tall and straight when the frame is torn away at maturity.

It was relatively easy for me to understand as wrong how school staff treated kids like Howard. More difficult was the decades-long process of learning how not to participate in the wrongdoing. I can look back now, through the lens of writers like Smith, to see how I degraded my own humanity by not challenging a system that denied other people their dignity. Instead of facing that fact, I looked for ways to justify my actions. Hadn't I displayed perfect southern manners for Jane? And, as for my flipping Mrs. Williams the bird, that was just me being a rebel.

*

Technically, everyone at Robinson Elementary was a Rebel. Our school mascot took its name from the men who fought, during the Civil War, for the Confederacy of states that seceded from the Union to form what Governor Wallace later called the "Great Anglo-Saxon Southland." Our colors were sky blue, like the infantry soldiers' pants, and red, like the field of their battle flag. After the school desegregated in 1970, our sports and cheerleading squads were made up of kids from different races, all rooting for the same team, the Robinson Rebels.

In fifth through seventh grade, I cheered for the basketball team. While the Black and white boys ran the courts, the Black and white girls yelled from the sidelines wearing our sky blue uniforms monogrammed with a big, white "R" and shaking our red and blue pompoms. My favorite cheer—because it ended with the one-leg-folded, one-leg-extended jump that I excelled at, the "herkie"—was "Victory!"

> Victory! Victory! That's our cry!
> V-I-C-T-O-R-Y!
> Will we win it?
> You're doggone right!
> Rebels! Rebels!
> Fight, fight, fight!

Cheerleaders from L. Frazier Banks, where we were zoned for high school, taught us the jumps and shouts. The all-white Banks squad also taught us their fight song, known as the "Southern Special."

> Oh I wish I was in the land of cotton,
> Old times there are not forgotten.
> Give 'em Hell!
> Give 'em Hell!
> Give 'em Hell!
> Frazier L!

When students sang the song during pep rallies for football games at Banks, then one of the state's best teams, a boy circled the gym waving a huge

Confederate battle flag that symbolized "Victory," never quite getting that the score remains USA-1, CSA-0. All students were expected to cheer and, as we had been told since *Know Alabama* in fourth grade, to tear up at the fight song's "Dixie" tune.

Memories of former Banks students vary on what happened during a riot that resulted from flying that flag, and even when it took place.

Some say it was 1971, the year after Mom wrote her letter and the schools finally desegregated. Others claim the riot happened in 1974, when tensions ran high because of football. That year, state champion Banks met its rival Woodlawn in a game with its own racial dynamics. The face-off between Banks's white quarterback, Jeff Rutledge, and Woodlawn's Black running back, "Touchdown Tony" Nathan, packed 42,000 fans into Birmingham's Legion Field. The match-up became the most well-attended high school football game the state has ever seen.

It's entirely possible that both years saw riots.

There is one point of agreement: the fight, whenever it occurred, started at a pep rally, with the Southern Special and the Confederate flag. But did a white football player really hurl a boulder? Did a Black male student really wield a knife? Who was the mysterious Black female with the large Afro, said to be nineteen or twenty, who allegedly stood on a lunchroom table rallying students to revolt? In the chaos, with teenagers pouring from the buildings into the street, no one can quite agree about what happened.

I do know that, by the time I started at Banks in 1975, the flag was gone, and the fight song was changed. And at some point after I left Robinson, my elementary school mascot became the Roadrunners. During the 1980s local demographics shifted. White families began moving out of East Lake, exercising their freedom of choice to send their kids to all-white or mostly white county schools. Robinson today is predominantly African American. Banks High School closed, graduating its last group of seniors in 1989. In 2021 demolition began on the abandoned, decaying building. Former students maintain an active Facebook page that is somewhat racially mixed yet sometimes reminds me of my mother's protest letter. Older white alums wax nostalgic over the Confederate "Victory" flag or complain in uppercase fonts that remind me of my mother's letters about how taking away the "Dixie"-based Southern Special is "REWRITING MY HISTORY." Other former students are glad to see the Confederate relics go. The Facebook page's moderator, a white woman who went into the ministry, reminds the ones up in arms about the fight song that not inflicting positive representations of slavery upon

African American classmates is "basic human decency." Some still do not get it. "Political correctness!" they shout back, and the battle continues.

Some of my classmates have mixed feelings about desegregation. One, a Black woman named Laurette, told me that the experience prepared her to deal with the many different kinds of people she encountered during a long career in corporate America. Conversely, she said that she attended a historically Black college because, after Robinson and Banks, she really needed a break from white people. Thinking back on what I did and what I witnessed during those years, I see her point.

Some white classmates, myself included, are glad that we spent most of our lives in integrated schools. A former neighbor named Connie and I spoke at length about the experience. We debated whether it planted the seed for the antiracist teaching we both practice today, or whether that seed, planted earlier, flourished under desegregation's sunlight. Either way, both of us agreed that when we find ourselves in all-white spaces today, they feel wrong. Connie described her feeling as "impoverished." For me, it's "trapped"—as if I'm stuck inside of Lillian Smith's warping, distorting steel cage.

Some of us also regret our past actions. A sister of a high school friend told me, "Yes, I sang it [the Southern Special]. Not proud now that I did, but I did. I was dumb and a follower. To say that I really didn't get it speaks volumes about my privilege." Like her, I really didn't get it either. If I could journey back to 1970s-era Birmingham, I would rewrite my history with Jane, Howard, and Mrs. Williams. After my experiences on the schoolhouse door's other side, I still had so much more to learn.

5 / "JUST A KID"

Sex, Salvation, and Unanswered Questions

I wish that I could say I was born woke. That I sprang from a line of superhuman beings who gifted me the powers to fight for truth, justice, and the American way.

A socially conscious Wonder Woman.

I certainly would not complain about looking smokin' hot, like Lynda Carter or Gal Gadot, in a gold tiara and a red, white, and blue bustier.

This book would have been easier to write if I could trace my development as a superhero through epic battles of good and evil that ended with me clocking the bad guy upside the head with my bracelets of submission.

But memoir binds the writer within another of Wonder Woman's weapons: the lasso of truth. I'm compelled to admit that I'm no superhero. I'm not even a regular hero. I'm more like a subhero: chunky, short, dorky, not at all a good person.

I did not come to study the Civil Rights Movement through a concern with racism. More accurately, the opposite happened: I became aware of racism, especially my own, through studying the Civil Rights Movement. Leading me there was a growing awareness of the history beneath the history, of stories that existed apart from official narratives. The route out of the *Know Alabama* world into which I was born was painfully slow. It started with the dangerous on-ramps of gender and sexuality, detoured through class and religion, wound circuitously around questions of right and wrong, and hit pothole after pothole of violence.

Being a Wonder Woman had nothing to do with it.

But in the beginning, Barbie played a starring role.

*

By September of 1971, my schoolmates and I had survived our first year of desegregation only to face the next challenge seeping up from Birmingham's dirty history: pollution. Smog from the city's steel industry settled on the skyline like a yellow-gray blanket. By the year's end, a federal judge would order the worst mills to clean up or shut down. In the meantime our class's handful of asthmatic kids had to play inside or, as I had many times, endure a hospital stay under an oxygen tent.

One day, a red-haired, freckled girl in a plaid jumper joined me on the gym bleachers during fifth-grade recess. She coughed. I wheezed. A friendship was set.

Soon Kelly was coming over to my house most days after school to play Barbies. I liked playing Barbies with Kelly because she had a Ken. I had two Barbies, one a bee-hived "Bubblecut," made in the early 1960s, that seemed to me hopelessly ugly and old-fashioned, and another new, early-1970s model with long blond hair stylishly flipped. This Barbie got to wear the latest outfits: the white go-go boots, the minidress in multicolored Day-Glo stripes, and the fur-lined gold lamé coat. Ken preferred her too. Poor Bubblecut spent most of her time shut inside the pink-and-white Barbie house, wearing the clothes hand-sewn from cast-off calicos and seersuckers that my grandmother taught me to make in order to save money.

During an early play date, Kelly and I sat on my bedroom's shag rug, in blue and green like a peacock's tail, sharing secrets that we vowed to keep forever. Most of mine I had inscribed on my closet door's back side:

8. A Birmingham steel mill emitting smoke. Image courtesy of the Birmingham Public Library Archives.

"Julie loves Donny" (Osmond)

"Julie loves Donny" (the drugstore delivery boy)

"Julie loves Ricky" (the paper boy)

"Julie loves Michael" (Jackson, my idea of taboo).

Kelly giggled that I was "boy-crazy." Then she asked if Ken and Barbie could screw.

"Sure," I consented. I thought "screw" meant he would take care of some Barbie-house chores.

"Here's how you do it," Kelly said, in a flurry of removing tiny high-heels and fluorescent polyester clothes. Soon Ken was atop the 1970s Barbie, who demonstrated the model's bendable leg function.

"Look. Ken puts his dick inside Barbie's pussy and moves it in and out, in and out." Kelly banged the two dolls together.

I scooted away, blue eyes wide-angled. "Why?"

"So Ken can shoot his jizz inside her."

"What? Why?" I did not like Ken and Barbie's actions. They were supposed to walk around a plastic house, hold plastic hands, and talk fashion—not smack into each other faster and faster.

"So Ken can shoot his jizz inside her. The white stuff that comes out of his dick. That's what guys do to show girls they're pretty."

"Who told you that?"

I wanted to vomit on the peacock carpet.

Kelly handed Barbie back to me and started dressing Ken.

"My brother Jimmy and I have been screwing since I was eight."

I had never met her brother. Kelly and I played at my house because she shuttled between the homes of parents, stepparents, and grandparents. I didn't know which house Jimmy lived in or which school he attended, only that he was older. I envisioned him looking like a life-sized plastic Ken doll, straight-legged and clacking on top of my best friend, her red hair coiffed in a Barbie flip, her freckled white face frozen in a plastic Barbie smile. I pictured myself hidden safely inside the plastic house, my face buried in scratchy homemade granny clothes.

Over the next couple of months, Kelly shared other secrets. She told me that I could make myself feel very good by putting toys into my pussy—the hard plastic ends of jump ropes or even Barbies. Thinking about doing these things made me feel curious, sometimes juicy, but mostly terrified. I imagined Bubblecut Barbie getting permanently stuck between my legs or, worse, growing in my stomach like a swallowed watermelon seed then sprouting tendrils from my ears, nose, and mouth. Kelly told me that Donny, the drugstore delivery boy, would take me riding in his car if I gave him something called a "blow job." Her description did not inspire me. Jizz sounded like mayonnaise left out after last summer's picnic, and it was not going into my mouth even for the promise of a Mustang ride. Kelly also told me how to catch boys' eyes using the cheerleader jumps and shouts we practiced in front of school each morning.

"Spot me," she would say when a member of the eighth-grade pack glanced at us during our "Victory!" cries. I readied my arms for a rescue if her standing backbend went wrong, but it never did. Kelly had perfected the art of arching backward until her palms met the sidewalk, her skirt flipping above her waist, her white cotton panties greeting the city's filthy air.

In early December, Kelly set us up with two of the boys to screw. I was scared but excited because I had been eyeing one of them, Lee, for weeks. He dared to wear his dark hair well past his collar. He had pale blue eyes like a wolf. Lee lived in a poorer neighborhood on the north side of our elementary school, just past a long block of houses that the city had condemned, bought out, and slated for destruction with giant red Xs to make room for a new interstate. The very thought of crossing that red, X-marked boundary, past a chain-link fence into a scrubby yard, and then into a shotgun house—the very phrase sounding like a place an outlaw might live—where I would transform into a naughty cigarette-smoking Barbie left to the mercy of a handsome boy unsupervised, left me breathless.

Lee and Mike, one of Kelly's boyfriends, sat behind me in study hall. As our planned screwing got closer, I practiced piano for the upcoming Christmas recital silently on my desk but could not make myself turn around to look at either of them. Each day for that classroom hour, I kept my eyes forward on the piano book's illustrated keyboard, my fingers furiously banging out the notes to "Good King Wenceslas" on the wooden desktop. I sensed the boys' eyes burning into my hunched-over back, heard their snickers and farts, and, finally one day, felt their spitballs pelleting the long blond hair that fell below my waist. Then a frustrated teacher exorcised them both to the principal's office for paddle licks and detention. They never returned to study hall, shutting the window on my naughty-Barbie opportunity.

When the time came for the piano recital, I sat again humiliated, parent and teacher eyes burning into my still-hunched-over back, my fingers recalling not one note of "Good King Wenceslas."

At some point before the school year ended, my mother informed me that Kelly and I could no longer be friends. I don't know what prompted Mom's decision. Maybe she overheard us sharing secrets. Maybe I shouldn't have told her that Kelly and I planned to be prostitutes when we grew up because men would pay us to go on dates. Maybe I shouldn't have shown my cousin Tracy, three years my junior, what dolls could do atop Barbie houses. Whatever happened, Mom put her foot down firmly using her most effective parenting tool.

"I'll buy you anything you want."

"Even record albums?" My mother usually refused me 45s, much less albums. She didn't want to waste her meager secretary's salary on the musical whims of a preteen. More to the point, her own mother, whose house we lived in, believed that rock and roll was Satanic. Perhaps Kelly and I had to stop being friends because Granny had caught us on the front-porch swing giggling at photos of David Cassidy in *Tiger Beat* and *Sixteen*. The worst offender was a May 1972 profile of Cassidy in *Rolling Stone*, where Annie Leibovitz photographed the teen idol nearly nude for the cover. Inside, the story "Naked Lunch Box" (a play on the title of a book by William S. Burroughs, also interviewed in the magazine) featured a shirtless Cassidy in low-cut jeans that showed off a thin line of hair running from his navel to where his thumbs pointed through his belt loops. Granny told us that looking at such magazines would send us to Hell, made me put them into the trash, and, after Kelly went home, burned the trash in a galvanized steel garbage can in the alley behind our house.

The Monday after my record-album Judas deal, I told Kelly at lunch that we could no longer be friends.

"But why?" she repeated, crying.

Mom didn't help me rehearse the part where I listened to my best friend sob while I blundered through excuses.

"Because my mom said so."

"Because you're not a nice girl."

"Because she bought me three albums if I promised not to be friends with you anymore."

"Fuck you, bitch," Kelly said, pushing her lunch tray across the table and into mine.

After she ran off, I sat alone, strawberry-red Jello dribbling down the front of my sky-blue cheerleader uniform, feeling Kelly's words flame up my neck and face. That afternoon, when I got home, both Barbies went into their plastic house and the back of the closet, along with never-listened-to copies of *The Osmonds*, the Jackson Five's *ABC*, and Three Dog Night's *It Ain't Easy*.

*

A few years later, I had many new friends at my grandmother's Southern Baptist church. Our charismatic youth minister, Bill, tapped into the national evangelical fervor known as the Jesus Movement and its young-adult spin-off, Campus Crusade for Christ, to build a large, active teen group. Campus Crusade, still operating today under the name "Cru," was founded in California during the 1950s as a ministry to college students. During the 1970s Campus Crusade grew exponentially as a conservative, evangelical response to the previous decade's left-leaning youth countercultural movements. The Cru website describes its watershed moment as "Explo 72," a 1972 evangelical conference in Dallas, which billed itself as the "Christian Woodstock" and drew more than eighty thousand attendees. The event paved the way for a Campus Crusade media blitz. According to Cru, the 1976 "I Found It!" billboard and bumper-sticker campaign—"It" being salvation—reached 85 percent of the US population, leading three million souls to salvation. Although such reports seem exaggerated, Campus Crusade drew from a wide, oddly diverse swath of Americans: former Black Panther Eldridge Cleaver was baptized at the organization's Arrowhead Springs headquarters, and former California governor/US president Ronald Reagan attended a Bel Air church pastored by a Campus Crusade convert. Such bedfellows were hardly strange in 1976, what *Newsweek* magazine called "The Year of the Evangelicals."

The movement worked by giving teens something to fill the hours and something to occupy the hormones. Our particular church rechanneled the era's celebration of sex, drugs, and rock and roll into Jesus, Jesus, and more Jesus. We had service twice on Sundays, not counting Sunday School, an extra teen-education session called Training Union on Mondays, another service with dinner on Wednesdays, choir practice on Thursdays, an open gym for playing basketball and hanging out on Fridays, quarterly youth retreats, and yearly mission trips to the sugar-sand beaches of the Florida Panhandle's "Redneck Riviera" to witness for the Lord.

Some of the ideas we learned in church were downright kooky. As fundamentalist Christians, our elders warned us away from alcohol and other vices. ("Why don't Southern Baptists have sex standing up?" goes the joke: "Because it might lead to dancing.") In Training Union, Bill explained how yoga and meditation similarly opened doors that allowed Satan inside to overtake the soul.

Some ideas were more pernicious.

In the early 1970s, our congregation voted that women should not wear slacks to church. God, in His infinite wisdom, had created clear divisions between the sexes, Bill said, that our clothing should reflect. Along with pants, off-limits for women were preaching, doctoring, lawyering, and any other jobs that God set aside for men.

Around the same time, another vote considered whether the church would allow nonwhite visitors. Behind all the hands raised for "no" were pews full of people who believed that race mixing—like rock and roll, Eastern religions, or women in britches—was a pathway to Hell.

Few of us questioned the racism and sexism that poisoned our minds as sure as Birmingham's filthy air fouled our lungs. In this instance my mom was the voice of reason. Hardly an integrationist, she did bristle at the skirts-only rule and especially at my pronouncement after one Training Union session that football fans, not evangelicals, were the real fanatics.

"You tell that church," she said, invoking a University of Alabama Crimson Tide cheer, "that they can 'rammer jammer yellow hammer' right up my ass."

Sometimes I agreed with her, but I still kept going to church—to a point.

The sense of community that it offered was powerful. Each youth group meeting began with teens standing, joining hands in prayer. Every prayer ended with heads bowed, eyes closed, and index fingers pointing up, "One Way!" We harmonized songs like "Kumbaya" and "Pass It On":

It only takes a spark
To get a fire going
And soon all those around
Can warm up in its glowing
That's how it is with God's love
Once you've experienced it
You want to share
You want to pass it on.

With "Pass It On," we lit candles from each other's flames. When the song was over, we extinguished the flames and hugged. The light burned in our hearts. As an outward sign of inward grace, we wore matching white jerseys with green letters that read "ΙΧΘΥΣ." The letters spelled out *ichthys*, the Greek word for "fish" and formed a pseudo-Greek acrostic, "Jesus Christ, God's Son, Savior." One sees them today most frequently on bumper stickers inside an outline referred to, derisively, as the "Jesus Fish." Bill ordered the shirts to remind teens that we, like Jesus's disciples, were to be "fishers of men." We wore our jerseys when we circulated around town to hand out religious tracts and give our personal testimony of salvation.

We had a Christian duty, Bill said, to counteract Satan's work by spreading God's word. As a group, we divided the Bible into sections to memorize so we could be ready to battle those forces in the end-times. The impending Apocalypse would bring book burnings and Christian persecutions. My selection was the apostle Paul's famous treatise from I Corinthians 13 ("love is patient, love is kind . . ."). I hoped that memorizing a passage on love would help my dating life, for I was hardly succeeding as a fisher of men.

At fifteen I remained hopelessly romantic and desperately unscrewed. Bill assigned us Hal Lindsey's bestselling *Late, Great Planet Earth* to show how signs pointed toward the end-times (a story that I did not quite understand involving the USSR, Israel, earthquakes, and tornadoes), and I did not want Jesus to Rapture me up to Heaven for eternal life as a lonely virgin. Make no mistake: Campus Crusade pushed Salvation Jesus, and Salvation Jesus was David Cassidy/rock-star hot. Young women and men alike hummed along to *Godspell*'s "Day by Day" and *Jesus Christ Superstar*'s "I Don't Know How to Love Him," while fantasizing about long-haired, poetic lovers who carried torturous burdens. A new name on the back of my closet door was Daniel, of the John Lennon glasses and pawn-worn guitar. I knew his personal testimony by heart. His downward slide began with disobedience, then smoking, then booze. He hit rock bottom with drugs, but Jesus lifted him up with salvation and music. He led us in "Kumbaya" and, when Bill was not around, the Eagles' "Peaceful, Easy Feeling." Following that song's lyrics, I very much wanted to sleep with him in the desert at night, and I worked actively at wooded youth retreats to get him alone so that we could swap testimonies. But Daniel was in college and uninterested in younger girls. His soulful brown eyes never came close to meeting my hopeful blues. A baby-voiced Beth or a lithe Lisa always beat me to him. I would be left standing alone, *Living Bible* in hand, while the two of them strolled off to a secluded spot beneath the pines to kneel down in prayer.

I resigned myself that it was not God's will that we should be together, for He knew that I contemplated sin in my heart. The Bible told me "The wages of sin are death" (Romans 6:23). I knew them viscerally to be fire—not the fire of Hell, but the blaze of guilt and shame, and the slow, dry smolder of emptiness inside.

During that year, a new figure slid into this hot mix of sin and salvation. He was tall, thin, about five years older, wearing flared jeans, paisley polyester shirts, blond curls cut short, aviator glasses, and a big wooden cross around his neck. The Jesus freak look didn't fool me. I knew that he was the Devil the moment I heard his name: Brother Jim.

Jimmy.

Brother of Kelly.

Bill loved him. Held him up as the kind of Christian we all should be: pious, abstinent. Jim was training for the ministry at a local Bible college. When Brother McKee, our televangelist-style preacher, frenzied himself up to the fiery-pits-of-hell part of each week's sermon, Jim shouted, "Praise the Lord!" louder than anyone else.

During Sunday Service, our youth group sat on the sanctuary's right side. Jim sat near the front, and I sat a few rows back. "Get thee behind me Satan," Bill taught us to say whenever we saw trouble coming. In this case I thought it best to avoid the Devil's sight lines.

Every "Praise the Lord!" that Jim shouted clacked like plastic on plastic.

Every "Amen, Brother!" he cried out burned like the slap of "Bitch!" against my cheek.

I'm certain that memorizing Bible passages for the end-times was supposed to have a different result. But there I was, like Paul himself on the road to Damascus: the fishy scales fell right off my eyes.

I could see that this church was a lie.

That the adults around me had been lying for all of my life.

That I, too, belonged to this vast network of liars.

I betrayed my friend when she needed a friend. And I lied about Jesus. I pretended to believe in the personal Lord and Savior, who stood outside my heart-door knocking to be let in. I never told Bill or Brother McKee, even when he dunked me under the water for baptism, that I opened the door many times, but Jesus stood me up.

When teens practiced giving our testimony at youth retreats, I said vague things about sassing my momma, snatching candy from Donny's drugstore, or fibbing to teachers about homework before Jesus taught me to walk the path of righteousness. And now that I had found the One Way! I was so Blessed! Praise the Lord!

But none of that was true.

I wanted to fit in. I thought the ΙΧΘΥΣ jerseys made me part of a team. I was a lonely only child: an awkward teen, sexualized too soon, desperate to be warmed by anyone's glowing. Donny, Daniel, God, whoever.

Face to face with my guilt and shame, I blamed Jim. If my Jesus-lie was bad, his sex-lie was worse. He was the Father of Lies.

God blamed Adam, Adam blamed Eve, Eve blamed the Serpent: I learned how to deflect responsibility from the Bible's first book.

My teenage ideas about justice were fairly simple: eye for an eye. While Jim sat in church shouting, "Amen, Brother!" at every pause, I lurked behind, wishing him into a fiery Hell, gripping the wooden pew, and chanting silently, "Die, Jim, die."

It took a few years.

I stopped going to church when Bill said that the end-times were just around the corner and we needed to throw our record albums into a bonfire to show Jesus we were ready to be Raptured out of the fallen world. I chose Bob Dylan and Bruce Springsteen, and because the apostle Paul made a lasting impression, reading.

So it was the newspaper, not my former church, that told me Jim was driving home from the Bible college one night when a drunk driver hit him head-on. He left behind a wife, a baby, and a sister.

I knew when I saw the obituary that God had listened, specifically, to me. How odd to feel a familiar, painful burn in my heart at the moment of answered prayer.

*

Today, the Barbies sit in my University of South Florida office. Bubblecut wears the Day-Glo minidress, Bendy-Legs the gold lamé. Nearby are the various Wonder Woman tchotchkes—an oversize coffee mug, a golden plastic tiara—that students have given me over the years. I'm no superhero, I remind them, although I do like wearing those socks featuring tiny blue capes. All I do is teach people to ask questions.

During the early 2000s, I began asking specifically about Kelly, Jim, and my experience with religion. The few church friends I remained in touch with didn't remember Jim. That isn't unusual. The 1970s evangelical fervor brought in dozens of passionate front-row Christians who soon moved on to other places—more liberal faiths or back into sin.

Bill moved on as well, to a new life as a motivational speaker and out gay man. I found his website, where he talks about surviving his harsh background in fundamentalist Christianity and apologizes for any harm he caused. He was battling cancer, so I emailed him. I didn't ask about Jim. I didn't feel like confronting a sick man who was already trying to atone for a difficult past. Instead, I told him that our youth group's study of the Bible—the memorizing and analyzing—ultimately led me to become a writer and a literature professor. I wished him peace, although I've hardly found my own.

I doubt that I could ever make amends to Kelly for not sticking by her when she most needed help. Still, I hope (pray?) that she found a way to heal.

A school friend told me she saw her a few years back eating lunch in a downtown diner. Kelly was sitting with a group of people all wearing the same polo-style work shirts. Her long, red hair had turned gray. She was wrinkled and smoking. "Rode hard and put away wet," is how we describe women like Kelly, the same words we use for a maltreated horse.

The classmate tried to convince me that I blamed the wrong victim, that the younger sister seduced the older brother. Thinking of Kelly that way felt grotesque and cruel, heaping more abuse onto what she had suffered. I already did that in elementary school and should know better now. Looking back, I can see that Kelly exhibited symptoms typical of children who have been sexually assaulted: keeping secrets, excessive knowledge of sexual topics, exhibiting age-inappropriate sexual behavior.

I can also see why someone of my generation might consider such acting out to be its own form of aggression. Attitudes about sexual abuse during the 1960s and 1970s differed from those of today. As girls we were encouraged from our first Barbies to make ourselves attractive and available, but not too much. Spread-eagle jumps that showed off your cheerleading bloomers were acceptable. Doing a backbend that showed off your white cotton panties made you a slut. Knowing how to navigate the line between naughty and nice was the girl's responsibility. It's not Humbert Humbert's fault for being a pedophile; it's Lolita's—the title character from Vladimir Nabokov's 1955 novel—for being a "nymphet." Dozens upon dozens of popular songs from the time period sent a similar message. Consider the 1968 hit from Gary Puckett and the Union Gap, where it's the "Young Girl" who needs to get out of the singer's mind, not the singer who needs to rein in his thoughts. A "baby in disguise," she is supposed to know that being alone with him is wrong, but she persists, with that "come-on look" in her eyes.

"Jailbait songs" is its own search-engine term, referring to music about girls under the age of consent who will potentially get the singer into legal trouble for succumbing to their "come-on" looks. Many of these songs suggest that doing time is worth the crime. "Fifteen may get you twenty," Jimmy Buffett sang in 1978, "but that's alright."

No wonder my grandmother thought rock and roll was evil. Maybe Bill was right to encourage me to burn those records. On the other hand, he also believed Brother Jim was a role model.

The refrain to the mournful hymn of Kelly and Jim is a question: what did the adults around us know, what did they cover up, and what did they pretend not to see because it was too ugly, or inconvenient, to confront?

As a child, I was taught about the stereotypical stranger with candy, but not how sexual abuse usually happens. One out of every six women in the US will be the victim of a completed or attempted rape in her lifetime. Over 90 percent of childhood sexual assault survivors know their perpetrators. I know very few women my age who grew up without an older male family member or a neighbor that they feared: the ones who called us "girlfriend," who wanted us to kiss them, sit on their laps, or give them hugs while they ever so lightly grazed their hands across our budding breasts. My mom used to fuss at me, call me "rude," for pushing away such men.

But adults back then knew better—or else "fifteen may get you twenty" would not have been a familiar saying in addition to a popular song lyric. According to Alabama laws on the books during the 1970s, anyone convicted for carnal knowledge of a girl younger than twelve should be sentenced to no less than ten years in prison. Even minors, like Jimmy, could have been prosecuted for statutory rape by engaging in sex with someone two years younger. Kelly told me that she and her brother had been screwing since she was eight.

One of my writer friends, Jesse, remembers Jim from back then. They used to play basketball in the church's gym.

"He was just a kid," Jesse said. "Then one day he changed. I thought it was all the Jesus stuff. He started wearing a big wooden cross around his neck."

They stopped being friends after that. Jesse couldn't tell me much more.

After talking to Jesse, I tracked down Jim's high school yearbook at the downtown public library. During my youth, when my grandmother didn't have me in church, my mom sent me here. The reading room is its own cathedral: two stories high, with a vaulted ceiling trimmed in gold leaf and supported by square columns of warm oak. Literary-themed murals—Don Quixote, King Arthur, Dante and Virgil, Faust, Krishna, Scheherazade—line part of the upper level. On the remaining side are picture windows that refract the southern sun. Surrounded by old-fashioned card catalogs, and the rows of bookshelves that contain Birmingham's history, I held Jim's senior picture up to the light. He looked exactly how I remembered him, and more: wooden cross, blond hair cut short, aviator glasses, sweet-faced, smiling. Just a kid, like Jesse said. I would use the word "innocent" if I didn't know another story. Even so, I don't have all the facts. If Kelly was acting out, then maybe he was, too. It's probable that they both were abused.

The thought brought to mind a sermon that my current priest gave on the Ten Commandments. Like many who walked through the valley of 1970s evangelicalism, I left the church but came back decades later, revolving through the Unitarian Universalists, the Quakers and, for now, Episcopalians. Shortly before my library trip, Mother Josie Rose spoke about ways of interpreting the fifth commandment, "Thou shalt not kill."

Mother Rose asked, "How many times have we destroyed someone's dream? Devastated their humanity?"

How many times, I asked myself in the library, did adults around me model soul murder? How did they teach me to become a killer myself?

Jimmy's picture provided me no answers, nor did the figures from the world's best literature—frozen in silence along the library walls. From the sunlight streaming through the windows, no illumination. Only motes floating in suspension of an old building's musty air.

6 / THE TRANSGENDER WARRIOR
JODY FORD

In the summer of 1973, just before seventh grade, my cousin Patti and I made a pact to be forever weird. The pinky promise was unnecessary, for we had been odd ducks throughout our childhoods and would stay that way into our adult years.

Patti and her two sisters, Vicki and Cindi, were the daughters of my mom's oldest brother, Walter, a corporate gypsy who moved to a different suburb every few years as he climbed the company ladder. Just when the girls made friends in Little Rock, the family moved to Kansas City, where another set of friends would soon be replaced by those in Indianapolis and, later, Memphis. They were the perpetual new kids in class, whose accents and fashion choices never quite fit what locals thought was normal.

Each summer Uncle Walter and his wife, my Aunt Janis, dropped off Patti and her sisters with the grandparents for two weeks so they could catch a break from three kids. Their visit was one of my few social outlets. I lived with my grandmother and mother in an eastern Birmingham neighborhood populated primarily by widows. Granny, still terrified of the "big city" after moving from a rural area thirty years earlier, confined my solo walks to a two-block radius in all directions. On my bike the limits were tighter: I could ride up and down the sidewalk in front of our house—but no turning corners or crossing streets. When I strayed, as I often did, to cruise past the houses of cute boys, the widow-network called my grandmother to fetch me. Thus, I spent a large chunk of my school years lurking furtively behind oak trees like a long-haired Boo Radley, hoping to glimpse my beloved before Granny drove up honking her Chevy's horn.

My redheaded cousins, whom I considered wild and worldly because they had lived "up North," helped me pass the time in other ways. With them I was allowed to walk each day to the drugstore (more than doubling my range), where we bought Cokes and Zotz, a fizzy candy that we would feed to a nearby German shepherd in order to watch his brow furrow when he bit into it. We double-dog-dared each other to ring the doorbell of Miss Buckley, the neighbor whose translucent white skin and red-lipstick-stained teeth led us to believe her a witch. We snuck Filter King Kools from Mom's purse then called high school boys on the phone and invited them to smoke with us on Granny's front-porch swing. From there it was a short slide into thinking of ourselves as outlaws.

Patti and I especially had trouble fitting in with our peers. We were both chubby, unlike our schools' slender prom queens in training. We had potty mouths, muttering "damn" and "shit" at church when the nice Christian girls praised the Lord. We liked music that other kids found weird, Todd Rundgren's deconstructed pop and Elton John's gender-bending stage get-ups. We laughed too much and too loud, refusing our parents' admonitions to act like ladies. That seventh-grade summer marked our refusal of ladyhood altogether. Instead, we would dress like boys—Converse All-Stars, T-shirts, and jeans (a radical decision given my church's stance on women wearing pants). Then, come next vacation, we would report back to each other on how kids at school reacted.

The experiment didn't pan out as expected. Our peers ignored us as the strange, socially marginal girls we remained. But we both grew up just fine. Patti married a Memphis rocker (with a Rundgren tune as their wedding song), divorced, dated a few women, raised a Nashville rocker, and climbed the corporate ladder like her dad. I wound up marrying the southern lady's sworn enemy, a Yankee, adopting a gay foster-care kid, and climbing the academic ladder, unlike anyone I had ever met before going to college.

Before seventh grade was over, however, my Patti-pact led me to encounter a real gender outlaw: the popular hairdresser known around Birmingham as "Ms. Sid."

*

Jody Suzanne "Ms. Sid" Ford was born Sidney McFerrin Ford on May 17, 1935, in Nashville, Tennessee. She died in Birmingham on April 4, 1977, from a close-range bullet to the chest. By that time she was a local celebrity and owner of a fashionable salon on the city's bohemian Southside, Ms. Sid's Coiffures.

My mother took me to Ford's salon just before school started in 1973, after I begged to get my waist-length blond hair cut. Mom had been getting bleach-and-bouffant jobs there for years, using a stylist other than Ford. She allowed me "short" hair, meaning just below my shoulders, only if I would sit through the stylist's lessons on blow-dryers and hot rollers. I also came away from the experience wearing glittery blue eye shadow and enough pink blush and lipstick to make me look, if not like a clown version of myself, then some quirky mashup of tomboy and pageant princess. I didn't mind, for the stylist (whose name I don't remember) called me "beautiful" and made me feel, like those cousin visits, worldly.

Mom prepared me ahead of time to enter the worldliness of Ms. Sid's Coiffures by describing it as "modern." Her notion of modern meant that the men who cut hair there carried purses. For southerners like us, such a notion was "funny," meaning a word we didn't use in polite conversation, "queer." But Mom said that people in places like New York thought that a man carrying a purse was normal, implying that I should think it normal, too. She also prepared me to see the shop's owner, whom she described as a woman who used to be a man. While this was out of the ordinary, she said, a lot of people in Europe were changing their sex. She told me that the process involved an operation, which I imagined being something like her recent hysterectomy, except afterward, instead of getting hot flashes, women grew "dickies" and men grew "boobies." Mom finished her explanation with a warning: "Don't stare; it's not polite."

Of course I stared, as Jody Ford—at 6'4" and well over two hundred pounds, with long, wavy hair, breasts, and high heels—emerged from a darkened back room, strolled past the hairdresser's chair, and then wafted out the salon door into the sunlight.

Locals remember Ford as intimidating and compassionate, but mostly as a larger-than-life presence who commanded the spaces through which she passed.

A former client named Michael told me, "I was always a little scared of Sid. She was the tallest woman I had ever seen and her hair was sort of Morticia Addams [from *The Addams Family* television show], dark brown with one white strip going down the side. She was also a little loud, and not one bit ashamed of who and what she was."

Once, Michael and Ford went out for dinner after a haircut. The server took Michael's drink order, gestured at Ford, and asked, "What does *he* want?"

Ford stood up, towering over the server, and screamed, "He, he . . . where do you see a HE?"

Ford then spent the next hour patiently answering all of Michael's questions about transitioning from male to female.

"She was very kind to a wide-eyed kid," he told me.

Another Birmingham resident named Jim recalls passing Ford striding purposefully down the city's main business strip, Twentieth Street, in the late 1960s, wearing a tailored woman's suit, high-heeled pumps, hair flowing down her back, and a full beard.

More than fifty years later, such a look is a staple for a television darling like *Queer Eye*'s Jonathan Van Ness. Back then it earned Ford catcalls and threats.

One former customer recalled on a social media site getting her hair cut at Ms. Sid's when a truckload of young men waving a Confederate flag passed by and threw a brick through the window. People in the salon tried to persuade Ford to call the police.

"No," she said. "They are just children. They learn this from their parents. . . . The ignorance doesn't begin with them."

Activist Leslie Feinberg calls people like Ford "transgender warriors." Ford insisted on being seen as fully human during a time that many Americans considered transsexuals and transvestites (words in currency then) to be mentally ill or, worse, criminally dangerous. Ford risked her livelihood and her life defending her right to be herself.

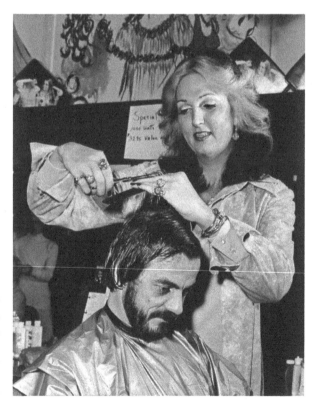

9. Jody Ford styling hair in her Five Points South salon. Copyright 1975. The Birmingham News. All rights reserved. Used with permission.

Still today, in a supposedly more progressive contemporary moment, being transgender means crossing an identity boundary—sex—that many believe to be fundamental, and fixed. As a result, even trans-warriors with fashionable hair salons face fear and misunderstanding.

An August 1973 newspaper profile shows Ford going public with her most effective teaching tool: humanizing her physical presence. Ford told the *Birmingham Post-Herald*'s Kay Kent that she knew from childhood she was female, even though her body was male.

She tried following a traditionally male path for the first decades of her life. As Sid she played basketball at the faith-based David Lipscomb College, married, had a son, divorced, and did a stint in the army. In 1962 she played briefly for the Miami Bombers, part of the semiprofessional Florida Football League. In 1965 she moved to Birmingham, via New Orleans, with the popular regional jazz singer "Big Freada" Wallace. Shortly afterward, she married a woman named Wanda and set up shop as Mr. Sid.

The *Post-Herald* article profiled Ford's process of undergoing what was then called a "sex change" and featured a photograph of her on a ladder installing the salon's new sign, which read, "Ms. Sid's Coiffures"—an image of a strong, proud woman that is, unfortunately, too grainy to reproduce. Another image, from a *Birmingham News* follow-up two years later, shows her cutting a client's hair.

Paralleling Sid's life was a countercultural explosion. In 1952 Christine Jorgensen's transition made headline news. Jorgensen traveled to Copenhagen for sex reassignment—or, more humanely, gender confirmation—surgery. By the 1960s Johns Hopkins University, Stanford University, and University of California Los Angeles (UCLA) established clinics in the US. In 1969 drag queen Marsha P. Johnson and others led an uprising at Greenwich Village's Stonewall Inn that became known as the opening salvo of the gay rights movement. Gay men and women, drag queens, cross-dressers, and other gender benders were living more openly, "out of the closet," not only in cities like New York but also in places like Birmingham.

Burgeoning acceptance did not mean that the living was easy.

Although "sex change" became a household term during the 1950s, people like Ford could not discuss their needs openly for at least another two decades. In *Crossing: A Memoir*, Deirdre McCloskey points to 1960s phenomena such as the magazine *Transvestia* and the clandestine organization Tri-Ess as lifesaving networks for people who felt as if their interior experience did not line up with the "M" or "F" a doctor assigned them at birth.

Finding a niche outside such early trans-networks was also difficult. Lumping together lesbians, gay men, bisexuals, and trans people into one LGBTQ+ acronym does not mean that all the letters get along. Ford said that she sought community, not always successfully, among artists and gay people.

"I went into the homosexual world and found right away that I didn't belong," Ford told the *Post-Herald*. "I was more of a misfit there than I am in the straight world, even with everyone knowing what I am."

Note the use of "what" in her statement, rather than "who." Ford was well aware that she was not perceived as a person, a "he" or a "she," but an "it"—an object of derision or, at best, morbid curiosity. *Don't stare*, Mom said.

No matter what the pronoun, Ford also did some jail time, according to her family and friends.

Crackdowns on Birmingham's LGBTQ+ residents were particularly harsh during the 1960s. As I read when researching information about Mom's cousin David, news accounts from the time describe the regular "pervert patrols" that Bull Connor ordered police to conduct at local nightspots and public restrooms. In early 1967 Alabama governor George Wallace appointed a commission to study sex crimes. Among the group's recommendations was a statewide registry to include those arrested for offenses as varied as rape, child molestation, obscenity, indecent conduct or language, and the more amorphous "disturbing women." On the books until 1975 was Alabama's Criminal Sexual Psychopath Law, which stated that a sex criminal could be confined to a mental hospital until cured. A scary prospect considering that "sex criminal" meant anyone from a murderous pedophile to a gay man to a heterosexual cross-dresser.

The brutal catch-22: one needed, at the time, a mental health diagnosis to qualify for gender surgery. Ford had hers at UCLA Medical Center not long after the *Post-Herald* article, between 1973 and 1974. The official journey began in a psychiatrist's office, where the doctor wrote, "mentally a normal woman—but an abnormal man."

That journey did not end, as most cis- (or not trans-) gender people imagine, with "the operation." Surgery, as McCloskey points out, is just one item that one can select, or not, from a very long list. Ford's looked something like this:

See psychiatrist
Take female hormones
Remove unwanted hair on face and chest with electrolysis
Live full-time as a woman for at least two years

Hire attorney

Change name (Jody Susan? Jody Suzanne?)

Change business name

Change business license

Get trans i.d. card (see *Trans Liberation Newsletter*)

Buy makeup (Dermablend works well on five o'clock shadows)

Learn to apply makeup that looks natural

Replace wardrobe (Cook & Love Shoes in Memphis for size 13)

Buy wigs

Get plastic surgery on cheekbones and Adam's apple

Lose weight

Replace penis with vagina

Dilate new vagina and new urethra daily

Buy lots of pads for bleeding

Get antibiotics for infections

Relearn how to sit

Relearn how to stand

Relearn how to walk

Relearn how to talk (tell stories not jokes, remember details about people, listen)

Relearn manners (let men open doors and pull out your chair, insist on being "ma'am")

Relearn unconscious gestures (smile at other women, pay attention to children, talk with your hands but not too exaggerated, close your legs when you sit, check your hair often, play casually with your jewelry, sit up straight, help clean up when the party is over, try not to take up space).

Aside from running a successful business, Ford found the work of following social codes for southern women to be its own full-time job. She failed in some aspects, like taking up space. In others she succeeded better than many of us who were raised, since birth, to be ladies. She made herself beautiful, walked in heels without tottering (a feat I never accomplished), and offered her story with style and grace to those who asked politely.

If the first question that people like Michael and the *Post-Herald*'s Kay Kent had about transitioning involved "the operation," a second centered on costs. This answer also gets complicated.

One level is financial. Now, as in Ford's time, transitioning costs don't differ too greatly from those of an automobile. The more one does on the list, the more expensive it gets, with prices running from used Ford to new Ferrari. Insurance companies rarely cover any part, especially if the transition involves what most plans consider to be "elective surgery."

Other costs are emotional. Ford's first wife left and cut off contact with their child. I tracked down Ford's son in another state. He said he did not want to talk about the past, and then we did for twenty minutes. A successful business owner and family man, he keeps the history of the woman he calls "father" a secret, even from those closest to him. The pain in his voice was palpable, especially when Ford's death came up.

The final cost Ford paid was her life. On Monday, April 4, 1977, a day the *Birmingham News* called "Black Monday" after a tornado did extensive damage across the city, she died in an altercation outside a Motor Lodge in an upscale suburb south of town, Vestavia Hills.

Jody and Wanda, still together after the transition, went to the movies that rainy night. After they left the theater, around 11:30 p.m., Jody exchanged harsh words with a man named Larry Maddox, the Motor Lodge's owner. Witnesses say Maddox started the ruckus by yelling homophobic remarks.

Maddox sped off, and Ford chased him for five miles from theater to motel in her yellow Cadillac. When they reached the Motor Lodge, Maddox ran into his office and came out with a 16-gauge automatic shotgun.

In the September 1977 trial, deputy district attorney Ken Gomany said Ford threw up her hands to surrender. Maddox claimed that the gun went off when Ford lunged. Defense attorney Russell McDonald argued that his client had to protect himself from a "242-pound gorilla . . . throwing people around like dolls," and that Maddox had the right to defend "his home, a man's highest ground."

The jury sided with Maddox, acquitting him of the manslaughter charge.

Just two months later another Birmingham jury would find Robert Chambliss guilty of murder for his role in the 1963 Sixteenth Street Baptist Church bombing. After the Chambliss trial, local newspapers spoke of the city's moment of healing.

Ford's family, and her lawyers, still wait for that moment. The attorneys were shocked at the Maddox verdict. They thought the D.A. had a win. Ford's first wife and son were shocked as well. They put aside anger and pain to attend the trial, hoping to see justice done. Ford's son said that, forty years later, he continues to hope.

Today, Ford's name appears regularly on lists for the November 20 Transgender Day of Remembrance. Groups such as the Invisible Histories Project, working to recover southern LGBTQ+ histories, view Ford as a pioneer in the struggle for queer equality.

*

In a city filled with civil rights historical markers, however, Ford's name remains conspicuously absent.

I often bring up Ford in my courses on movement literature. Some students consider it ludicrous to wedge a white trans person into a story of Black freedom. Whatever Ford's views on race or the movement might have been, placing her within that context seems a clear example of whiteness co-opting a Black narrative.

On the other hand, overlaps exist: the fight for inclusion into a society clearly divided along lines of race, class, and gender; a death that many local residents see as an unpunished hate crime; and the Confederate flags that circled any challenge to the status quo. Even Bull Connor and George Wallace make appearances.

Examining those overlaps is important for several reasons. First, they show how different movements for civil and human rights intersect. Second, they provide insight into the ways that violence operates as a form of social control. Finally, they illustrate how, despite violence, individuals from marginalized groups insist upon their humanity, their dignity, and their freedom.

An underlying issue is how two stories converge and diverge. Television, film, and other forms of popular culture typically present bifurcated movements, where civil rights equals "Black" and LGBTQ+ rights equals "white." Anyone who has heard of Bayard Rustin and Pauli Murray knows a different story. Rustin, a Black gay man who advised Martin Luther King Jr., was a target of smear campaigns because of his sexuality. Murray, who coined the term "Jane Crow" to describe how discrimination impacts Black women, was a Black lawyer and an Episcopal priest who identified as male. For people like Rustin and Murray, the fight for justice did not stop where one aspect of identity met another.

To better understand how an LGBTQ+ story like Ford's intersects with Birmingham's movement for African American civil rights, one might start with Howard Cruse's 1995 graphic narrative *Stuck Rubber Baby*. I came upon the book while researching my mother's cousin David Armstrong and returned to it while trying to wrap my mind around Jody Ford. Cruse's thinly veiled autobiography, set in a fictional town very much like Birmingham, recounts the story of a white protagonist, Toland Polk, who comes of age as a gay man during the civil rights era. Many of the book's characters—including its white bohemians, Black and white gay men, an older Black lesbian couple, and a Black drag queen—are based upon people that Cruse knew from his own experiences growing up in and around the city. *Stuck Rubber Baby*'s plot also draws from familiar movement events. Toland joins a protest in a park where demonstrators are attacked by police dogs. He and a friend march on Washington. Another friend is injured in a church bombing. Some of the book's settings, unfamiliar but very real, complicate what readers think they know about civil-rights-era Birmingham. A bar that Cruse calls The Rhombus is based upon Tito's, a club on downtown's fringes where, during the 1960s, men defied the city's draconian Jim Crow and sodomy laws. Another bar, *Stuck Rubber Baby*'s Alleysax, pays homage to the Sand Ridge Country Club, a versatile space southwest of Birmingham, that served, by day, as a gathering spot for African American families and, by night, as a juke joint that saw a clientele as varied as the colors on a rainbow flag.

Such is the Birmingham that Ford moved to in 1965 while making the shift from Sid to Jody: a place thought of in terms of strict (and highly policed) lines between Black and white, straight and gay, male and female, but one that was in practice much more fluid. As Cruse explained to me in a 2014 telephone interview, "We benefited from the naïveté of most Birmingham people, who didn't know what was going on."

In that interview Cruse told me that he "knew of" but didn't know Ford. The author left Birmingham in 1969 for graduate school, dropped out, came back home, and then left for good in 1977, the year Ford was killed. *Stuck Rubber Baby* does not touch on Ford's death, although the book does depict an unpunished LGBTQ+ hate crime: Toland's friend Sammy is murdered for his support of Black civil rights. What Cruse focuses on are the human interactions that often get overlooked in mainstream movement stories. He stated, "When I decided to do this book, one of the things I thought I could contribute was this sense of various subcultures that existed and how they intermingled. . . . There's a tendency people have of trying to make it [the movement] a morality play of a battle between good and evil, Black and white. The South was full of much more nuance."

LGBTQ+ oral histories collected by James T. Sears and E. Patrick Johnson also address the nuance. Sears interviewees Quinton Baker (an African American) and Pat Cusick (who is white) were heavily involved in southern civil rights activities. Baker, who at the time had a white boyfriend named John, explained that the couple faced more problems for their activism than their sexuality: "If there were negative reactions to us it was because we were civil rights agitators. Everyone in the movement at that time knew that John and I were gay and in a relationship." Cusick confirms, noting, "There were more gays than people ever realized in the civil rights movement." There were more gay men, more lesbians, more trans people—from different races, ethnicities, and walks of life—than traditional movement narratives depict. As lesbian activist Pat Hussain tells Johnson, "There are so many stories. The civil rights movement in textbooks has been reduced to two lines, and there are three-dimensional people who are part of that, and I want to be part of the excavation to make that so." Another African American that Johnson refers to using the pseudonym "r. dioneaux" speaks pointedly to misconceptions about binary divisions between "Black" civil rights and "white" LGBTQ+ struggles: "We need to de-romanticize movements and realize that there were a whole bunch of people, not our color but our kind. And there were a lot of people our color that sat on their rusty butts and did absolutely nothing."

The historical record does not indicate whether Jody Ford engaged in the kind of activism, such as marching or boycotting, that one associates with civil rights and similar social protest movements. She might have sat on her rusty butt doing nothing. Then again, one might argue that Ford's highly visible public presence during a transphobic time was itself a form of protest, one that she paid for with her life.

In an article titled "Love in Action: Noting Similarities between Lynching Then and Anti-LGBT Violence Now," scholar Koritha Mitchell outlines how violence works as a tool for policing race and sex. Mitchell asserts, "Both forms of brutality [Jim-Crow-era lynching that targeted African Americans and current hate crimes against LGBTQ+ individuals] emerge from an investment in denying citizenship." Consider, for example, the Confederate-flag-waving hoodlums who tossed a brick through Ford's salon window and those who, on the 1963 eve of desegregation, circled Birmingham schools dragging noosed effigies of Black people. Both groups intended to strike fear in those that they believed should not have the same rights as they did to occupy public space—whether it was a bus or a classroom or a beauty salon.

Consider, too, how acts—and threats—of violence go unpunished. As Mitchell explains, violence gets normalized when it happens so often that it becomes routine and when authority figures condone it. Such was the case in post–World War II era Bombingham. Robert Chambliss, one of the men responsible for numerous dynamite attacks on Black homes, went unpunished for those crimes and later played a major role in a 1963 church bombing.

Chambliss was not prosecuted for what happened at Sixteenth Street Baptist until 1977, the same year that a different jury refused to find Larry Maddox guilty for shooting Jody Ford point blank.

The racist rhetoric that Maddox's attorney used in his client's defense is worth noting. McDonald's description of Ford as "a 242-pound gorilla" evokes longstanding stereotypes of African Americans as "monkeys," and of Black men especially as "brutes." The latter term was frequently employed in justifications of lynching that relied on images of Black male "savages" attacking innocent white "ladies." McDonald argued as well that Maddox had the right to defend "his home, a man's highest ground," a concept that more recently has inserted itself into "stand your ground" laws (such as one in Florida) that disproportionately impact Black men. Although Ford was white, McDonald's words sent subtle, racially coded messages to the mostly white jury, allowing them to see her as the enemy and her death as acceptable—and to let Maddox walk free.

McDonald's words linked Ford to racist stereotypes, further marginalizing a figure already perceived as an outcast because of gender. The point was to reassert a social status quo rooted in heteronormative, white-supremacist notions of whose lives matter and whose do not. One of Mitchell's most salient points is that success makes certain people targets. Such was true during the Jim Crow era when, more generally, a rise in lynching numbers followed African American political, economic, and social advancement or, more specifically, when Birmingham's Black families moved into middle-class neighborhoods reserved for whites and found themselves on the wrong end of a dynamite fuse. Such is also true for today's hate crimes, where statistics continue to spike despite the fact that LGBTQ+ identities seem to meet growing mainstream acceptance. Television shows such as *Queer Eye*, *Ru Paul's Drag Race*, or *Transparent* can become commercial or critical successes, but that doesn't mean everyday queer kids can avoid getting beaten up in high school. The visibility, the refusal to stay quietly in the closet, draws the slur, the fist or, in Jody Ford's case, the gun.

"Know-your-place-aggression," as Mitchell describes it, "ensures that an unmistakable message continues to be sent, that 'those people' do not belong and should not expect to be treated as if they do." Messages about knowing one's place, Mitchell explains, "are created and conveyed with microaggressions and bullying, but they are also sent and received when someone is beaten or murdered and the response of authorities is to blame the victim." A server calls Ford "he" instead of "she." The newspaper prints a photograph of a smiling, proud "Ms. Sid," and then bullies hurl a brick through the window of her salon. Jody takes Wanda to the movies, gets called "faggot," and a Birmingham jury says she is wrong to fight back.

*

Ford's insistence on her humanity, on her right to have her *female* body included in Birmingham's body politic, made her both a transgender warrior and a local civil rights legend. Telling her story is a way of validating her life and the lives of others like her.

Although queer visibility can increase the likelihood of antiqueer violence, the alternative—invisibility, silence—remains untenable. Who among us, no matter how we describe our identities, would deny our own right to exist? What kind of person, what kind of society, denies that right to another? When I think about the young LGBTQ+ people that I know, including my own child, I also have to ask what kind of society we hope to create for future generations.

In the ongoing tug of war between oppression and resistance, each of us chooses a side of the rope.

At the time of this writing, politicians like Alabama's governor Kay Ivey have made their positions clear. In May 2022 Ivey signed two laws: one bans students from using bathrooms consistent with their gender identity; a second law makes it a felony to prescribe hormones to minors wishing to transition, even if they have parental approval. "I believe very strongly," Ivey stated, "that if the Good Lord made you a boy, you are a boy, and if he made you a girl, you are a girl."

Positions like Ivey's are echoed in more than forty antitransgender bills filed recently in fifteen other states. In Florida (where I now teach), a controversial bill dubbed "Don't Say Gay," which prevents discussion of sexual orientation or gender identity in grades K–3, set the stage for bills like Alabama's and other, similar legislation across the country (175 anti-LGBTQ+ laws filed in thirty-two states). The Human Rights Campaign describes this recent surge of legislation an "unprecedented onslaught."

But Jody Ford's warrior spirit lives on. Each semester, I walk into the first day of classes with the university-provided roster and ask students which names and pronouns they actually use. Kim has transformed into Billy. Alejandro, Alexa. Jabari, the letter "Z."

"We're here! "We're queer! Get used to it!" goes an LGBTQ+ protest chant. I pull out my pen and mark the students "present."

7 / "CALL IT IGNORANCE"

A 1963 Church Bombing, a 1977 Trial

Uncle Bobby sat on my grandmother's couch with a hangdog look and a brown paper sack. He seemed like a different man from the one I knew. Tall, lanky, bearded, and gruff, Uncle Bobby usually dispensed orders and opinions. On Monday, November 14, 1977, he delivered tampons.

His wife, my Aunt Nell, was sequestered for a jury. A bailiff called with her request: clothes, her Bible, and a large bag of feminine hygiene products.

Trying to square my memory with facts, I search through the Birmingham Public Library archives forty years later. There, I find a photograph of Aunt Nell, Juror 149, leaving the courtroom of the biggest case in the city's

10. Martha Wynell Hughes and other jury members leaving courtroom during the *State of Alabama vs. Robert E. Chambliss* trial, 1977. Image courtesy of the Birmingham Public Library Archives.

civil rights history. I note first that Uncle Bobby brought her a menstruating woman's worst nightmare: white slacks. Next, in her right hand, I see a crumpled tissue. She's crying.

At sixteen I didn't think about the situation's severity. I thought only of myself. Nell was the cool aunt, the party aunt who packed a large green Impala full of giggling teenage girls each Friday night and drove to football games, past cute boys' houses, or to rock concerts. How long was this sequester? Would we miss KISS?

My cousin Tracy, thirteen, and I pestered her dad to let us ride to the courthouse with him. We wanted to see the sights. Just before downtown were the old, rusty Sloss Furnaces, which used to make iron but now, we heard, housed the ghosts of men who fell into the melting ore. Just past that was our all-time favorite billboard, advertising Penny Pet Food, with a mechanized spotted dog that lolled its tongue and wagged its tail.

Maybe, at the courthouse, we could be on television!

"No!"

Uncle Bobby dashed our hopes with a bark. He wasn't taking girls to any courthouse where Dynamite Bob was on trial.

*

On the morning of September 15, 1963, Addie Mae Collins, Carole Robertson, and Cynthia Wesley—each fourteen—and Denise McNair, eleven, were busily primping in the basement ladies' room of Birmingham's Sixteenth Street Baptist Church for a special Youth Day program when a dynamite blast tore out the church's east side. The explosion's force blew off their frilly Sunday dresses and left their bodies damaged beyond recognition. Denise's family identified her by her ash-covered patent leather shoe.

A local Ku Klux Klan faction targeted the church for its visible presence in the Civil Rights Movement. Protestors had gathered at Sixteenth Street multiple times earlier that year for mass meetings of the Birmingham campaign to confront one of segregation's most violently defended bastions. In April Martin Luther King Jr. penned "Letter from Birmingham Jail" after his arrest in a downtown march. In May a protest called the "Children's Crusade" left from the church to face Jim Crow. Birmingham's commissioner of public safety Bull Connor ordered police to attack the young demonstrators with dogs and firemen to hit them with water cannons. Photographs and video footage shocked the world. Embarrassed civic leaders agreed to hire Black workers and desegregate downtown stores and businesses.

But the chaos was not yet over. In early September, not long after the March on Washington and King's "I Have a Dream" speech, a few city schools admitted the first Black students. A violent backlash ensued. White students at three high schools rioted. Local civil rights activists' homes were fire-bombed. Gov. George Wallace did nothing to help. Earlier that summer he famously blocked the way of two Black students trying to integrate the University of Alabama, making good on words from his inaugural address, "segregation now, segregation tomorrow, segregation forever."

On Tuesday, September 10, President John F. Kennedy bypassed Wallace, federalizing the Alabama National Guard and sending the troops to schools to keep order.

On Friday the thirteenth, the city remained awash in hot rods flying Confederate flags on their radio antennas and hanging signs from their windows that said things like "Keep Birmingham Schools White."

On Sunday the church exploded.

Along with the "four little girls," as the primary victims were collectively known, more than twenty other people were wounded.

The blast resonated far beyond Sixteenth Street, inspiring poetry, fiction, visual art, and music across the nation and around the world. The church bombing galvanized support for the movement, leading to passage of the 1964 Civil Rights Act and the 1965 Voting Rights Act.

Back in Birmingham, the FBI and local police chased each other's tails around a slipshod investigation that went nowhere. Fourteen years passed before Robert "Dynamite Bob" Chambliss, the Sixteenth Street bombing's ringleader, was brought to trial.

*

Like many white children who grew up in Birmingham, I was insulated from the city's racist violence by the adults around me.

Uncle Bobby wasn't about to let Tracy and me ride downtown with him to deliver my aunt's sequester care package. I don't remember what, if anything, I knew about the church bombing before that day—although I certainly knew more by the end of that week as trial coverage dominated the local and national news.

Because I listened to rock stations on the radio, I knew that Neil Young railed against the "Southern Man," but I didn't know why—only that, as Lynyrd Skynyrd fired back at the Canadian singer, a "Southern man don't need him around anyhow." Those same rock stations would not have played

Joan Baez's protest anthem "Birmingham Sunday" or John Coltrane's jazz hymn "Alabama." I didn't know the latter, I have to confess, until Spike Lee's 1997 documentary, *4 Little Girls*.

I didn't know during the 1960s and 1970s that my hometown had a long history of racial terror bombings. We didn't exactly learn about the Civil Rights Movement in my Rebel-mascot elementary or my Confederate-flag-flying high school. Nor did my family discuss such things at home, other than occasional comments about "Communists" and "outside agitators," which could have referred to anything from Martin Luther King Jr. to labor union organizers, hippies, and feminists. My grandmother and her children lived for a short time just blocks away from Dynamite Hill but never talked about (and claimed when asked that they didn't hear) any explosions.

Only much later in life, when I asked my grandmother directly, did she tell me what she recalled about the Sixteenth Street Baptist Church bombing. She didn't work at her nursing job that day, but friends from the hospital called to warn her not to come downtown. The dead and wounded had come there, and "they"—meaning Black people—were rioting. Granny said that she gathered me, a toddler, into her arms and headed to the hallway in the middle of her house, where we sheltered during tornadoes, covering ourselves with homemade quilts and singing hymns while the storms passed.

I get that. Who doesn't want to protect their children and grandchildren from life's dangers and hard facts? That's why we make up stories about storks bringing babies and missing pets moving to farms. My husband Tom and I have hunkered down in a tiny bathroom with our son for "family game time" during many a Florida hurricane or tropical storm. In the first years after we adopted him when any trouble reared its head, I used to sing, "Adopto-Mom's got it taken care of / Adopto-Mom's got it under control." More than anything, I wanted him to feel safe and to live without fear.

That's what the parents of Addie Mae, Carole, Cynthia, and Denise wanted for their kids, too. And they believed their daughters were safe on a Sunday morning at Sixteenth Street Baptist—until an explosion cratered the church's eastern wall and blew out the face of Jesus in the balcony's stained glass window.

What I don't get is this: why did my grandmother believe that white children like me needed to huddle under quilts for protection, when Black families were the ones facing such horrific violence? Why didn't our parents and grandparents shield us from the racism that perpetrated and condoned it?

I cannot count the number of Sunday dinners where white male relatives or family friends spouted off about the [insert any number of racial slurs here]. Racism in Birmingham was as common as sweet tea.

Granny's coworkers were right to warn her away from downtown during the civil unrest that occurred the day of the church bombing. Cars were being overturned, bricks and bullets were flying.

But little old white ladies and their grandkids were hardly the ones in danger.

Even after the church bombing, white people continued killing Black kids. Later in the day of September 15, a white police officer shot Johnny Robinson, sixteen, in the back. White teenagers shot Virgil Ware, thirteen, at random.

What frightened the adults around me more: the possibility of dodging bullets or of facing up to their own complicity?

*

White complicity was a major theme of King's "Letter from Birmingham Jail," written five months before the bombing. The civil rights leader was responding to eight white clergymen who published an open letter on April 12, 1963, decrying the Birmingham Campaign's demonstrations as "unwise and untimely." The ministers, priests, and rabbis described their letter as "A Call for Unity," claiming that racial unrest in the city was the fault of protestors, not the racism they fought against. King's reply dismantled their argument piece by piece in what since has been recognized as one of the most effective examples of persuasion ever written. About halfway through his letter, King expresses his disappointment that the clergymen, and the moderate white people that they represent, do not see their actions as part of a larger problem. "I have almost reached the regrettable conclusion," King states, "that the Negro's great stumbling block in the stride toward freedom is not the White Citizens Councillor or the Ku Klux Klanner but the white moderate who is more devoted to order than to justice." King's words point to a basic ethical question. Who bears responsibility for violence and injustice: the perpetrator only or those who stand by, watching in silence?

The church bombing made such a question tragically clear to two white moderates who responded in the days following the attack.

On September 16, 1963, attorney Charles "Chuck" Morgan Jr., spoke out publicly at a lunch meeting of the Birmingham Young Businessmen's Club, an all-white organization. His address, known since as "A Time to Speak," raised the issue of responsibility. "Four little girls were killed in Birmingham yesterday," Morgan told his audience. "A mad, remorseful worried community asks, 'Who did it? Who threw that bomb?' . . . The answer should be, 'We all did it.' Every last one of us is condemned for that crime and the bombing before it and a decade ago. We all did it." For the roughly five minutes that he talked, Morgan spelled out specifically who "we" meant. White elected officials who fueled the fires of violence with their words. White courts that moved too slowly against injustice. White lawyers who pointed fingers at everyone but themselves. White police officers who failed to serve and protect. White businesses that refused to desegregate. White educators who taught prejudice rather than civics. White clergy presiding over segregated houses of worship. Ordinary white people who voted for racist candidates, supported racist institutions, or laughed at racist jokes. Everyone, Morgan emphasized: "every person in this community who has in any way contributed during the past several years to the popularity of hatred, is at least as guilty, or more so, than the demented fool who threw that bomb."

Eugene Patterson, editor of the *Atlanta Constitution*, also focused on white complicity in a column published the same day as Morgan's speech and read later that night on the *CBS Evening News* with Walter Cronkite. In "A Flower for the Graves," Patterson argued that responsibility for the bombing lay not only with the act's perpetrators but also with the white southerners who "created a climate for child-killing." Patterson's column drew much of its emotional energy from an Associated Press photograph of Denise McNair's grief-stricken grandfather, F. L. Pippen, running from the church carrying Denise's shoe after pulling the girl's body from the rubble. Patterson used the image to create a sense of empathy—and shame—in his white readership. "Every one of us in the white South holds that small shoe in his hand," Patterson stated:

> Let us see it straight and look at the blood on it. Let us compare it with the unworthy speeches of Southern public men who have traduced the Negro; match it with the spectacle of shrilling children whose parents and teachers turned them free to spit epithets at small huddles of Negro school children for a week before this Sunday in Birmingham; hold up the shoe and look beyond it to the state house in Montgomery where the official attitudes of Alabama have been spoken in heat and anger.

Patterson urged his readers to do better, to "plant a flower of nobler resolve" on the girls' graves. "We created the day," he said. "We bear the judgment."

*

At the time, Morgan's and Patterson's words did little (to echo a phrase often attributed to King) to bend the universe's moral arc toward justice.

Morgan's speech received polite applause and, later, death threats. He closed his law practice and moved his family to Atlanta. Patterson received over two thousand response letters: some in agreement, others not. Roy Peter Clark, former director of the Poynter Institute for Media Studies, recalls that his mentor kept a ball-peen hammer in his desk for protection.

Meanwhile, in Birmingham, investigations into the church bombing dragged on, even though the FBI and local police knew who did it.

11. Robert Chambliss mug shot, 1963. Image courtesy of the Birmingham Public Library Archives.

Robert Chambliss topped everyone's suspect list. A craggy-faced drinking and fighting man, Chambliss learned the explosives trade in Birmingham's iron ore mines. In 1963 the fifty-nine-year-old Chambliss officially worked in Birmingham's city garage. Unofficially, he worked for Bull Connor setting fuses on Dynamite Hill.

The FBI had been monitoring Chambliss and his KKK cronies through an informant, Gary Thomas Rowe. A Black female eyewitness named Gertrude "Kirthus" Glenn reported seeing a 1957 Chevy (later traced to Chambliss's friend Thomas Blanton Jr.) near the church the night before the bombing, and a man matching the description of either Chambliss or another suspect, Bobby Frank Cherry, inside the car. But Glenn's testimony alone could not be the foundation for a trial against white men, especially considering that another potential eyewitness, the white police officer on duty that night, was Floyd Garrett, Chambliss's nephew. Chambliss and two other men, John Hall and Charles Cagle, were picked up for possessing and transporting dynamite. They paid a $100 fine and received a suspended sentence. No other arrests were made. In 1965 local authorities would name Cherry, Blanton, and another man, Herman Cash, as primary suspects, with Chambliss as the ringleader. Yet in 1968 the FBI closed the case, and director J. Edgar Hoover sealed the files.

In the months following the church bombing, as investigations continued to yield no results, younger movement activists such as Diane Nash and James Bevel grew frustrated and angry. The continuing miscarriage of justice fueled their desire to take the universe's moral arc into their own hands. For a time, they challenged King's stance on nonviolence. But after much soul-searching debate, they decided to fight for the right to vote and get men like Bull Connor out of office.

The strategy worked. The tangled emotions—the grief, the shame, the rage—that prompted men like Morgan and Patterson to speak out, and thousands to converge on places like Mississippi in 1964 and Selma in 1965, manifested themselves in two pieces of civil rights legislation. Both put Dynamite Bob on a collision course with a Birmingham courtroom.

The 1965 Voting Rights Act changed who voted, which changed who served on juries, and who got elected to judge and prosecutor positions. A young white law student named William "Bill" Baxley vowed in 1963 that he would one day do something about the church bombing. When he became the state's attorney general in 1970, Baxley immediately started digging into the case.

12. *Four Spirits*, a memorial to the four girls who died in the 1963 church bombing, by artist Elizabeth MacQueen. Image courtesy of the author.

The 1964 Civil Rights Act changed who had access to public space. The church bombing sent a message that Black citizens had no rights to public facilities, no rights to stores, no rights to schools, no rights to the most sacred places. Voting shifted the city's demographics from majority white and dominated by Jim Crow violence to primarily Black and ready to tell a new movement story. That storytelling process would start with the 1977 Chambliss prosecution and reach its fruition in 2013 with a monument to the four girls on the fifty-year anniversary of their murders. *Four Spirits*, by locally born artist Elizabeth MacQueen, features bronze statues of each girl—one beckoning visitors, another releasing doves—and a bench for rest and reflection. The monument sits at the center of a large memorial complex that includes the church, the Birmingham Civil Rights Institute, a walking tour, and multiple works of public art in a park that used to be famous for police dogs and fire hoses. Such a space sends a very different message from that of 1963: that the story about the fight for justice, equality, and freedom will occupy a significant portion of the city's newly defined civic identity.

*

The 1977 Chambliss case was shaky, but Baxley pushed ahead because the time was right. Old-guard civil rights warriors tired of justice too long delayed. New Birmingham looked forward to healing and redemption.

The trial opened on November 14. The charge was the murder of Denise McNair. Baxley told me in an April 2013 interview, "You can murder someone without knowing them if you set a bomb intending to do harm." The state made four separate murder indictments, one for each girl. The judge, Wallace Gibson, ruled that the trial would go forward on one indictment only, an odd decision that would prove decisive. The jury was made up of nine white and three Black members.

Juror 149, Aunt Nell, was an unlikely choice. She went to high school with defending attorney Art Hanes Jr., and Hanes's secretary Suzy was my mother's best friend. "Six degrees of Mississippi," my husband Tom calls the phenomenon of southerners who always seem to know somebody that knows somebody else that knows you. It's like the once-popular party game Six Degrees of Kevin Bacon—with the title coined from John Guare's 1990 play (and, later, a film) *Six Degrees of Separation*—where participants try to find the shortest path of connection between any random actor and the ubiquitous movie star. The only difference: in a place like Birmingham, one is never too far removed from someone who played a key role, for good or ill, in the Civil Rights Movement. Both Hanes and Baxley returned my phone calls within a matter of minutes because they remembered my legal-secretary mother and me as a child.

I interviewed both in Spring 2013 about the trial, especially their jury selections. Hanes said that because his father had been Birmingham's mayor (from 1961 to 1963), it was hard to find jury members he didn't know. Baxley did not remember Aunt Nell specifically, but he had a definite trial strategy that she fit. She was a Christian, a homemaker, and a mom. Her daughter, my cousin Tracy, was in 1977 about the same age as Addie Mae, Cynthia, Carole, and Denise when they died.

The evidence against Chambliss: he purchased a case of dynamite; he knew how to construct the specific, and rare, kind of fishing-bobber and metal-bucket detonator used at Sixteenth Street; he was seen near the church the night before. But more important than any of that was Chambliss himself.

Aunt Nell said she based her decision to convict on "his arrogance, his hatred, and his niece."

For Aunt Nell, the niece Elizabeth Hood Cobbs's testimony was the trial's turning point. In 1963 Elizabeth Hood was in her early twenties. By 1977 she was divorced, a mother of one, and a Methodist minister named Elizabeth Cobbs. (A few years later, Cobbs underwent gender transition surgery to become Petric Smith.) Cobbs testified about being at Chambliss's house during the school riots and finding him noticeably agitated, cursing, and using racial epithets. "Just wait till after Sunday morning," he said. "They will beg us to let them segregate." He had enough dynamite "to flatten half of Birmingham," he confessed. Cobbs was at the house after the bombing, when news reports stated that murder charges might possibly be filed. "It wasn't meant to hurt anybody," Chambliss told the television. "It didn't go off when it was supposed to."

On November 17, 1977, Baxley made his closing argument. He noted that the day would have been Denise McNair's twenty-sixth birthday, and by then she likely would have been a mother herself. He told the jury that it was their "duty" to convict.

At 4:10 p.m. they went into the jury room to begin deliberations. Five hours went by with no verdict. The judge allowed them to retire for the evening so they could get some sleep and start fresh the next morning. What happened during those five hours?

Aunt Nell told me that she had no doubt how she would vote.

"Baby, that man was guilty as sin," she said. "You could see it in his face the minute he strolled into that courtroom like he owned it. You could see it in the way he stared at his niece."

Not all jury members saw what Aunt Nell did. They spent their five hours reviewing the evidence piece by piece: witness testimony, intricate details about bomb building, Chambliss's whereabouts in September 1963, morgue photos. Then they voted: 11–1. One white man remained unconvinced. The deliberations were exhausting and painful, Aunt Nell remembers, but not acrimonious. The man needed more time. The jury ate dinner: something from room service that Aunt Nell doesn't remember. She does recall marking her Bible, Jeremiah, chapter 29, verse 11: "'For I know the thoughts I think toward you,' saith the Lord, 'thoughts of peace, not of evil, to give you an expected end.'" Aunt Nell slept well trusting that her Lord had a plan. The jury started up the next day a little after 8:00 a.m. Two hours later they voted again.

On November 18, 1977, at 10:40 a.m., the jury returned a guilty verdict and set the sentence at life in prison. Chambliss served his time in a solitary cell.

The conviction established a new precedent for civil rights era crimes. Cold case prosecutions became increasingly common over the next few decades. In 1994 a Jackson, Mississippi, jury convicted Byron De La Beckwith for the 1963 murder of Medgar Evers. In 2005 another Mississippi jury found Edgar Ray Killen guilty for the murder of three voting rights activists during 1964's Freedom Summer. Such "atonement trials," as historian Jack Davis calls them, were important to people in places like Birmingham who wanted to leave a violent past behind.

Some people have a different take on redemption. Chambliss died in 1985, still saying his Klan brothers did it, not him.

Ten years after Chambliss's death, the FBI reopened its investigation files. With new evidence unavailable to Baxley in 1977, Doug Jones, then the US attorney for Alabama's Northern District, successfully prosecuted the co-conspirators who remained alive: Thomas Blanton in 2000, and Bobby Frank Cherry in 2002. The other suspect, Herman Cash, had died in 1994. After Cherry's conviction newspapers nationally spoke of "healing" and "closure."

Not everyone in Birmingham sees it that way.

*

Both Morgan and Patterson claimed that the moral responsibility for the church bombing lay with men like Chambliss, who planted the dynamite at Sixteenth Street, and with white southerners who, by their overt actions or their silence, created fertile ground for violence.

Interviewing Art Hanes taught me a lot about justice and accountability.

Hanes said that he lost the case in the defense. During the prosecution he was aggressive, objecting to anything related to the use of words such as "dynamite" or "bomb." He even got the judge to cut those words out of the coroner's report with a penknife. The trial transcript shows that during the defense, as Hanes called up one motley character witness after another, his attitude shifted. He stopped pushing. He stopped objecting. He seemed resigned. I asked him what happened. He told me that he had planned to call only one witness: Chambliss himself. When it came time, Chambliss said, "I ain't gettin' up there." Hanes said that was his epiphany.

One needs his backstory to understand. Art Hanes Jr. was a Princeton-educated partner in his father's law firm. The firm defended what he called the "worst of the worst": Chambliss, the white men who killed Selma civil

rights worker Viola Liuzzo, and, briefly, James Earl Ray for killing Martin Luther King. Hanes claimed that he came out of law school "idealistic." He told
me, "Jefferson says that 'you judge a society not by how it treats its privileged
but how it treats its meanest wretch.' I came out of law school saying, 'I can
represent the meanest wretch.'" But in that courtroom, he said, he changed
his mind: "I was not going to spend the rest of my life bleeding on those
counsel tables." He still worked in murder trials, but when Medgar Evers's
murderer Byron De La Beckwith tried to hire him in 1994, Hanes declined.
No more being, he told me, "on the wrong side of history."

I asked Hanes if he thought that Birmingham had redeemed itself from
that wrong side of history. Not nearly enough, he said, despite the prosecutions and the memorials: "We can't adjust to a new society until all of us who
were raised in a segregated America are gone. . . . To me, all those things are
current events. You can't put them behind you and think of them as past."

His words remind me that history is never tidy. Too often the story of
Birmingham, and of the US Civil Rights Movement more generally, is cast
in terms of progress. People want closure, healing, redemption. We want to
believe that however bad the past might have been, the present marks an improvement. We also want to believe that removing the "bad apples," prose-
cuting men like Chambliss and waiting for their cronies to die out, destroys
the process of rot. I disagree with Hanes on this point. Racism doesn't go
away with the "worst of the worst." It operates more like the mythical, many-
headed monster known as the Hydra: chop off one head, and more grow
back in its place.

I do agree with Hanes about something else: the past is a current event.

A month after our 2013 interview, the US Supreme Court's ruling in *Shelby
County v. Holder*—a case originating from the county just south of Birmingham, where the city's white population took flight after integration—set voting rights protections back five decades.

Two months after I interviewed Hanes, a Sanford, Florida, jury found
George Zimmerman not guilty of murdering seventeen-year-old Trayvon
Martin. The incident was one of several that helped to launch the Black Lives
Matter movement, drawing attention to the persistence of racist violence.

Five months after my Hanes interview, the Sixteenth Street Baptist
Church's "fifth little girl," Addie Mae's sister Sarah Collins Rudolph, pe-
titioned the City of Birmingham for financial assistance with the ongoing
health problems she faced after the bombing. Rudolph, in the basement that
day along with her sister Addie Mae and the other girls who died, lost an eye,

spent months in the hospital, and endured decades of physical, emotional, and economic distress. Birmingham's mayor at the time of her request, William Bell, declined to help. In 2020 Alabama governor Kay Ivey issued an official apology to Rudolph, stating that "there should be no question that the racist, segregationist rhetoric used by some of our leaders during that time was wrong and would be utterly unacceptable in today's Alabama." Ivey, however, would not discuss any financial restitution.

It's always someone else who needs to plant what Patterson called the "flower of nobler resolve"—someone "back then," "over there," separated by far more degrees than six—but never "us."

*

Aunt Nell and I also talk a lot about the past. She likes to ride with me around the city to see how it's changed. Sloss Furnaces are now a National Historic Landmark, where visitors can rent bikes and follow trails that once were rail beds (as I am doing in this book's author photograph). The Penny Pet Food dog has been relocated to the city's new, beautifully landscaped Railroad Park, where this fond icon of many a Birmingham childhood presides over the minor league baseball Barons, named after a historic Negro League team. Sometimes Aunt Nell and I drive by the lavish malls and sprawling gated communities of Shelby County's northern suburbs. We compare their wealthy extravagance to the empty storefronts and crumbling buildings where we each grew up, the now predominantly Black neighborhoods of Elyton Village and East Lake.

Who needs KKK dynamite when you can just turn your back?

Yet Birmingham's civil rights memorial complex, just west of the city's central business district, is lovely—all green space and public art. Aunt Nell and I visited near the church bombing's fiftieth anniversary.

Now in her early eighties, Aunt Nell is the kind of southern lady that calls me, and everybody else, "baby." The kind that cooks supper for her Baptist church on Wednesdays, prepares the programs for Sunday service on Thursdays, and visits shut-ins on Saturdays. Still the cool aunt, but no longer the party aunt, Nell has silver hair, which complements her steel blue eyes. Her walker, named "Mr. Walker," goes with her everywhere after Uncle Bobby's 2010 passing.

Aunt Nell and Mr. Walker have been through all Twelve Steps of the Alcoholics Anonymous recovery program. Like Chuck Morgan, she does not shy away from honest reckonings.

I asked her what she was doing while the famous "dogs and fire hoses" incidents were taking place downtown.

"I cared and I didn't," she said, "because it didn't affect me. I was into my own life, doing my own things. I was a young mother. But when I sat on that jury, it really opened my eyes."

We stood at the corner where *Four Spirits*, the memorial to Addie Mae, Cynthia, Carole, and Denise now stands, diagonally across from the church. Off to one side, the artist set a small pair of bronze shoes.

Denise's mother, Maxine McNair, kept the ash-covered patent leather shoe that her father retrieved from the rubble in a box for decades after she lost eleven-year-old Denise. Today, visitors can see it in a Birmingham Civil Rights Institute display on the bombing, near a large picture window that overlooks the church.

My cousin Tracy and I survived our teens, went to plenty of rock concerts and football games, and both had children of our own, enjoying all the rights and privileges Birmingham daughters—no matter what their race—deserve.

As Aunt Nell and I talked, she looked over at the church, then out at Birmingham's sleek skyline and sighed, "It makes you wonder how all that could go on and you just didn't know. I guess you could call it ignorance . . .

"But it wasn't."

8 / THE GREAT AMERICAN HAMBURGER AND THE WHITEWASHING OF MEMORY

During the 1960s my mother and I spent most every Saturday shopping downtown. Our weekly ritual began with getting dressed. First, Mom teased and Aqua-Netted her beehive, twisted herself into a tight girdle, hiked up pantyhose, and finished with a smart, drop-waist shift and low-heeled pumps. Next, she wrestled her squirming daughter away from *Bugs Bunny* and into a blue sailor dress, white bobby socks, and shiny black patent leather Mary Janes. With purses in white-gloved hands, we made one last mirror check— *Is my face on straight? Smile!*—then walked out the front door and across the street to catch the bus downtown. We hit Mom's favorite department stores: Loveman's, Pizitz, Yielding's, and Parisian, the latter's very name evoking the sophisticated fashion choices that she craved. The day was not complete until she purchased at least one new outfit and forced me to try on frilly dress after frilly dress until I bolted underneath a clothing rack to pitch a wailing temper tantrum. Then Mom would pull me out by an arm and half drag me to the bus stop, fussing the whole time about my refusing to act like a lady. Back at home she plopped me in front of the television, where I had wanted to be all along, and donned the day's new clothes for the date who would take her out to drink and dance at the Cane Break Supper Club, again downtown.

The Civil Rights Movement changed our ritual, not in ways that most people would guess, but because it forced my mother and grandmother to learn how to drive. The story of desegregation on Birmingham's city buses did not follow the plot that conventional wisdom associates with Montgomery.

Then again, neither did Montgomery. The short version of the conventional story casts Rosa Parks as an unassuming seamstress who one day in 1955 decided that she was too tired to give up her seat in the white section of a Montgomery bus. Her arrest prompted the city's African Americans to unite in a boycott of the local bus system, under the leadership of a new, young minister, Martin Luther King Jr. The boycotters remained steadfast for over a year, until a November 1956 US Supreme Court ruling in *Browder v. Gayle* declared segregation on city buses unconstitutional. Civil rights historians generally agree that the story was much more complicated. Parks—a seasoned NAACP activist trained in nonviolent civil disobedience at Tennessee's Highlander Folk School—was hardly unassuming. Her action—one of several instances where African American women refused to obey Montgomery's bus segregation laws—was hardly spontaneous. And Montgomery's bus system—despite the boycott and the Supreme Court ruling—hardly integrated.

Neither did Birmingham's. What happened, more accurately, is that some local activists, including the ACMHR's Fred Shuttlesworth, continued testing desegregation on public buses well into the 1960s until eventually the point became moot. Once the "Colored" and "White" signs came down, white people stopped riding. In an oral history, Birmingham civil rights activist Bernard Johnson describes his excitement about testing the bus laws, only to find that everyone on the bus with him was Black. "I wanted to sit across, next to or in front of a White person just to let them know that I was just as equal as they were," Johnson states. "So, here I am sitting on the bus, my objective, and there is no one on the bus but Black people." Looking out of the window, Johnson discovered that the white people were below him, riding in cars. In an article on bus desegregation in Birmingham, historian Sarah Frohardt-Lane explains that the years between 1956 and 1962 saw a 30 percent increase in Alabama's automobile registrations. With ridership down, bus routes got clipped to bare-bones service, which forced people, if they had the means, into cars, thus continuing the cycle. Frohardt-Lane notes that "white Birminghamians chose to sacrifice the bus itself rather than integrate it."

My family was among those who gave up on the bus—and ultimately on shopping in downtown Birmingham. By the time I started school in 1967, my grandmother was chauffeuring me the three blocks in a blue and white, 1950s-era Bel Air. By the time Mom got her license, a few years later, Granny had a new, frost-green 1969 Malibu. Later, Mom got her own car, a used 1972 Chevelle, in forest green. On Saturdays, instead of hopping onto the bus with our white gloves and a smile, Mom and I now pointed a Chevrolet toward Eastwood Mall.

Eastwood opened in 1960 as the city's first indoor shopping center, conveniently located on a major intersection near the Atlanta Highway and close to what would become, a decade later, Interstate 20. After the 1963 Birmingham movement paved the way for integration in downtown stores and businesses, white customers like us gradually moved our dollars from the city's center to the mall's famed "air-conditioned sidewalks" east of town. Soon, in 1969,

Western Hills Mall would open to service shoppers on Birmingham's west side. By the time Brookwood Village, in the southern suburbs, opened in 1973, downtown had gone the way of the city's once-thriving buses: empty and dead.

Eastwood Mall replaced downtown's ghosts with so much new life. Its fifty-five-acre space held Mom's beloved Parisian, where the smart shifts soon gave way to mod-patterned miniskirts and polyester jumpsuits, and the Pioneer Cafeteria, where we could grab a plastic tray and select our favorites from a long line of meat loaf, turkey and dressing, mashed potatoes, fried okra, banana pudding, and other delights that Mom claimed made her need the girdle. Surrounding the mall was a movie theater, a bowling alley—its sign a multicolored star upon a pole, towering above the mall and visible for blocks—and, around back, another local icon: Kelly's Hamburgers, a building designed to resemble a giant chuck wagon with a cowboy driver. Mom and I spent every Saturday at the mall, with me morphing from a shopping-averse, tantrum-prone child to a teenager finding stores of my own, especially Oz Records, with its trippy spiral-patterned tunnel entrance and, overhead inside, plastic monkeys "flying" along guide wires to deliver merchandise to the cash register. So it was inevitable that, by my sixteenth birthday—time, in Armstrong years, for one to buy her own Chevrolet, records, and clothes—I would get an Eastwood Mall job. I wound up waiting tables, for $1.50 per hour plus tips, at The Great American Hamburger and Soda Fountain Restaurant.

The locally owned Great American was a knockoff of a national chain, Farrell's Ice Cream Parlor. Like Farrell's, the style was turn-of-the-twentieth-century Americana. Both restaurants had menus printed like a broadside newspaper in a rustic, Old West–style font, and illustrated with images of people in American Gilded Age fashion. Employee dress mirrored the illustrations, with females wearing white, ruffled shirtwaist blouses, males sporting bow ties, and all of us in straw boater hats. Great American, like its Farrell's precursor, focused food offerings around sandwiches (menu front) and ice cream (menu back). Each side featured its own version of the "The Kitchen Sink," served in a large, sink-styled metal dish atop a wooden stand. Anyone ordering a Kitchen Sink sandwich would receive a bacon cheeseburger surrounded by chili-cheese fries. The ice cream equivalent mixed hot fudge sundae with banana split. Both were served by the full waitstaff clapping or blowing kazoos while the fountain staff sounded a siren. Such antics drew families in big, intergenerational parties, kids celebrating birthdays in their own special room that featured (for an extra fee) a magician, and teens making their own magic on Saturday-night dates. If one could tolerate listening for hours to pseudo-ragtime, player-piano music and fishing the occasional dime tip from an overturned water glass, Great American was a fun place to work.

The mall's location, maximizing customer access from multiple areas in eastern Birmingham, meant that the restaurant drew its staff of teens and twenty-somethings from disparate neighborhoods. Most of my high school friends, blue-collar white kids from East Lake and Roebuck, worked at Great American. Neighborhoods north of the mall—Gate City, Zion City, and Airport Hills—supplied Black employees. Mountain Brook, to the south, brought in Jewish kids and wealthy WASPs. From the west came an ethnic mix from the Catholic high school, John Carroll, mostly Italians, with a sprinkling of Southeast Asians. For the first time in my life, I had not only bosses but bosses who were Caribbean, Hispanic, or openly gay. In my memory the restaurant was its own kitchen sink: a great American mix of flavors working together in a messily perfect concoction. In reality the mix was more often a window into the perfect mess that was post-civil-rights-era Birmingham.

The Great American Hamburger had its own hierarchy of race, gender, class, and space. Smiling white girls worked the host/cashier station up front that doubled as a candy and stuffed-animal shop and that also housed a small to-go window, primarily serving Oz's hippies and Parisian's lunching ladies. The waitstaff was mainly female, with another set of smiling white girls getting the best-for-tips tables down the restaurant's middle and right aisles. Other girls, like the Vietnamese whose families had recently immigrated to the US after Saigon's 1975 fall, practiced their English at the less-populated tables on restaurant left. Clearing tables was for males, except Jenna, who some called the girl-busboy. White males, especially the Mountain Brook WASPs, manned the soda fountain—a U-shaped spot for making ice cream treats—at the restaurant's center. Behind the soda fountain, close to the rear entrance, and hidden behind large swinging doors, was Great American's kitchen, where Black males made the rules. Julius, a tall, heavy dishwasher about my age, controlled the music. On a metal shelf high above the water, Julius kept a large boom box that played only Parliament/Funkadelic—the psychedelic, futuristic, funk band whose 1970s-era hits included "P-Funk (Wants to Get Funked Up)," "Flashlight," "Give Up the Funk (Tear the Roof off the Sucker)," and "Chocolate City." Pete, who had a gold right incisor and looked to be in his early thirties, controlled the flow. Order tickets got clipped to the spinning wheel at the left of the food prep area. When orders were up, Pete rang a bell and paged servers by their Great American name. (I was "Greedy" for filching bacon and french fries.) Completed tickets got stabbed to a counter spike, then servers stacked their plates onto trays, carrying them one-handed through the swinging doors next to the reminder sign, "The Customer Is Always Right."

No matter where we were on the restaurant hierarchy, our prime directive was working together to ensure that every moment of customers' experience, from front door to food to check, made them smile. Once we donned boater hats and red aprons, we ceased being individuals from East Lake, Gate City, or Mountain Brook. We became a team dedicated to maintaining the illusion that we occupied a space apart from any real place or time, an idyllic "great" America where the food was bountiful, the kazoo-party never ended, and we all got along. If we had a slow section, we did not grumble over another server's full tables and extra tips but cleaned and restocked the salad bar—and we certainly tried to avoid thinking about how many times we piled new garbanzo beans on top of old garbanzo beans, or what might lie at the bottom of the garbanzo-bean crock. If the scowling, growling customer we called Raw Onion Rosie sat in our section, we met her request for the burger rare, not medium, with onions raw, not grilled, and no lettuce, no tomato, no pickle, no nothing else with a hearty "yes ma'am." If a small child running the aisles slammed into our tray full of milkshakes, we did not stalk back to the kitchen and yell "goddam brat!" Or, if we did, then our tough-talking, cigarette-smoking manager Sharon made us choose whether to move into a job without customer contact or to leave the Great American team.

Truthfully, many reasons beyond that goddam brat led me to become a soda jerk. I was a terrible server, easily frustrated by low tips and naughty kids. I was so anxious about messing up orders that my underarms dripped with sweat, staining the white shirt yellow, and my hands shook, sending far too many plates into customer laps. Hovering over ice cream freezers kept me sweat-free. Making malts and banana splits did not require steady hands. And the soda fountain placed me with the cooler, richer kids at the restaurant's center, where, like the guys in the kitchen, I could make my own rhythms, claim my own space of power within Great American's flow.

Working the soda fountain make me feel equal to the ice cream boys like Jack. He was all Mountain Brook High School preppie, from his pressed Izod polo to his polished Sperry topsiders; I was all working-class Banks, with feathered hair, blue eye shadow, and scuffed-up, off-brand sneakers. Jack laughed at me when I confessed to finding his friend Trip cute.

"You?" he said. "Ha!" Then he told Trip.

When I was a server, they snickered when I placed orders or put caramel where chocolate should be. A couple of times, they followed me to one of the restaurant's large, walk-in freezers so they could lock me inside, laughing while I yelled and cursed to be let out. When the manager let me try the soda fountain job, Trip quit, refusing to work with "some girl." Jack stayed on for my soda jerk initiation.

During my first week of working with Jack, he had a pimple on the tip of his nose so bright red that I could not look at his face. I forced myself instead to focus on his Izod alligator.

One slow night he asked me if going to school with Black kids was better or worse than going to school with Jews.

"I don't know what you mean," I said.

I dropped my eyes from Jack's alligator to his topsiders.

He asked again. "I mean that they talk funny. And they look funny. And they smell funny. And they all sit together at lunch. It's like they gang up. Are Black kids like that, too?"

I stood there for what seemed like minutes, as frozen—and as silent—as the ice cream tubs. I vowed to myself that for the rest of my life, I would avoid people who wore Izod and Sperry. I swore that, cross-my-heart-forever, I would stay away from ice cream and happy restaurants and shopping malls and even the people who liked such things.

Cathy, our assistant manager—large-boned, dark-haired, and fierce—ended my line of promises with a slammed hand on the counter and a bark.

"Look alive back there! Jack, we don't pay you to be a jackASS! Jules, you look like someone stole your lunch money! Restock something. Wipe a counter. Get to work."

*

Great American's hierarchies seemed to grow more fluid during my two years there. White girls like me, and eventually Black boys, moved to soda-fountain jobs, and the hardworking Vietnamese girls claimed the coveted center tables. But what really mattered more than being a server, busboy, cook, or soda jerk was whether or not one had a car. Bus desegregation, suburban shopping centers, and, in the mid-1970s, a new interstate system drove local residents like my mother and grandmother into individual automobiles and out of public transportation. In turn, ridership, then routes, dropped, making cars necessities rather than luxuries. Like many teens at the restaurant, I worked to afford my own ride.

Pre-car, I relied on high school friends to get me to and from the restaurant. Or Mom and I shared her Chevelle. Not long before I started working, she and I moved from my grandmother's house to an apartment just outside Birmingham's eastern border, near Center Point. That meant Mom and I got up Monday through Friday at 5:30 a.m. so that we could get ready in time for me to drive her to her legal-secretary job downtown and then get back east by 8:00 for school. In the evenings I was supposed to pick her up at 4:30 so she could get me to work by 5:00, then come back by 10:00 after my shift was done. In reality that meant I waited in the mall parking lot outside the closed, darkened restaurant until 11:00 or later, because Mom and her new boyfriend, Glen, were out drinking.

Like her shopping, Mom's partying moved east after the 1960s. She and Glen liked to dance at a Roebuck honky-tonk, The Mousetrap. Sometimes they waited for me at the mall's T.P. Crockmier's, a Great American Hamburger for grown-ups. Like the restaurant where I worked, Crockmier's printed its menu in a saloon-style font that harked back to an earlier (though different) time. The food and beverage options came with a story of the legendary Thaddeus P. Crockmier, a mustachioed man in an ascot, and a "loyal southerner who fought with General Lee's army" to defend his father's Virginia plantation. "After the War Between the States," the menu continued, "young Crockmier moved south" to open a chain of restaurants, first in Atlanta, then in Birmingham.

One time Pete stayed outside with me until Mom and Glen wobbled the Chevelle over from Crockmier's. On the long drive home, Glen crossed back and forth over the pavement's white lines and berated me for talking to "some jigaboo." How stupid could I be, he yelled; I could have been killed.

A week or so later, Glen found me a car. Before dating Mom he worked as a Mountain Brook police officer. After he was fired, for reasons I don't know, he worked at one of the many used car lots that dotted the road from East Lake to Center Point. One day he picked me up from school, drove me to an aluminum-sided building behind a chain-link fence, and parked next to a silver 1973 Chevy Vega. I got a quickie lesson on how to operate a manual transmission, wrote a check for $200, and hit the road. My first stop was my best friend Mary's house. We needed to give the Vega a name. Mary's Datsun 510 was "Baby Cakes." Our friend Shawn had an Austin Marina called

"Tallywacker." After a short trip through the neighborhood around our high school, filled with hills that kept stalling the Vega's transmission, Mary christened my new car "Dingleberry," little piece of shit.

Dingleberry transformed my Great American Hamburger days. No more waiting behind a darkened restaurant for a drunken-driver ride. Now I had the power (when Dingleberry started) to chauffer myself and my friends. I drove anybody anywhere. The farther the better, because staying out later meant I got home after Mom and Glen fell asleep. Mark lived in Mountain Brook, Cedric by the airport, and Sarah near John Carroll, where the hills rolled into downtown's flat valley. Sometimes after dropping them off, I got lost, accidentally or on purpose. I drove along unfamiliar streets half hoping that Dingleberry would stall permanently somewhere that I could live out my own Great American dream: move to a new world, change my name (but not to Greedy), erase the past, and make a fresh start.

My favorite drop-off was Mark, who lived in a garden apartment down the four-lane road from Eastwood Mall, just past the Mountain Brook city limits sign. Afterward, I kept driving toward the old-money mansions with the British-sounding street names—Carlisle, Argyle, Wellington, Stratford— that topped out at a ridge overlooking the city. Part of me ached to live there. Another part wanted to slam down the gas pedal, screaming and crashing Dingleberry through a mansion's iron gates.

I started working at the Great American Hamburger and Soda Fountain Restaurant in the late summer of 1977—a few months after the killing of Birmingham's transgender warrior Jody Ford and two months before the November trial of Robert "Dynamite Bob" Chambliss. I quit near the end of my high school senior year, 1979, after Dingleberry's clutch and master cylinder conked out, leaving me again at the mercy of friends, Mom, or Glen. Not long after I stopped working there, a white police officer shot an unarmed twenty-year-old Black woman, Bonita Carter, outside a convenience store in Kingston, not far from where I used to take a coworker home. Protests over the incident helped to propel Richard Arrington Jr., the city's first Black mayor, into office. Birmingham was well on its way to becoming, as it is today, nearly 70 percent African American—or, as Parliament/Funkadelic might sing about it, a "Chocolate City."

In my memory of the time, I saw the city's power dynamics shifting as sure as Great American Hamburger's.

But then, while writing this book, I started tracking down people who worked there. I found a few through Facebook groups that traffic in nostalgia for local high schools, Eastwood Mall, and Birmingham history.

It turns out that most of us see Great American Hamburger as a microcosm of our larger world. But not everyone agrees that this vision is positive. One man, a white guy whose personal Facebook feed focuses on far-right screeds and gun collecting, remembers the restaurant's kitchen as a dangerous place. He told me a story about the Black guys working there seeing a white busboy filching tips and then taking him out back to beat him up. One woman, also white, who went on in life to work for a corporate culture that valued "color blindness" challenged my view of the restaurant's racial hierarchies, especially among the female servers. She remembers the Vietnamese girls getting the better tables, but not because they outworked the white girls with immigrant hustle. Instead, she said, they were cuter and smiled more.

Mark, whom I found not through Facebook but from a rabbit-trail-like Google search, confirmed my sense of the place. Yes, absolutely, he said; the restaurant's manager promoted Black boys to the soda fountain and the cashier stand, but only the ones who went to John Carroll, the Catholic school, not the poorer kids who lived in Gate City or by the airport. Yes, he said, we had nonwhite managers, but only over the kitchen, not over the restaurant front. And, yes, said Mark, who was raised Jewish in Mountain Brook, his WASP-y classmates were "complete jerks." Mark told me that after he got his own car, he sometimes gave kitchen guys rides home. Buses stopped running at midnight, and if they had to stay late, as they often did to do the dirty work of making the restaurant health-department safe, they'd have to walk home, navigating a busy four-lane road that had no sidewalks, or cutting through white neighborhoods where police lay in wait. Mark said they routinely got stopped in Woodlawn, with white cops sometimes pulling him and the Black guys out of the car to frisk them or rough them up. "Where's the liquor?" the cops would demand. "Where's the drugs?"

I didn't realize, until talking to Mark, the extent to which I had whitewashed my own memory. I didn't consider that Pete, by waiting with me after hours in the restaurant parking lot, put himself at risk for something worse than being called a racial slur. I didn't think about the ways that the city's dismantling of its the bus system created a de facto sundown town, unsafe for Black people to be on the streets at night, even as the city became more "chocolate."

As with that bus system, Birmingham's white people eventually opted out. The city's vanilla suburbs expanded alongside interstates and malls.

The process involved its own form of whitewashing. In 1975 another mall, called Century Plaza, opened just up the hill from Eastwood. Century Plaza eventually drew away enough customers to drive Eastwood out of business, as the latter mall helped do to downtown. In 2006 Eastwood Mall was demolished; Century Plaza closed three years later. Both malls gave way to the Riverchase Galleria, which took shoppers farther south and outside of Birmingham to Hoover. This residential community, incorporated in 1967, was named after William H. Hoover (1890–1979), who cofounded the white-supremacist American States' Rights Organization. After the city of Hoover annexed the land around Riverchase in 1980—to build the mall, an office park, and some upscale, gated-housing communities—its population grew exponentially, from 18,995 to today's 85,700—with over 70 percent of its residents identifying as white, like Birmingham in reverse. The growth was part of a larger explosion in Shelby County, which became famous in 2013 when the US Supreme Court ruled, in *Shelby County vs. Holder*, that federal election monitors were no longer necessary, even in places with a history of Jim Crow. The ruling, people like journalist Vann R. Newkirk II argue, "set the stage for a new era of white hegemony," negatively impacting voters who are poor, elderly, Black, and Latinx.

Around the time that the Riverchase Galleria was getting built, Mom broke up with Glen, and we moved again, this time to the garden apartments where I used to drop off Mark. I helped her pay for the place by working full-time at a law firm during my University of Alabama at Birmingham college days. The job also afforded me a new, not used, Honda Civic (the one that eventually would carry me away from Birmingham). Sometimes after work I drove the Honda through the British-sounding streets to the ridge. Instead of fantasizing about a screaming crash through iron gates, I listened to a lot of loud punk rock, smoked a lot of weed, and stared a lot at the roads intersecting through the valley.

I still go back there today on my yearly trips home. Looking down on those intersecting roads, I consider how they pave the way from past to present. I consider, too, how the words of people like Jack and Glen create paths to the actions of those who would decimate a whole bus system or create a whole new city so they can cut themselves off from anyone they perceive as different. Working at Great American Hamburger helped me see those connections, and I look back fondly on my days as a soda jerk.

Then I remind myself that spaces of nostalgia are never true and rarely safe—and that far too many of us, as Cathy ordered, need to stop being jackasses and get to work.

9 / CRAZY MARY ANN AND THE DELUSIONS PEOPLE TAKE FOR TRUTH

When my mother checked into a Florida psychiatric hospital in 2010, at age seventy-two, an RN named Lisa reviewed her symptoms over half-rim glasses and a clipboard chart: depression, anxiety, paranoia, delusions, and hallucinations.

Mom looked like a tiny child version of herself: slumped in a wheelchair, wearing pink cotton pajamas, fuzzy white slippers, and, because she knew the hospital would be cold, a white faux-fur coat.

"Sometimes I see things that aren't there," she told the nurse.

"It's good that you know they're not real," Lisa said as she turned her back to pull out a blood-pressure cuff. "A lot of people who come here don't."

Good psychiatric nurses have the gift of responding with neutral-voiced efficiency to the most extreme human actions. Before we made it back to see Nurse Lisa, we spent two hours in the pale-yellow waiting room with Mom stomping imaginary cockroaches and me watching other patients with wide-eyed worry. Lying splayed on the floor was a drunken twenty-something woman whose father brought her in for the rehab unit. Periodically she would stand up, yell, "I don't want to be here," charge the exit door, and fall down. Another twenty-something who looked anorexic sobbed in the corner and clawed her arms bloody. The admissions coordinator, tucked behind bullet-proof glass, took a call from a former patient whose boyfriend beat her up, stole her meds, and threw her out of the car in a Walmart parking lot. A taxi that the coordinator sent delivered her later, bruised and toothless. Following her was a man who dragged his wife in through the automatic front door and screamed at her in the lobby. A staff member came out to ask him calmly if he wanted to yell outside or have a hospital room of his own. After two hours of waiting, I felt as if I needed one, too.

During a previous stay in a Birmingham psychiatric ward, when she was seventy, Mom had been one of those patients to put visitors on edge. I once watched all 135 pounds of her take down a football-player-sized orderly. She believed that she was being held hostage and forced into prostitution. She told me that people were doing "unspeakable things" with knives and spiders to her private parts. When she couldn't take any more of the imaginary torture, she sprang out of the metal restraint seat like a mad cat from a wet box. The Geri Chair slid across the floor, and a few seconds later, so did the orderly who tried to catch her.

Two years later, in 2010, Mom had moved to an assisted living facility a few miles from my Florida home and was sleeping most of the day. She told the staff that she stayed awake all night watching the "Negro" drug dealers across the street who kept coming in to rape her roommate. Typically, an abuse report meant that the state sent in an investigator. A few weeks earlier I found myself going through Mom's finances with an eldercare agent after she complained that I stole her money. At the time, my husband Tom and I were in the process of adopting our son, then nine, from foster care. I was terrified that any suspicion of elder abuse would get the boy, Zack, taken away. I was angry at Mom, impatient with her delusions, not at all a level-headed nurse. Every visit to her room, every trying-to-be-compassionate review of her checkbook left me yelling and cursing.

"No one's stealing your fucking money! Look!"

Then I'd pull out whatever bills I had in my wallet to fling at her before stomping out. Later the aides would return the money to me after Mom tried to tip them. "It's hard to find good help," Mom said to me. "You have to be generous with them. Not like you. All you think about is yourself."

After a few rounds of money circulation, the facility manager realized that Mom had more trouble than other patients navigating reality. When she didn't have her own cash, she tipped the aides with items she took from other people's rooms. As for the people across the street, they were not African Americans but working-class white guys who stayed up late drinking beer and fiddling with their project cars. The roommate said that her problem wasn't getting raped each night but Mom making so much noise pacing the room in her walker.

Thus, we found ourselves in the psych ward, waiting for a meds evaluation.

I was surprised to hear Mom talk openly, for her, about what she experienced. No, she said, she never felt like hurting herself or others. People often tried to hurt her, but only in her imagination.

"Has anyone ever hurt you in real life?" Lisa asked.

"Well, you might say that I was abused," Mom said. "I had this boyfriend that was mean to me."

"Abused how—physically or emotionally?" Lisa continued.

My mother had a beautifully circuitous way of telling-not-telling. She stared into space for a few seconds, then replied in a voice like a winding country road, "Well, how many ways can a man be mean? You might say that Glen liked them all. But he's dead now. After me, he got mixed up with the wrong people, and they were mean to him."

Lisa looked at me for translation. I told her that Glen was a man Mom dated when I was in high school. He was a former police officer from a ritzy white suburb who got fired and started selling used cars from a tiny corner lot in a crumbling part of town. An alcoholic prone to rampages, Glen hit us routinely with words and hands. He was not her first abusive boyfriend, or the last, but he was certainly the worst. Mom didn't want to break up with him, though. When Glen wasn't being mean, she enjoyed having him around. Her friends thought him a good ol' boy, the life of the party, and a good Christian: when he wasn't hung over, he went to church. Mom depended on Glen financially, too. He bought her a car and helped her out with rent and the substantial credit card debt she racked up from compulsive shopping—a behavior that many people don't realize is symptomatic of bipolar mania. Another of Mom's symptoms, making poor relationship choices, manifested itself through men like Glen. Without him, she said, we were a paycheck away from living on the streets. (An exaggeration, as we had plenty of family members to take us in, but nevertheless an exaggeration that we both believed.) When I was in my early thirties and living in New York, Mom told me that Glen had been killed. She said his new girlfriend was connected to some organized-crime figures, and after he abused her too, he died mysteriously when she was out of town. The official ruling was "natural causes"—maybe a heart attack—but he supposedly had bruises all over his body that pointed toward a more violent end. I told Lisa that I didn't know what's true, but I preferred Mom's version.

The nurse smiled and nodded. "Whatever helps you heal, right?"

*

The first time that Glen went wild, I was fifteen. Mom and I had recently moved from my grandmother's house to a ticky-tacky apartment farther east of downtown, toward Center Point. We came home long after dark from a Memorial Day weekend at Aunt Nell and Uncle Bobby's Smith Lake cabin. I stumbled into the door of my tiny room, kicked off my Earth shoes next to the single bed, plopped the suitcase onto the desk chair at my left, crumpled my new Levi's on top, and then crawled under the covers in a yellow Bob Dylan T-shirt and white cotton panties. I don't remember anything unusual before going to sleep. The adults around me partied hard. Alcohol, cigarettes, and chaos were facts of life. Whoever drove home from the lake was probably drunk. In 1977 the rules were as lax as the social conventions. Getting pulled over for drinking and driving no more occurred to anyone than wearing a seat belt.

Around midnight, I woke up to the sound of something in my room. Running water? No. I sat up wide awake to articulate a fifteen-year-old girl's worst gross-out nightmare: *my mother's drunk boyfriend was peeing in my suitcase.*

I got up, walked into Mom's room and shook her awake. "Get your boyfriend out of my bedroom."

By that time Glen had stumbled back to his pass-out couch. I jostled him. "Glen, wake up. The bathroom's on the right."

He had no idea what he had done, and my mom thought he did something else entirely. While they yelled at each other, I ran back to my room, threw the wet Levi's and the suitcase into the hallway, shut the door, and locked it. I grabbed the pink Princess phone from the floor next to the bed. As I dialed my aunt and uncle, Glen charged down the hall after me.

"You goddam cunt, you goddam cunt!" he screamed, pounding on the door.

"Come get me!" I screamed to Aunt Nell when she picked up the phone. Then Glen kicked in the door.

I don't recall how long the fight lasted or even all the details about it, but I remember (truthfully or not) that I won. Glen slapped me and threw me up against the wall, demanding that I tell my mother he didn't touch me. I remember thinking quite clearly, and seemingly in slow motion as Glen slammed me repeatedly against the drywall, that to defend herself, a girl should kick a man in the balls, but I did not want to get any part of my body, even my stinky teen-girl feet, anywhere near his man-parts. Then something in me thought of the Earth shoes that I wriggled free an arm to grab. In my memory, I took time between drywall slams to ponder how such a shoe, worn on the right hand of a 120-pound girl can be an effective weapon against a drunken 200-plus- pound man, even an enraged one, for then the shoe becomes an effective club. Glen retreated to nurse his bruised head, and soon after, Uncle Bobby showed up with a shotgun.

He Dirty-Harry-dared Glen to move while I packed clothes in a black trash bag.

*

That summer would not be the last time Aunt Nell and Uncle Bobby took me in. Their house became part of the finely honed coping strategy I developed over two years of facing Glen's whiskey tempers. Smile. Agree that I had a fat ass. Agree that I was a slut. Pull out the keys I kept hidden in my bra so that Glen wouldn't take them. Walk out the door and drive to my aunt and uncle's. To my grandmother's. To my best friend Mary's. Anywhere the road might go.

One night in 1979, during a bone-cold March rainstorm, Mom and I were watching television when someone knocked on the door.

"Don't open it," Mom cautioned. "It's Glen. He's mad."

She told me later that he had gone through her purse and found a $500 check from a lawyer friend—a loan to help with that month's credit card bills. Glen believed she got the money as payment for sex.

I looked out the peep hole and, seeing no one, told Mom that it must be Mary and her boyfriend playing a trick. They often dropped by after dinner to goof around. I expected to open the door and see Mary mooning me.

Instead, a soaking-wet Glen jumped out from the stairwell.

I slammed the door in his face, fumbling with the deadbolt and chain. A cheap apartment's hollow-core entrance was no more a match for a rampaging drunk than the Geri Chair was for my traumatized mom decades later.

Glen crashed through in a few cop-kicks.

I ran to call 911. Glen grabbed Mom off the couch, dragged her outside by the throat, and slammed her against the stairway's metal railing.

Then he pulled the gun.

I saw him dig the pistol into the side of Mom's face and heard the trigger clicks over her sobbing.

"Cheating whore," Glen growled.

"Hurry! Please hurry!" I screamed into the phone.

The 911 operator asked, "Do you *know* the man with the gun?"

I watched myself throw down the phone and move to the kitchen. I remember thinking that I needed just a few minutes to boil water in the tea kettle so I could scald Glen to death.

The next thing I remember is seeing our neighbor Johnny—a skinny, shirtless man with his name engraved on his belt buckle—at the stairwell's bottom with a shotgun.

"Goddam, girl," Johnny said, snapping me into realizing that I stood behind Glen clutching a butcher knife.

Glen let go of Mom, slung the pistol down the stairs, and ran off in the rain.

"It's not even loaded, you dumbasses," he yelled before climbing into the red Buick he had left running.

As Glen screeched and fishtailed out of the parking lot, Uncle Bobby and Aunt Nell drove up. Johnny had called them before coming to us. They also had a Glen routine. Uncle Bobby patched up whatever got broken, this time the door. Aunt Nell wrapped Mom in a blanket and helped me, again, fill a trash bag with clothes.

Two policemen arrived thirty minutes later. They ran their hands along the cracked door frame, talked to Johnny and Uncle Bobby, but not Mom or me, then headed back out.

A cop friend told me years later that some officers took their time when the call was domestic.

"They try to wait it out," he said. The men usually calm down, the women rarely press charges, and "nobody wants to face down some crazy mother-fucker with a gun."

*

Years later, when Mom called to say that she saw a Black man across the street, the police came within a minute.

By that time, 1984, she had broken up with Glen, and we lived in a differ-ent apartment, this one just inside the city limits of an elite Birmingham sub-urb, Mountain Brook. I had first seen the small, brick garden units when tak-ing a coworker home from my high school mall job and drove by them often during my hide-from-Glen rambles, fantasizing about a better life in a nicer part of town. In college I worked full-time, for the lawyer who lent Mom the $500, to put a deposit on the garden apartment we called our "Over the Mountain Ghetto." We distinguished our home, on a four-lane by the mall, from the old-money mansions closer to the Birmingham Country Club, and especially from the projects at the bottom of the long, downhill road into the city.

We were used to seeing African American domestics getting off the bus and climbing the winding streets up to the mansions. But one day Mom saw a man walking past them, toward the mall.

"You can't just call the police because you see someone walking down a road!" I yelled at my mother when she told me she had just dialed 911.

"Yes I can," she said, as a cruiser's blue lights flew by outside.

Mom was right. The immediate response of police in affluent Mountain Brook versus the delayed response in blue-collar Center Point was related in some ways, as my cop friend indicated, to domestic violence. But those response times also had their roots in race and class. Years later I would nod in recognition when Flavor Flav chanted, "You better wake up and smell the real flavor/Cause 911 is a fake life saver" in the 1990 Public Enemy song "911 Is a Joke." Later still, my recognition shifted into cringe mode at the cutesy nicknames devised for white women who called 911 on Black people doing ordinary things in public: BBQ Becky, Permit Patty, the ubiquitous Karens. The bottom line is that zip codes play a significant role in how quickly someone gets help in a real-life emergency (the wealthier the better), and that white women have a long history of perceiving Black people as threats when no actual emergency exists.

13. Mary Ann Gamblin, ca. 1968, with the Birmingham Legal Secretaries' bowling league. Image courtesy of the author

I used to think that my mom was her own unique nut. She called 911 many times from her Mountain Brook apartment: when she saw, or thought she saw, an African American outside her window, giant spiders crawling up her bedroom wall, or the man who lived behind us, who had died, come back to life to beat his girlfriend.

It would be 2008, the year Mom busted the Geri Chair and took down the orderly, that I discovered she had an actual mental illness. Diagnosed variously until her death as Bipolar II, borderline personality disorder, and early-onset dementia, her problems were compounded by living through the trauma of domestic abuse. For most of my life, friends and family thought of her as "Crazy Mary Ann," who loved shopping, drinking, dancing, gambling, dirty jokes, good fights, and bad men.

Mom had her own temper—one that flared up like fireworks and just as quickly fizzled out. Glen's violence, on the other hand, was chronic: daily insults, weekly outbursts, and periodic, life-threatening explosions. Few people knew what took place in our home and how it pushed my mother over an emotional precipice from which she would never return.

I also learned later that schizophrenic symptoms like paranoia and delusions are culturally specific. The Bible tells many stories of people hearing the voice of God. Joan of Arc saw angels and saints telling her to liberate France. In Africa and India, people who hear voices describe them as friendly or benign. In the United States, delusions typically threaten and frighten. At the New York Public Library, I did my graduate-school studying across from a wild-haired, wild-eyed patron I called "Cutting Board Man." He filled page after page with tiny, cramped handwriting, while clutching a cutting board to his chest. Next to him he kept a sign saying that the CIA had implanted a chip into his brain—a frequently experienced delusion in our technology-dependent society.

After Cutting Board Man, I did not find it surprising that Crazy Mary Ann, who came of age in the Jim Crow South, perceived her terrors through the lens of race and violence. As southern white women, we both lived with the delusion that Black men intended us harm. The belief—rooted not in mental illness but in racism—emerged after the Civil War, as the former Confederate states developed postslavery strategies for maintaining white supremacy. Between 1877 and 1950, white southerners lynched more than 4,500 African Americans, most of them men, under the guise of protecting white ladies from a violent, hypersexualized stereotype, the "Burly Black Brute." Such lynchings were not mere hangings but often involved torture, shooting, stabbing, and burning. Some lynchings occurred before large crowds—hundreds or thousands of men, women, and children—who took photographs and, occasionally, "souvenirs" from the dead person's body. Yet even by 1892, activists such as Ida B. Wells were describing the "rape myth" that justified such gruesome violence as "a threadbare lie." Wells's research, corroborated by contemporary scholars such as Stewart E. Tolnay and E. M. Beck, found that fewer than 30 percent of all lynchings resulted from accusations of rape, and most of those accusations were, at best, spurious.

During the 1970s and '80s, the women in my family weren't reading Ida B. Wells. Instead, we persisted in believing the old threadbare lie. We avoided African American areas of town. We locked our car doors or, if walking, crossed the street when a Black man came near. When we heard stories of white women assaulted, we whispered of the alleged perpetrator, "Was he Black?"

All the while we knew that the men insulting us, hitting us, raping us were white.

*

Mom's 2010 stay in the psychiatric hospital with Nurse Lisa got her a medication cocktail that kept her relatively stable. She moved to a different assisted living facility, where she lived until her 2015 death, far away from the imaginary drug dealer rapists. This new facility, which specialized in patients with mental illness and dementia, installed Mom in a sunlit corner room that looked out on live oak trees and gave her what she believed was a job. Each morning after she woke up, an aide dressed her in the bright, color-coordinated blouse-and-capri outfits she loved, topped with the faux-fur white coat. She wheeled down to the television room through a long corridor lined with people of different ages and different hues, some of them dozing, others conversing, aloud, with their memories. Mom spent her days in the television room or outside the nurse's station, believing she was at work, holding onto the empty manila folders that the nurses gave her to organize. She told me that she liked her new job even though, she said, getting there meant walking through that Over the Mountain Ghetto.

Her delusions often had factual roots. In her mental landscape's instability, she tried to set right the uncertainties of her past. Mom was a legal secretary for thirty years in a US bankruptcy court, rising up from the typing pool to supervisor. Her work was her pride and her life. She was active in her professional organization—the Birmingham Legal Secretaries Association—established a scholarship in her name, and once won Alabama's Legal Secretary of the Year.

But Mom's office manager pushed her to retire in her early fifties because she insisted that two of her coworkers, Pete and Sue, were sabotaging her career, angry at her for breaking a glass plate of fudge from the office Christmas party. Mom kept boxes of notes—in a script that looked like Cutting Board Man's—where she ranted about Pete and Sue, and corruption in Alabama's federal court system. Of course she would spend her last years on earth trying to order her files.

I visited her assisted living facility a couple of times each week. We would eat lunch, go outside to sit in the sun, or work together at her imaginary job. I tried to stay calm when she accused me of stealing her money, cheating on Tom, or beating Zack. I let her drone about the good old days of living in the country or her phone conversations with my grandmother, long distance to Heaven.

On one visit in 2012, I sat with Mom in the television room as she took a break from her make-believe job and watched the news. I was partially listening to her and partially scrolling through Facebook on my phone, when I realized that she was getting agitated. She shifted around in her wheelchair and dropped her files to the floor.

"Call 911!" she yelled at me.

The news report was covering the recent charges filed against George Zimmerman in Sanford, Florida, for the shooting death of seventeen-year-old Trayvon Martin. Zimmerman, like an earlier version of Mary Ann, had a history of calling the police on Black males walking through the streets of the gated community where he lived. On the night of February 26, 2012, Martin, visiting his father, walked to a nearby convenience store. Zimmerman, a volunteer neighborhood watch coordinator, dialed the local nonemergency number to report a suspicious person walking down the street. Against police advice, Zimmerman began to follow the teenager. A confrontation soon ensued that led to the unarmed Martin's fatal shooting. In a later murder trial, Zimmerman's self-defense plea resulted in a not-guilty verdict.

What bothered Mom was George Zimmerman's mug shot on the television room's big screen. With his beard, chubby cheeks, and balding head, he looked much like her ex-boyfriend, whose given name was George Glen. Mom's mind conflated the two men as one.

She insisted that we call Glen's deceased mother. We needed to ask why her son shot a teenager who wasn't doing anything but walking down the road.

"Call 911!" she screamed again.

Glen had been hiding in the woods for years, Mom said. He was building her a house, but she didn't want to live there. Instead, she wanted the police to take her to live with my grandmother. She wanted to move to Heaven, as far away from Glen—and Hell—as she could get.

"9-1-1!" Mom bellowed.

An aide intervened.

"Miss Mary," she said in a calm, even nurse-voice, "Julie can't call 911 with you making so much noise. Let's go down the hall and give her some quiet."

The aide wheeled Mom away from the coverage of Martin's death and Zimmerman's arrest. Mom went back to putting her files in order and soon forgot what she saw on television.

Driving home afterward, I thought about the different ways that, throughout her life, Crazy Mary Ann folded truth and delusion into an odd origami of sense. The former legal secretary became a wheelchair file clerk. George became Glen. Trayvon became all Black men deemed suspicious for walking down a road.

I realized, also, that I am grateful for my mother's crazy vision. If not for Mary Ann, I might never have looked closely at the delusions, especially about race and gender, that far too many people take for truth. If not for the trauma that the two of us survived, together, I might never have seen how capable I am of fighting back.

10 / LEARNING FROM BIRMINGHAM

At the time of this writing, I've lived away from Birmingham for more than three decades and, for just over two, I've been teaching civil rights movement literature.

A typical course begins with students stumbling into my University of South Florida classroom and blinking their eyes to readjust from the outside's blinding St. Petersburg sun. They sit down in caster-wheeled orange desks scattered across the blue-and-gray-tile carpet in an unruly circle. The lights are dimmed so the students can focus on the jumbo screen up front, where a video plays John Legend and the Roots' 2010 remake of Harold Melvin and the Blue Notes' 1975 "Wake Up Everybody." The song sets the stage for the semester. It begins with Legend's clear tenor singing, "Wake up everybody, no more sleeping in bed/No more backward thinking, time for thinking ahead." As I organize handouts and greet the incoming students, Canadian chanteuse Melanie Fiona pipes in: "They're the ones who's coming up and the world is in their hands." A white millennial, pierced and tattooed, takes a seat next to an equally tattooed Latinx veteran of Iraq and Afghanistan, who sits behind a thirty-something Jamaican Christian, who in turn sits next to a gender-fluid atheist wearing earbuds. By the time that rapper Common finishes his lines, "in this generation living through computers / Only love, love, love can reboot us," the students have settled and quieted, and I fade out the sound to introduce the course.

"The wake-up call opens a long history of civil rights cultural productions," I tell them. Most link the idea to a social media hashtag, #staywoke, popularized with the rise of Black Lives Matter protests during the early-to-mid-2010s, but they aren't familiar with the term's lineage. Some recognize the refrain "I stay woke" from Erykah Badu's 2008 song "Master Teacher." Rarely does anyone in class know that the term goes back decades before Badu. William Melvin Kelley brought "woke" to the attention of white audiences in a 1962 *New York Times* article on "Negro idiom": "If You're Woke You Dig It." But the concept goes back before 1962, and forward from 2008. Some of the more familiar iterations in film and literature include an alarm clock's "*Brrrrrrriiiiiiiiiiiiiiiiiiinng*" in the first line of Richard Wright's 1940 novel *Native Son*, Ruth yelling for Walter Lee Younger to "do some waking up in there" at the start of Lorraine Hansberry's 1959 play *Raisin in the Sun*, and Mister Señor Love Daddy crying, "Waaaake up! Wake up, wake up, wake up!" to introduce Spike Lee's 1989 film *Do the Right Thing*. In fact, most every film Lee ever made—including, more recently, 2018's *BlacKkKlansman*—features a character challenging another, or looking directly into the camera while challenging the audience, to "wake up." Scenes like these set the stage for the transformative experience of becoming politically aware, or "woke."

During the later years of the Donald J. Trump presidential administration, conservative commentators began declaring war on "woke," employing the term as a catch-all for ideas deemed too liberal or progressive, like critical race theory or white privilege. The irony is that by the time white conservatives began saying "woke," the word had become passé among progressives. Like that blond Afro my mom sported during the 1970s and 80s, once white people catch on to, and co-opt, a trend from Black culture, it loses potency. If William Melvin Kelley wrote his article today, the title might read "If You're Woke You Don't Say the Word." More than the word, however, what white conservatives seem to fear most is a situation like the one that takes place at least once a year in my classroom: a bunch of people from a diverse range of backgrounds coming together to ask why things are the way they are, and how they might change.

But the idea of waking up—of moving from ignorance to insight—persists.

Perhaps someone should tell those "antiwoke" conservatives that a similar theme exists in the writings of white southerners from the twentieth century, with roots that go back even further than that. In a 1999 book titled *But Now I See*, literary scholar Fred Hobson identified a story pattern that he called the "racial conversion narrative," where characters progress, in terms of racial consciousness, from blindness to awareness. As Hobson describes it, the racial conversion narrative has its origins in Puritan stories of religious awakening. Anyone raised in a Protestant evangelical tradition knows the narrative well. The Southern Baptist church trained—and repeatedly encouraged—young people like myself to map our lives around the moment of salvation. The racial conversion narrative's arc similarly moves from sin to enlightenment and repentance as the storyteller confesses, then hopes for absolution from her racist ways. Hobson traces the pattern through multiple writers from Lillian Smith to Katharine Du Pre Lumpkin, James McBride Dabbs, Willie Morris, Larry L. King, and others. One might also see resemblances between these authors' autobiographical writings and fictional works such as Mark Twain's *Huckleberry Finn* and Harper Lee's *To Kill a Mockingbird*, where characters struggle to locate their own sense of ethics in a society that deems slavery and segregation acceptable. Hobson takes his book's title from the hymn "Amazing Grace," penned by the eighteenth-century slave-trader-turned-clergyman John Newton: "I once was lost, but now am found / Was blind, but now I see." It's worth noting how the conservative reaction against "woke" culture emerges from the fear of a Black challenge to a white status quo. White writers have pointed out that racism is a sin for hundreds of years without politicians and pundits declaring a war on "Amazing Grace."

Both the Black wake-up call and the white racial conversion narrative involve moments of rupture, a powerful departure from one way of seeing and being to another. *Native Son's* Bigger Thomas tumbles into the rat maze of Chicago's Jim Crow North after he accidentally kills his white employer's daughter. Walter Lee Younger gets conned out of his late father's life insurance money, which was supposed to put his family on a better path toward the American Dream. Huck Finn reaches a moral crisis after he thinks his river-raft partner, Jim, has been sold back into slavery, deciding, "All right then, I'll go to Hell," rather than do what slaveholding society tells him is right. In one of the most popular civil-rights-era books of the last half century, *To Kill a Mockingbird's* Scout realizes what her father, Atticus, means about seeing the world from other people's perspective only after she meets face-to-face the violence that structures the scenery of the small southern town in which she lives.

In both the Civil Rights Movement literature course and others I regularly teach, we talk a lot about that moment of rupture and its place within broader journey stories. Many of the characters we read about, or that students know from other places, undertake journeys that are both literal and metaphorical. Twain's Huck learns about life, and himself, after he runs away from his abusive father to raft down the Mississippi River. Lee's Mookie takes trips that are more limited in breadth, circling his Bedford-Stuyvesant neighborhood delivering pizzas, but certainly not in depth, plunging into a lesson on racist cruelty that culminates in his friend Radio Raheem's death at the hands of local police. Students recognize such journeys and how they work from a lifetime of books and movies where the protagonist leaves (or is forced from) home; undertakes a quest for knowledge, treasure, or both; encounters mentors and helpers; battles demons inside and out; and then returns wiser and more empowered. Anyone unfamiliar with Huck on the Mississippi probably knows Dorothy on the Yellow Brick Road; those who haven't seen Mookie with his pizza box have watched Luke Skywalker with his light saber. Traditional-age college students especially are interested in the journey and the rupture. Most are living away from home for the first time, trying to learn who they are and what they think apart from what they've been taught. They're facing the demons and meeting the helpers that will shape the directions their life paths take. Those who sign up for a Civil Rights Movement literature course typically (unless they want only to fill three hours of elective credits on Wednesdays) come in thinking of themselves as "woke." Even if they no longer use that term, they remain concerned about the world they've inherited. Whether liberal or conservative, they hope to figure out in college what it is that they truly, authentically believe, for those beliefs to be guided by some form of moral compass, and for that compass, in turn, to guide their actions. As much as students tell me they want to think "outside the box," they also want structures to help them organize the messiness of their changing lives.

Most every semester, someone in class asks how my own racial awareness developed. They imagine their white professor's journey to have a familiar arc: the rupture of leaving Birmingham, moving to New York to get woke, coming back south to cure others' blindness with new insights. I want to be a good helper, not a demon my students must battle (although that happens occasionally, at least according to what they say in end-of-semester evaluations), so I try to tell them my version of the truth. In some ways that journey story is correct, but it leaves out a key piece of information. As much as traveling the world helped me see Birmingham, Birmingham taught me to see the world.

When I left home in 1985, I knew, intimately, the physical and emotional violence of living in a highly stratified society that was deemed natural—our "southern way of life"—but was in fact constructed to benefit a select few, mostly men, mostly affluent, mostly white. I learned this in my integrated schools and my integrated jobs. I saw it in my church's warped ideas of good and evil. I experienced it when moving from a poorer part of town to a wealthier one. I felt it in my body every time I had to stay silent around men like Glen to keep from getting hurt. What I didn't understand then but discovered in the decades after leaving home was how I sometimes benefited from social hierarchies. I got jobs through my mother's connections to lawyers and judges. I rebelled against gender norms but didn't have to fear, like David and Jody, getting beaten up or killed because of it. No matter how often I did something wrong—and, trust me, that happened way more times than

I'm confessing in this book—all I had to do was open my blue eyes wide, turn on my Barbie-doll smile, and shake my long blond hair to become the perfect picture of innocence. These things I learned to acknowledge from continuing my education, in school and out, and then turning that new awareness back to where I've come from and forward to where I need to go.

The most important part of the journey story that I want my students to know is that the waking-up process is recursive, not linear, and most important, ongoing. The potential for rupture—to be shaken out of my comfort zone into new knowledge—happens every day that I walk into a classroom, every time I open a book.

*

A frequent refrain in classes that focus on civil rights, race relations, or political awakening has students asking, "Why didn't I learn this in school?" The answer is multilayered.

To begin, today's public K–12 classrooms often aim for the acronyms. In Florida we have, at the time I am writing, the FSAs (Florida Statewide Assessments), the EOCs (End of Course testing), and the other barrage of assessments students undergo yearly to measure their supposed learning. Other states have their own versions, all designed to hold teachers "accountable" for students' educational progress. In practice, little actual learning takes place. For example, Florida schools "teach to the test," making sure to cover, from August to March, all the content snippets that students need to regurgitate through multiple choice at the school year's end. By early April testing season begins. When students are done, usually by mid-May, they watch movies in class or go home early until the final bell rings just before Memorial Day. Brazilian educator Paulo Freire describes such a practice as the "banking concept" of education, where teachers make "deposits" into the heads of passive students and then make "withdrawals" come test time. Students in my classes who tell me that they never learned about the Civil Rights Movement are partially correct. They likely were exposed to the topic in grade four, where they studied Florida's role in the movement, and again in high school, where they looked at such subjects as "key figures and organizations in shaping the Civil Rights Movement and Black Power Movement" or "the freedom movements that advocated civil rights for African Americans, Latinos, Asians, and women." Exposure does not necessarily mean learning. Although Florida's legislature mandates coverage of the movement as part of the general US history curriculum, the state also explains that history "shall be viewed as factual, not as constructed . . . as knowable, teachable, and *testable*" (emphasis mine). For Florida students, and I suspect for those in other states, a small civil rights deposit was made and withdrawn, leaving their mind-banks empty. They learned and promptly forgot.

Beyond the testing culture lie problems of teacher preparedness. First, classroom content offers a self-perpetuating cycle: teachers pass on to students what they learned in their own K–12 and college experiences. The organization Learning for Justice (formerly Teaching Tolerance) explains that Civil Rights Movement education across the country can be summed up as "two names and four words": Martin Luther King Jr., Rosa Parks, and "I have a dream." Teachers who did not learn more-complex content are unlikely to provide their students with more-complex content, especially if it takes time away from material on a state-mandated test. Second, focusing on the familiar "two names and four words" provides what historian Jacquelyn Dowd Hall describes as a triumphant, although not necessarily accurate, story of American progress. The dominant, or "master" narrative, tells us that Jim Crow was bad, heroes like Parks and King fought back, and racism went away. Many teachers don't feel ready, comfortable, or motivated to engage students in a process of busting that myth, especially when the process involves connecting the past to highly charged issues of the present. Classroom conversations about topics such as white privilege, racial disparities in the criminal justice system, or the link between political rhetoric and racist violence provide an almost certain recipe for parental, administrative, or community outrage. Consider the controversy that emerged in 2021 over critical race theory. In an offshoot of conservative "antiwoke" battles, several states, including Florida, outlawed the teaching of a subject rarely, if ever, covered in K–12 classrooms, because it was misconstrued as unpatriotic and divisive. In a social climate where thought censoring and school shootings have become the norm, how much easier and safer to stick to a noncontroversial script that everyone thinks they know.

Even though I later became a civil rights educator, my formal schooling provided little training in the movement or race relations. Instead, most of my knowledge came from outside-the-classroom reading and other learning opportunities, from colleagues and friends, and especially from students. As a young woman named Corey told me pointedly during my first tenure-track job in Georgia, "white people invented this mess, so it's your responsibility to learn how to fix it." The "mess" she referred to—how racism structures, often invisibly, our foundational institutions, our language, and even how we think—was not something I considered seriously until I began teaching and writing. Growing up in a postmovement-era Birmingham gave me a vantage point from which to perceive those invisible structures. But for much of my life I didn't look too far beyond the "script" I was given. Like many, I fell into the trap of believing in "color blindness": the notion that ignoring race makes racism disappear. A legally blind woman in one of my classes once called out a peer who argued that looking closely at race is the real problem. "I can't see," Paula said, "but I still know when I smell a rat."

How to see, or sniff out, the rat in the room has been my pedagogical focus for more than twenty years. At some point I had to consciously break the cycle of passing along the easy, familiar stories passed along to me. First I had to recognize that the cycle existed, that it could be broken, and that doing so was both a social benefit and a moral imperative. That process involved both journey and rupture.

*

I wasn't supposed to go to college, much less become a civil rights educator.

As for going to college, my high school did not have official tracks back in the 1970s, but students did meet with guidance counselors to outline goals and plan courses. My assigned counselor terrified me. She was tall and angular, all hacksaw arms and hawk face. She frequented the same grocery store where I helped my grandmother shop for her weekly cans of salmon and peaches. Once Ms. Counselor stood behind me in line while I paid; Granny's back gave out in the middle aisles, so she went to the car to rest while I finished the shopping. I had not been self-conscious before about paying with food stamps, but this time Ms. Counselor hovered behind me with one brow cocked above a beady gray eye. As I tried to tear the coupons from their perforated book, my hands sweated and shook so badly that the cashier had to help. After we finished the transaction, I gave the counselor a weak smile and a "see you at school" before pushing the cart out of the store so quickly that I nearly slammed into the automatic door. Within a few weeks, I found myself in Ms. Counselor's office while she turned the beady eye upon what students are taught to fear from first grade: my "permanent record."

I had a ready answer for her question about life after graduation: college.

What I didn't expect was her response: "Why? I don't think you can afford it."

My family figured that I was probably college-bound from the time, prior to starting elementary school, I used to line up my stuffed animals before a toy chalkboard for reading and writing lessons. Granny did a two-year nursing program, and Mom did a stint in secretarial school—but beyond that I knew few people who made it past twelfth grade. I was a fluke, but one whose educational ambitions were nurtured by the adults around me. My fourth-grade teacher had me tested for a gifted program, which I got accepted for but did not attend. Going meant changing to a school where Mom couldn't drive me and still make it to work on time. But I knew that she was proud: she saved every report card, every "A" assignment, every glowing note that teachers sent home.

In fairness to the counselor, she had hundreds of students to place. If our school did not have official tracks, we did have unofficial ones that guided her decision making. Four K–8 elementary schools fed into Banks High (we didn't, at the time, have junior high or middle schools). Kids from South East Lake and Christian, set in the green hills behind the high school, typically took the academic courses that would send them to the state's flagship universities, Alabama and Auburn. Kids from the grittier side of the Fourth Avenue South dividing line—Robinson, where I attended, and Barrett—typically went directly to blue-collar and service jobs. (A Barrett-to-Banks student named Jerri reported an experience similar to mine with the same guidance counselor.) What was Ms. Counselor to make of a gifted kid on food stamps that she couldn't fit into a box? I wound up my junior year with a schedule that included Career Explorations, Distributive Education (a vocational program where students get on-the-job training), Advanced Composition, and Latin.

Ultimately the counselor served me well, even though I chafed at being challenged about college. The odd mix of courses clarified what I could and would do—and what I would not. On our Career Explorations field trips, typically to the city's iron and steel mills, I hid in factory bathrooms or skipped school altogether. Through Distributive Education, I got the Great American Hamburger job, building the work history that eventually helped me pay for college. Ms. Counselor was right: we couldn't afford it, and I wound up working full-time all the way through graduate school. She knew her demographic. Although the neighborhood where I grew up has changed over the years, it has never offered high predictability for success. A Harvard University research team assembled a database using census information, the Opportunity Atlas, that shows the population from our zip code on the economy's lower end: in the United States' sixth percentile for income. (The hillside neighborhoods behind my high school, conversely, fall right in the median.) As a young woman growing up in Birmingham, chances were almost double that I would have a baby in my teens (40%) than graduate from college in my twenties (21%). And I did *not* want a baby.

With regard to a working-class white girl from Birmingham going on to teach and write about the Civil Rights Movement, well, Harvard doesn't yet a have data-set to predict those odds. But here I was not the only fluke. *Birmingham News* columnist John Archibald, a schoolmate two years my junior, went on to win a 2018 Pulitzer Prize for his writing on Alabama politics and, in 2021, to publish a book called *Shaking the Gates of Hell* about his Methodist-minister father in civil-rights-era Birmingham. Banks High School, before it graduated its final class in 1989, saw many star football players pass through, but award-winning writers were in short supply. If anyone can be held responsible for helping students like John and me defy the odds, it would be the teachers.

Two in particular pointed me down this path, Mary Bowie and Sidney Moore.

Mrs. Bowie—thin, prim, no-nonsense—taught English. I took several courses with her, including the senior-level "On to College," where we learned to write term papers and read Great Books. More important than class was what happened outside of it. When I had to leave home after Glen's drunken rampages, Mrs. Bowie drove me to school. She lived near Aunt Nell and Uncle Bobby, who took me in several times during my teen years. Our fifteen-minute rides from Center Point to Banks carried us down Parkway East—a road filled with fast food, used car lots, churches, big-box stores, and billboards—where Mrs. Bowie made sure the learning didn't stop. "What's wrong with that sign?" she asked at every plural that incorrectly used an apostrophe, every confusion of "its" and "it's" or "your and "you're." Moving from spelling and grammar faux pas to the Civil Rights Movement might seem a long stretch of intellectual highway, but Mrs. Bowie ultimately taught me to pay careful attention. Do that enough times in Birmingham, and you notice a few things: the connection between faulty words and faulty logic, for instance, or the deep structures of race and class that many believe are as God-created as the local topography.

If Mrs. Bowie covered the details, then Mr. Moore, who taught psychology, mapped the depths. The two were opposites in many ways. Mr. Moore was a favorite teacher of almost everyone at Banks; Mrs. Bowie was the tough presence we feared but didn't appreciate until long after graduation. She was all about the rules; he had a twinkle-in-the-eyes naughtiness that encouraged students to ask who made the rules and why. In another place and time, Mrs. Bowie would have been a white New England schoolmarm. Mr. Moore would have been in a Harlem bar, theorizing the Black revolution. For one of his first lessons, on operant conditioning, I sat across from another student in the middle of our class circle (disrupting authority from the start, he organized students not into orderly rows but into the circles I use for teaching to this day). When Mr. Moore rang a bell, my partner clapped her hands together millimeters from my nose. I jumped back, startled. After a few repeats, he rang the bell, and the other student, whom he coached for the experiment ahead of time, didn't clap. I still flinched. "What have you learned in life," he posed to the class, "that's just habit, muscle memory? You know that you can also unlearn those things." He rang the bell again. I made myself not flinch.

*

Like many white students educated in public schools after desegregation and before the 1990s "culture wars," I had several nonwhite teachers, most of them females, but little nonwhite curriculum. (Those culture wars were a precursor to today's battlefield of wokeness, with their own rhetorical bugbear: "political correctness.") Classes meant learning that Columbus discovered America, the Pilgrims invented Thanksgiving, the cowboys defeated the Indians, southerners gave Africans jobs, and then the United States brought democracy to the world. Literature meant Shakespeare, Hawthorne, and Hemingway. If any teacher tried to give me a different perspective, I probably would not have listened, even after my lesson from Mr. Moore. I loved making construction-paper turkeys each November, could not get enough *Macbeth*. I was the one weird kid who enjoyed "The Custom House" preface to *The Scarlet Letter*, who finished Margaret Mitchell's *Gone with the Wind* during a three-day binge weekend because a teacher said that someone else read the thousand-page book in a week. Organizing my K–12 years was a trinity of beliefs in the South as a superior region, America as a superior nation, and white people as a superior race. Nothing I read challenged that godhead.

The only change that college and graduate school brought was more white males in charge. All of my professors at the University of Alabama at Birmingham (for a BA in English), the University of Memphis (MA), and New York University (PhD) were white, and five were female. Granted, university faculties grew more diverse between 1979, when I first entered college, and 1997, when I finished a PhD, but the demographics certainly did not reflect US society as a whole—and still do not. Statistics from the

American Academy of Arts and Sciences show that, as of 2015, roughly 90 percent of humanities doctorates are earned by white people, with the remaining 10 percent composed of all other racial/ethnic categories combined. The curricula from the schools I attended reflect their faculties' racial dynamics. Consider, for example, textbooks in my field of study, American literature. The widely used *Norton Anthology of American Literature* first came out in 1979. Only two of the writers in Volume I (*Beginnings to the Civil War*) are not white: Phillis Wheatley and Frederick Douglass. Ten of the writers in Volume II (*Civil War to the Present*) are not white, though all of those non-white authors are male: Booker T. Washington, W. E. B. Du Bois, Charles Chesnutt, Jean Toomer, Countee Cullen, Langston Hughes, Richard Wright, Ralph Ellison, James Baldwin, and Malcolm X—the latter a surprisingly radical choice for the time, over Martin Luther King Jr. Note the absence, too, of writers who don't fit into a Black/white binary division. Today's Norton differs quite a bit. The anthology has expanded into four volumes, with writers from a wide range of backgrounds. Even more diverse are the Heath Anthologies, which began appearing in 1989, and focus on what editor Paul Lauter describes as the "heterogeneity and richness of American culture" missing from previous books.

In college, I don't remember reading any of the Norton's Black writers. If I did, the material did not stick with me. Much like high school, college meant sitting silently in rows taking notes while the professor lectured, and then filling in the correct bubbles with a No. 2 pencil come test time. (The only real difference being that in college, after tests, classmates went out drinking—which might also explain any faulty memory occurring in this book.) Occasionally we wrote five-paragraph essays on topics such as the features that made Hemingway's *The Old Man and the Sea* a "classic"—a paper that I actually wrote and still hang on to for reasons of humility. An A- for spelling the author's name "Hemmingway" reminds me that many very good students still have a lot to learn. In retrospect, that "Hemmingway" essay also tells me something else: that students do not stray too far from familiar paths of knowledge. I wrote on *The Old Man and the Sea* because I read the book in Ms. Bowie's class and did very well on my first term paper, a study of Hemingway's Christ imagery. Today, when I teach Introduction to Literature to first-year students, I ask them to pick course readings; steering them away from their *Great Gatsby* and *To Kill a Mockingbird* comfort zone takes effort. Part of the problem for all of us is laziness—reading something new means work—but another part is that students in their late teens and early twenties are, with the growth of their frontal lobes, just starting to think critically. As their brains develop, they begin figuring out who they are and what they know apart from what they've been told.

*

Ultimately, that brain science thing is what happened to me. I discovered African American, and especially Black women, writers about the time that my frontal lobe started connecting the dots. And doing so effectively rewired my brain circuitry.

It happened casually. In Memphis a teaching-assistant colleague gave me Alice Walker's 1982 novel *The Color Purple* to read around the time that the film version came out. I recognized in Celie my own story of healing from violence through writing, of educating myself through books. But *The Color Purple* also provided images of whiteness that contradicted what I had been taught—in school and out. If I identified with the African American Celie, I also saw myself (to my chagrin) in the white Miss Millie's condescending ignorance. The experience offered what great literary works do best: provide an entryway, through connection and empathy, to a world that takes readers outside of themselves into new ways of seeing and being.

From Walker I moved on to Toni Morrison, then James Baldwin, then Richard Wright, and so many other writers not on my high school or college reading lists. However, I didn't quite become an antiracist civil rights educator overnight. Writing my MA thesis on Flannery O'Connor in 1987, I earnestly went to the University of Memphis's new African American hire in English to ask him whether I should capitalize "Negro," a term that was, by then, no longer appropriate. A few years later, when I was teaching part-time at Lehman College in New York, a Black male student in Malcolm X glasses greeted me with "As-Salaam-Alaikum," Arabic for "peace be with you," and I reminded him to speak English. At issue was the clash between the segregated world in which I lived as a humanities graduate student, first at UM and later at NYU, which reinforced ideas about race that I grew up with in Birmingham, and the integrated world of my teaching and reading, which was edging its way, slowly, into my consciousness. On the one hand, in 1994, I made up a reading list for my PhD oral examinations and had a white, male professor chide me for including so many women and Black people. When I turned in a dissertation proposal, the director of graduate studies laughed at me for misspelling Toni Morrison's name. "He spells it T-O-N-Y," he told me, oblivious to the Nobel laureate's gender. On the other hand, just before graduating I audited a feminist theory class with a new professor, Carolyn Dever (now at Dartmouth), who had me reading works by figures such as bell hooks, Kimberlé Crenshaw, and Birmingham native Angela Davis, giving me the language to understand the unevenly distributed relationships between race, class, gender, privilege, and power that I had observed growing up but did not know how to articulate. When Professor Dever discussed the "matrix of domination," a term coined by Patricia Hill Collins to explain those power dynamics, a map of Birmingham flashed before my eyes. When another student in class quoted Audre Lorde, saying "the master's tools will never dismantle the master's house," it was as if someone had taken a sledge hammer to my mind. Still, I was first in line to ask Prof. Dever to recommend more books by "Audre Lordy" (the surname's "e" is silent). I hadn't strayed that far from my "Hemmingway" days.

Ultimately, Lorde was right. I needed a completely new set of tools to begin dismantling the master's house that was my mind. And still, nearly every day, I bump up against the edifice that is my own ignorance.

Today, when students ask me why they never learned "this" before, I tell them that the answer is complicated. We live inside structures that determine how we see, think, and act. Moving beyond those structures entails a lot of work. I might never have started that process had I not left Birmingham for Memphis and, then, New York. But the inverse is also true: growing up in Birmingham laid the foundation for the work of waking up that needed to be done.

11 / "JUST DOING MY JOB"

The Desegregation and Resegregation of Public Schools

Uncle Bobby wouldn't talk about 1957. In September of that year, he was a young army recruit, stationed at Kentucky's Fort Campbell, a member of the 101st Airborne Division. The prestigious "Screaming Eagles," as they were called, were known for their ability to mobilize quickly and work effectively under extreme circumstances. Before my uncle's time with them, the unit's paratroopers dropped from the sky on June 5, 1944, to prepare the way for the soldiers who would, the following day, storm the beach at Normandy. Now, thirteen years later, a Screaming Eagles force deployed to Little Rock, Arkansas, to keep nine high-school students safe. Known as the "Little Rock Nine," the students—Minnijean Brown, Elizabeth Eckford, Ernest Green, Thelma Mothershed, Melba Pattillo, Gloria Ray, Terrence Roberts, Jefferson Thomas, and Carlotta Walls—were the first African Americans to attend the city's all-white Central High School. On September 4, the first day of school, Gov. Orval Faubus sent the Arkansas National Guard to keep the nine from entering. By September 24 the students were still facing down both the Arkansas Guard and the local residents who threatened them with verbal and physical violence. To make the state comply with the US Supreme Court's 1954 *Brown v. Board of Education* decision to desegregate public schools, President Dwight D. Eisenhower federalized the Arkansas troops, changing their mission from prevention to protection. As an added layer, Eisenhower sent in the Screaming Eagles. Private First Class Bobby D. Hughes, at twenty-one, was not much older than the students he would walk among for the next two months, armed with a fixed bayonet rifle.

Just over forty years later, fresh out of a 1998 National Endowment for the Humanities Summer Institute on teaching the Civil Rights Movement, I tried to get Uncle Bobby to tell me about his time in Little Rock. I was eager to connect my family past with a larger story. Both he and his wife, my Aunt Nell, played small roles in significant historical events: she, as member of the 1977 Chambliss jury, and he, as one of the soldiers assigned in 1957 to Central High School. I became a civil rights educator, in part, because of my aunt and uncle. In my youth, during the 1960s and 1970s, the movement was rarely, if ever, a conversation topic among Birmingham's white people. Most of my knowledge came, as it still does for many, from what I stumbled across on television or in books. The result was an incoherent, incomplete, often inaccurate story about good and evil, heroes and villains. Aunt Nell and Uncle Bobby's experiences—although I knew little about them at the time—opened a tiny window onto the ways that ordinary people met extraordinary events. The older I got, and the more I learned about civil-rights-era Birmingham, the more I wanted that view enlarged. But, when interviewing Uncle Bobby in 1998, I felt the window shut and the blinds fling down with a thud.

Uncle Bobby and I sat down for the interview with him in his usual place, the head of a large cherry-wood dining room table, my Aunt Nell's Christmas china gleaming from the cabinet behind him. His salt-and-pepper beard covered the dimples of his youth, and he wore a faded red University of Alabama cap atop the combover his nieces had teased him about since our childhood. "Uncle Yul" we called him, after Yul Brynner, the bald stage and screen star. Truthfully, he reminded me more of Clint Eastwood or John Wayne: tall, tough, silent. He was even less talkative with a voice recorder between us, although I tried to lubricate our conversation with glasses of Wild Turkey.

"Oh Gawd," he said in his deep-voiced southern accent. "I cain't remember back that far."

"Can you tell me anything that happened?" I pleaded.

He didn't offer much. "Them people were nuts."

That I knew. One of the most frequently reproduced photographs of the Little Rock Nine shows fifteen-year-old Elizabeth Eckford walking through a group of white people, mostly women, who taunt and threaten her. Eckford had missed a communication with the other eight students and their parents saying that they would go as a group to the first day of class. When she walked, alone, along the sidewalk to campus, she endured the taunts of students and other locals, chanting, "Two, four, six, eight, we ain't gonna integrate!" and "Lynch her! Lynch her!" Later in the school year, someone pushed her down a flight of stairs. The violence that the students faced was relentless and routine. Melba Patillo (later, Beals) had acid thrown in her face and was held down in a bathroom stall while white girls threw lit matches on her. The boys reported being hit with baseballs during gym class and walking over broken glass in the showers. All students spoke of their white peers harassing them "under the radar": spilling ink on their clothes or stepping on the heels of their shoes as they walked through crowded hallways. The troops were limited in how much they could intervene. They could protect the nine students from immediate harm, but they could not serve as official witnesses to misconduct; only another nonsoldier adult could make a claim against a teen. Troops were not allowed in certain spaces—such as the gym, restrooms, and classrooms—where white students soon learned that they could harass, threaten, and harm Black students with impunity.

Troopers helped as they could. Beals, in her memoir *Warriors Don't Cry*, writes about the steady, understated guidance that she received from Danny, the Screaming Eagle assigned to protect her. When someone threw a lit dynamite stick at her in a stairwell, Danny and another soldier put their bodies on the line. Danny stomped out the flame, and the other soldier ran to carry the dynamite outside the building. Perhaps more important than Danny's courage under fire, according to Beals, was how he modeled the "warrior" behavior that allowed her to make it through each day:

> I could see Danny's face, his expression was blank. But his posture was so erect and his stance so commanding that no one would dare to challenge him. Seeing that made me think about my own posture. I had to appear confident and alert. I squared my shoulders, trying not to show how frightened and timid I really felt. I told myself that I had to be like a soldier in battle. I couldn't imagine a 101st trooper crying, or moping when he got hurt.

I want to imagine my uncle being like Danny, but I don't know what he did or how he acted. Uncle Bobby never told me anything about his interactions with people in Little Rock. Instead, he told me that racial tensions were so high that only white troops got sent to the school. His commander feared that the seeing the division's Black troops would provoke even more violence. One Hawaiian man—Uncle Bobby pronounced it "high-WAH-yun"—went with them to Little Rock, but his dark skin kept him confined to the base camp. Another man picked up crab lice from a night on the town, spreading them through the division's toilets and laundry. Uncle Bobby pointed to a soldier from a picture I brought to help jog his memory.

"See him standin' still, no expression," he said. "He's thinkin' 'bout how bad his pecker itches."

"What were you thinking?" I probed him for more.

"Nothin,'" Uncle Bobby said. "I was just doin' my job."

*

Uncle Bobby's words recall the lines poet Cyrus Cassells uses to describe Eckford as she walks, alone, through a crowd of whites, their faces contorted with angry yelling:

> Thick at the schoolgate are the ones
> Rage has twisted
> Into minotaurs, harpies
> Relentlessly swift;
> So you must walk past the pincers,
> The swaying horns.

"Sister, sister," the poem's speaker inquires, "Where are you going?" Eckford—expressionless, a "pioneer in dark glasses" who "won't show the mob" her eyes—remains opaque: "I'm just going to school."

Uncle Bobby, likewise "just doin' his job," refused my pincer-questions.

Perhaps he offered me little because he couldn't find the right language to convey his experience to a military outsider—which is not to say that he ever struggled for words. Uncle Bobby, self-taught, was highly intelligent. He read dictionaries and encyclopedias for fun. We had a long-standing Trivial Pursuit competition, and another one involving the Sunday *New York Times* crossword puzzle: who finished first, who used pen. He usually won. But in Little Rock, Uncle Bobby was ultimately on a mission. "This here is a battle if I've ever seen one," Beals recalls Danny telling her. How does the soldier adequately describe the battle, the parachuter the jump, the pioneer in dark glasses the walk through gusts of fear and fury? As Zora Neale Hurston's character Janie tells her friend Phoebe in the 1937 novel *Their Eyes Were Watching God*, "You got tuh *go* there tuh *know* there."

Perhaps Uncle Bobby didn't want me to "go there," to know what he remembered. I was the family's token liberal, teased lovingly yet relentlessly about wanting to save the world and leaving the South for graduate school in Manhattan. Before I left, Uncle Bobby borrowed a post-hole digger from his across-the-street neighbor Gooch. They took a picture of me in the front yard, posing with my "free PhD" from the "University of Gooch." Uncle Bobby also bought my Honda for well above its value so that I could go "up

North" with $5,000 in the bank. When I graduated, he came up too, whooping and hollering alongside the rest of my aunts and uncles as I walked across the Carnegie Hall stage, the only one of my family to receive a doctoral degree after being the first to finish college. In high school I lived off and on with Aunt Nell and Uncle Bobby, because my own home often became too violent. Twice he came armed with a shotgun to keep my mother's boyfriend Glen from hitting or shooting us. When I was born, Aunt Nell said, my father left town, and Uncle Bobby drove me home from the hospital. From that moment on, he was my stand-in dad and my hero. But I became a civil rights scholar, and Uncle Bobby, I thought, remained a man of his place and time: a working-class white guy raised during the 1940s and '50s, when our hometown of Birmingham was becoming infamous for its persistent, and devastating, racial violence.

Just before Uncle Bobby went to Little Rock, his alma mater, John Herbert Phillips High School, was undergoing its own integration attempt. During the summer of 1957, four Black teens, including two daughters of the ACMHR leader Fred Shuttlesworth, sought local school board permission to enroll at the all-white Phillips. For Shuttlesworth, education was a major front in the battle against Jim Crow. "When kids go to school together, and play together, they won't be unknown and they won't be enemies," he told biographer Andrew Manis. Local Klan members thought otherwise. On Labor Day (September 2), a group of six Klansmen attempted to deter Shuttlesworth and the other families from pushing desegregation by picking up at random and torturing a Black man named Judge Aaron. "Stop sending nigger children and white children to school together," they told Aaron to tell Shuttlesworth, "or we're gonna do them like we're gonna do you." Then the men beat Aaron, carved "KKK" into his chest, castrated him, and poured turpentine into his wounds. Aaron survived, barely. When hearing what happened to him, Shuttlesworth was shaken, but he pushed forward. On September 9 Shuttlesworth and his family drove to Phillips, where they were met by another mob of Klansmen, including Bobby Frank Cherry (convicted, in 2002, for his role in the Sixteenth Street Baptist Church bombing). The thugs beat Shuttlesworth nearly to death with chains, brass knuckles, and tire irons. His wife, Ruby, was stabbed in the hip. Their daughter Ruby Frederika came away with a broken ankle. Despite their injuries, the family showed up that night for a heavily bandaged Reverend Shuttlesworth to lead a mass meeting at New Hope Baptist Church, encouraging the packed house to keep the fight going. Phillips, however, would not desegregate until 1964.

14. The Rev. Fred Shuttlesworth escorts Dwight Armstrong (9) and his brother Floyd (11) from Birmingham's Graymont Elementary School, 1963. Image courtesy of the Associated Press.

As with Little Rock, Uncle Bobby kept mum on Shuttlesworth and Phillips. If he was not just doing his job, would he have supported the angry, unruly, dangerous whites bearing down on the Little Rock Nine? What did he think about Shuttlesworth trying to enroll Black students at his white alma mater as he stood, rifle at the ready, amidst a civil rights showdown? I'm certain that he wouldn't have joined the mobs. Uncle Bobby was the kind of soldier who looked for the excitement of jumping from a plane and the challenge of fixing a problem—not the power of wielding a weapon. Unlike many of his male relatives, he didn't even like to hunt. But I also find it hard to imagine him saying, "Them people are nuts," and then parachuting downtown like a civil rights superhero to set his bayonet, or his body, between Bobby Frank Cherry's brass knuckles and Fred Shuttlesworth's face.

When I was younger, in elementary and high school, Uncle Bobby freely shared his opinions about race. He served an integrated army, worked an integrated railroad job, and palled around with a Black man named J.T. Yet he wanted no part of integration.

"If a Black man moves next door to me," he said, "I'll be the first to leave." He never did.

Birmingham's demographics shifted after the movement. Center Point, the community where Uncle Bobby and Aunt Nell lived northeast of Birmingham, remained predominantly white through the 1980s. During the 1990s and early 2000s, Center Point grew smaller, Blacker, browner, and poorer. Many of its former white residents helped fuel growth spurts along the interstates that head out from the city. Gardendale, up I-65 north of Birmingham, nearly doubled in size, going from eight thousand residents in 1980 to over fourteen thousand in 2020. In the same time span, Trussville, east of the city off I-59, grew more than sevenfold, from 3,500 to 23,000. Both towns hover around 90 percent white. Center Point's population, meanwhile, decreased from twenty-three thousand to sixteen thousand, with less than 30 percent reporting as white. No matter what their race, Center Point's residents must drive to Gardendale or Trussville if they want amenities other than fast food, used car lots, pawn shops, or bail bonds.

While many of their neighbors joined the white, middle-class flight that followed the interstates and the shopping, Uncle Bobby and Aunt Nell remained in their house. They stayed in their Baptist church as it, too, integrated.

A year or so before Uncle Bobby died from a heart attack in 2010, I asked him why they never moved. We were talking politics over a Thanksgiving turkey. I was surprised to learn that he, like me, leaned left. We both belonged to unions. We both voted for a Green Ralph Nader in 2004, and a Black Barack Obama in 2008.

"You used to tell me that you wouldn't live next door to a Black man," I confronted my uncle, "but now you're telling me you voted for one to be president?"

"Girl," Uncle Bobby said, shaking his head. He often started sentences by calling me "girl," as if to emphasize his wisdom over my naivete.

"Girl," he repeated. "If a man cain't change, then he ain't fully human."

*

I want to believe in change. I want to believe that individuals grow, develop, see the light. I want to believe that when they do so, then they work together to make the world a better place.

But then I hear Uncle Bobby's voice in my head, asking me, as he often did, "Girl, how can you be so smart *and* so dumb?"

The year before he died, I edited a collection of writings about the movement, *The Civil Rights Reader: American Literature from Jim Crow to Reconciliation.* The title alluded, in part, to Mississippi's William Winter Institute for Racial Reconciliation, where I spent a year from 2005 to 2006 gathering materials for the book and learning how communities across the US made amends for their segregation-era sins. Through the institute's then-director, Susan Glisson, I met members of the Philadelphia Coalition, a multiracial group of Neshoba County, Mississippi, residents who worked toward the 2005 prosecution of Edgar Ray Killen for his role in the 1964 murders of civil rights workers James Chaney, Andrew Goodman, and Michael Schwerner. I got to know the Rosewood, Florida, descendants who, in 1993, successfully sued the state for reparations over the loss of their town during a 1923 massacre. I broke bread in Georgia with the Moore's Ford Memorial Committee, which put up in 1999 one of the earliest historical markers to commemorate a lynching. Groups like these showed me how individuals can come together—despite different backgrounds and fraught pasts—to listen, talk, see each other's humanity, and strive toward the betterment of all. The 2008 election of Barack Obama to the presidency, the last entry in *The Civil Rights Reader's* chronology, convinced me that what I saw happening through the institute was taking place everywhere, that our society was bringing to fruition the Beloved Community of justice and equity that Martin Luther King Jr. had envisioned.

Then, over the next eight years, I watched a New Jim Crow rear its head. Voting rights took a hit with the US Supreme Court's 2013 *Shelby County vs. Holder* decision. Police violence and mass incarceration disproportionately targeted Black and brown communities across the country, with the US prison population jumping from 300,000 in the late 1980s to more than two million in 2010.

Schools resegregated.

One example can be found in Gardendale, the upstart white community just west of Uncle Bobby's Center Point. In 2013 Gardendale tried to secede from Jefferson County Schools to form its own system. Local residents admitted their race-based reasons for doing so. Gardendale students, mostly white, attended school with the surrounding area's mostly Black students, who white parents believed brought down educational quality. Gardendale followed a precedent set by other Jefferson County communities in the wake of the US Supreme Court's 1954 *Brown vs. Board of Education* ruling that paved the way for school desegregation. In many cases white parents avoided *Brown*'s changes by putting their children into private schools. In others entire communities opted out. The wealthy white suburb of Mountain Brook left the Jefferson County school system in 1959. Other white towns—Pleasant Gove, Midfield, Homewood, and Vestavia Hills—soon followed, using as their battle cry "local control" over education, an idea that seems to miss that all the county's schoolchildren are, in fact, local. As for Gardendale, the US 11th Court of Appeals ultimately denied their petition, but their actions reflected a larger pattern of school resegregation nationwide. According to Nikole Hannah-Jones, who reported on the story for the *New York Times*, "Laws in 30 states explicitly allow communities to form their own public-school systems, and since 2000, at least 71 communities across the country, most of them white and wealthy, have sought to break away from their public-school districts to form smaller, more exclusive ones." As civil rights attorney and author of *The New Jim Crow* Michelle Alexander notes, "We have not ended racial caste in America, we have merely redesigned it."

Alexander would recognize the Pinellas County, Florida, system from which my son, Zack, graduated in 2019 as part of that redesign. In 2007 Pinellas County stopped busing students to achieve racial equity. Just out from under federal monitoring, the Board of Education voted in favor of "neighborhood schools" that would keep students closer to home. The problem, however, is the county's history of neighborhood segregation. Built into the 1931 charter of St. Petersburg, Pinellas's largest city, were provisions outlining where African Americans could, and could not, live. Black people who ventured north of Central Avenue, the city's main east-west drag, put their lives at risk. Remnants of such provisions endure. "South St. Pete" is code for "Black neighborhood," while "north county" remains predominantly white. The school board thought that sprinkling the county with "magnets"—arts, technology, or international baccalaureate (IB) programs—would give students "choices" that superseded busing to create integrated schools. What happened instead, reports the 2015 *Tampa Bay Times* Pulitzer Prize–winning series "Failure Factories," was "de facto segregation." The five elementary schools south of Central Avenue—Campbell Park, Fairmount Park, Lakewood, Maximo, and Melrose—now predominantly Black, plunged into a downward spiral of failure to teach basic skills such as reading and math, high rates of staff turnover and violence, and an unequal share of resources—some schools receiving almost $1,000 per pupil less than their north county counterparts.

So smart and so dumb, I wondered about but did not question how the demographics changed at the schools my son attended near our South St. Pete home. His K–8 IB magnet started as a beautiful bubble of rainbow-like diversity, where students earned medals for being open-minded, caring, thinking risk takers. By the time Zack started sixth grade, in 2012, that rainbow had bleached out. School staff explained that students who left, some white but mostly Black and Latinx, could not meet academic requirements (maintaining a C average). Zack made Ds and Fs, but his dad and I were told not to worry. We were "involved parents," the principal said, so Zack could stay in. Less involved parents (whatever *that* meant) could send the twelve-year-olds who refused to take responsibility for their learning (whatever *that* meant) to neighborhood schools. By the time Zack started high school, the *Tampa Bay Times* article gave us the words to understand without a doubt what *that* meant: we were caught up in our local system of Failure Factories.

High school made the connections to a New Jim Crow even more direct—and frightening. Zack used strong test scores to slide into another exclusive magnet program, the Center for Advanced Technology (CAT) in our neighborhood school, Lakewood. The demographics are revealing: Lakewood, where many students from the elementary Failure Factories attend high school, is just over 65% Black; its CAT program is nearly 80% white. CAT had its own entrance, so parents who lived north of Central Avenue could easily access the car circle from Interstate 275. CAT students rarely took courses—only Honors and Advanced Placement (AP)—with those in the "traditional" program, referred to as "general population" or "gen pop." The term is also used to describe those who don't merit any special treatment, perks or punishment, in jail.

Our family might have overlooked the terms' similarities, except that when Zack ran late to school, as teens with ADHD often do, he lurked by the CAT entrance, locked to outsiders, waiting for a sympathetic student to let him in so that he wouldn't have to join the gen pop latecomers in IC. "IC," officially the Intervention Center for problem students, had an unofficial nickname among the CAT kids: Incarceration Center.

Our family might also have overlooked "Incarceration Center," as we had "gen pop," except that when Zack started failing the CAT program, as he had IB, the staff called a meeting with my husband and me, the concerned, involved parents. One white, male teacher scoffed at Zack's learning disability, saying that he needed "to take more responsibility." Maybe, the teacher suggested, we could give our son some "tough love," even take him on "a tour of prison." The teacher meant letting him visit classes in Lakewood's traditional, and predominantly Black, program, gen pop.

The high school ultimately has a decent graduation rate, over 90 percent, but coded words like "gen pop" mentally prepare its students to enter what activists refer to as the "school to prison pipeline." That system, according to the American Civil Liberties Union, reveals a "disturbing national trend wherein children are funneled out of public schools and into the juvenile and criminal justice systems." Many factors create the pipeline. Chief among them are "failing schools," with inadequate, poorly funded resources to attend to students' educational and social needs. Another is zero-tolerance policies, harsh disciplinary practices that punish students, through suspension, expulsion, or court involvement, often for relatively minor crimes. Such practices hit hardest those students who are Black, brown, or, like Zack, special needs. Each time he got into trouble (usually for truancy), guidance counselors cautioned us, "You do not want your child to go into the system. He'll never get out."

What parent wants their child sucked into a pipeline to prison rather than mentored through a track to success? We considered private schools, even looked at a couple where diversity was more a theory than a practice. We pleaded with Zack to go to a local Catholic high school, where he had a few friends. But Lakewood, and gen pop, was ultimately Zack's choice. "I'm a Spartan," he told us, claiming his identity from the school's mascot. "I don't want a special program. I just want to be a kid."

His words resonated across space and time—through Elizabeth Eckford's "just going to school," through Uncle Bobby's "just doing my job"—as he walked across the graduation stage in 2019, one of a few white faces alongside his Black, Latinx, South Asian, and Middle Eastern friends. So much has changed in sixty years, I thought, and so much has not.

During the NEH Institute where I began learning how to be a civil rights educator, I argued about change with another professor, an African American woman who taught in Vermont. I believed, sincerely, that our contemporary moment differed from the 1960s of my childhood.

"It's like a game," Willi told me. "We might have moved our individual pieces around, but we're still playing on the same board."

"Girl," I hear Uncle Bobby schooling me.

*

The Screaming Eagles stayed in Little Rock through November of 1957. One of the Little Rock Nine, Ernest Green, graduated from Central High School in May 1958. Later that year Governor Faubus closed the schools rather than integrate. The African American students who returned to Central High after it reopened faced harassment and violence not much different from when they started. Eckford wound up taking correspondence courses to get her degree. She went to college and did a variety of jobs, including a stint in the US Army.

15. Private Bobby D. Hughes, US Army, at Fort Campbell, Kentucky, ca. 1957. Image courtesy of the author.

Uncle Bobby served out the rest of his army time at Fort Campbell, until 1959. Six years later, his unit deployed to Vietnam. When antiwar protests were fashionable during the late 1960s and early 1970s, he gave me an army jacket, which I embroidered with peace signs, flowers, and smiley faces. He didn't say whether or not he wore the jacket while protecting the Little Rock Nine. Perhaps if I had known the jacket potentially had a place in history, I wouldn't have lost it.

A few years after Uncle Bobby's 2010 death, Aunt Nell gave me a second army jacket that I pretend is from Little Rock. The jacket is classic Uncle Bobby. There's a palm-sized splotch of blue ink by the right pocket: what other paratrooper on this planet would carry a cartridge pen? The left epaulette hangs to the side, but the right one remains somewhat intact, held on by a kind of rusted contraption that might once have been a safety pin and that only a southerner would rig up. I'm surprised there's no duct tape. Even though the pin sticks me every time I put on the jacket, I wear it with pride, especially when teaching literature about school desegregation. I chose a snapshot of me in the jacket as my author photo for this book—for the same reason, pride in what my uncle did right.

Around the same time that she gave me the second jacket, Aunt Nell also dug out a military memorabilia folder that Uncle Bobby never showed me. In it was a commendation letter from his commanding officer, Col. William A. Kuhn, dated November 30, 1957, shortly after the unit departed Little Rock. Colonel Kuhn's letter does not specify any actions but does praise Uncle Bobby's "outstanding performance" and his "continued, unselfish devotion to duty" in Little Rock. "That performance," Kuhn explains, was "especially commendable in view of the long hours, irksome living conditions and other hardships." The only hardships Uncle Bobby told me about were the crab lice and standing all morning outside a math class. He didn't say which student he accompanied, only that he wondered why he learned to jump out of an airplane just so he could go back to high school.

A photograph in the folder shows Private Hughes standing in front of an airplane in full combat gear, his left shoulder bearing the Screaming Eagle patch. His right hand holds the carabiner that tethers the jumper to solid plane before the leap into open sky. Poised on that precipice between fear and freedom, Uncle Bobby is all lanky limbs and goofy smile.

He's ready to do his job. Because of him, I'm better equipped to do my own.

12 / TWO DAYS ALONG VILLAGE CREEK

If my grandmother uttered any words more frequently than biblical quotations when I was a child, they were, "Stay away from that ditch!"

The ditch in question channeled runoff from Ruffner Mountain to the creek that bordered East Lake Park. It was very close, less than half a city block down the alley that ran next to our house. Granny had to warn me away because the ditch fascinated me. A rock bridge passed over it, and from that vantage point I could watch the water bubble over the stones below, catch glimmers of minnows, see the occasional snake looping over a tree branch, or busy myself trying to grab blue jays or mockingbirds.

Sometimes I deliberately disobeyed my grandmother to leave the bridge's safety and walk alongside the ditch. I liked to peep inside the windows of Old Joe, who lived behind us in a shotgun house. Old Joe, a bachelor, did yard work for the neighborhood's "widda-wimmin," as Granny described herself and her friends. In return they gave him a few dollars and hot plates of leftovers to eat for dinner. Otherwise he survived off catfish he caught in the lake that gave our neighborhood its name. Old Joe didn't talk a lot, because he stuttered, but he whistled day and night. I imagined that he was communicating with the birds I hoped to bring home as pets, so I wanted to know his secret. But all I saw inside his house was a rickety chair, a worse-looking table, bottles of a brown liquid that I suspected was not sweet tea, and, nailed to the wall, dozens of old calendars with naked-lady pictures.

Then there was the gang of roving neighborhood boys that Granny called the "Statler Brothers," though that was not their name, they weren't all brothers, and they didn't sing country or gospel. According to my grandmother, all they did was skip school to hide in the ditch, take drugs, and wait for me to walk by so that they could pull me by my long, blond hair underneath the bridge and "rake" me. I didn't know what she meant by "rake" but suspected it had something to do with Old Joe's garden tools, which sounded painful and not fun. I also suspected that my grandmother might be right, because once, while clambering off the bridge to walk along the water, I found a plastic baggie full of something unfamiliar that my mother called "grass" and flushed down the toilet.

"Stay away from that ditch!" she said, repeating Granny's warning.

As a child I never connected the ditch to Village Creek, a waterway that runs forty-four miles across (and beyond) Birmingham's width. Village Creek was often in the news for the flooding that displaced those who lived in the city's lowest-lying areas. After big storms I had seen the ditch rise from a trickle to a torrent, jump its banks, and turn Old Joe's yard into squishy marsh. But houses on television with water up to the windows seemed distant, even though they were just a few minutes away in Birmingham's northern and western industrial areas. We rarely drove through those neighborhoods, because they smelled like rotten eggs and aggravated my asthma, so they weren't on my mental map.

When I began, during the early 2010s, to learn more about the Birmingham of my youth, I thought that the flood-prone creek might be worth investigating, even though I knew little about it or even where to find it. Rather than rely on my faulty knowledge, I bought an actual map, a 3 x 4-foot AAA city overview, and then looked north and west until I located the thin line labeled "Village Creek." I traced it out with a blue marker to its terminus, at the Warrior River's Locust Fork, and then to its headwaters. I was shocked to find that it began in Roebuck Springs, a little over a mile from my grandmother's old house, and that it was the same body of water that skirted the edge of East Lake Park, where Old Joe caught his catfish. As a child I crossed Village Creek multiple times each week when Granny and I went to church. The ditch that she warned me away from was a tributary.

So I decided, as I did many times in life, to ignore my mother's and grandmother's "stay away" warnings—and follow the water's path to find out what all the fuss was about.

*

Village Creek, like Center Street, offers a microcosm of Birmingham history and geography.

Village is one of several creeks—including Valley, Five-Mile, and Turkey—that drain the mountains lining Jefferson County's southern border. Important side note: Birmingham is nestled in a valley that runs northeast to southwest between a range of small mountains and a series of ridges. This Appalachian foothill topography makes the city look slanted on a map. In person, getting lost is easier than one imagines. Drivers who think they're heading due east might instead be heading more toward the north; what seems like west is closer to south. I don't think I'm wrong in seeing this wonky geography as a metaphor of so many things Birmingham. Village Creek's history seems particularly awry.

Prior to the 1810s, the area known today as Jones Valley was a hunting ground for the Creek (Muscogee) Indians. White settlers began moving in after Andrew Jackson's forces defeated Native ones at the 1814 Battle of Horseshoe Bend. For these early settlers, like John and Jeremiah Jones (for whom the valley is named), and Williamson Hawkins, who owned a 3,000-acre plantation alongside its banks, Village Creek functioned as a source of irrigation and drinking water. According to John Milner, whose 1850s survey of the area for possible railroad routes led to Birmingham's founding, Jones Valley was "one vast garden as far as the eye could reach," and Village Creek was one of its "beautiful, clear running streams found gushing out everywhere."

The creek and its watershed also contained coal.

The mineral that, along with iron, would make those Birmingham founders rich, lay all over the valley. It outcropped on Hawkins's land. A seam of it followed the streambed from Village Creek's mouth.

Birmingham was incorporated in 1871 to take advantage of the seemingly unlimited stores of mineral wealth. But coal and iron changed the area's relationships to its waterways, especially Village Creek.

During the late nineteenth and early twentieth centuries, city leaders realized that this one stream would not be sufficient to support both drinking water and local industry needs. Iron production takes enormous quantities of water: blast furnaces use an estimated twenty-five thousand gallons per ton of ore. In 1910 the Tennessee Coal, Iron, and Railroad Company—just one of the many iron and steel companies to set up shop along Village Creek—used 400 million gallons each day. To feed the growing need for water, channels were built from other local sources, including Five Mile Creek and the Cahaba River (southeast of Red Mountain, the latter is now the city's primary municipal water source). West of the city, TCI dammed Village Creek to create Bayview Lake, capable of holding 3.5 billion gallons of water on reserve. The problem, however, was not only finding enough water for iron and steel production but also what to do with that water once it had been put to industrial use. The solution for the latter was simple: dump the untreated water back into Village Creek.

Thus began the pollution problems that would, along with flooding, continue to plague parts of the city that lie along this historic waterway.

As Birmingham grew, exponentially during the twentieth century's first half, it built paved roads, an airport, more manufacturing, and concrete channels to straighten and reroute the creek into a more industry-favorable flow. Worker housing went in as well, varying by race, class, and zoning laws. Before the civil rights movement, the city's Black labor force was, for the most part, confined to unskilled positions and shacks or shotguns in low-lying areas close to the water. White workers got better, skilled jobs and more breathing room, in cottages and bungalows on higher ground. I saw the class, though not the race, divide up close with Old Joe: poor laborer = shotgun house on the ditch, working-class family = bungalow farther away and higher up. But that racial divide was implicit in what I did not see: how intricately my life was connected to the creek.

The upshot of such divides was that, in some parts of Birmingham, Village Creek functioned as a natural boundary reinforcing human-made laws or customs; in others, the creek bisected predominantly Black neighborhoods. Here, heavy spring rains meant that a toxic, and now overtaxed, waterway would overflow its banks into family homes. A Birmingham Historical Society report notes that flooding "became more damaging and more deadly" during the 1960s and 1970s. That's when Interstate 59 went in, ferrying automobiles across the city atop a concrete river that parallels and sometimes abuts the creek. What local "flood veterans" recall as the worst instance occurred in 1979 when, in Ensley, the waters rose up to the rooflines.

Over the past twenty years, the Federal Emergency Management Agency (FEMA) helped to relocate nearly a thousand households from the areas most affected by Village Creek flooding. But relocation does not solve all the environmental problems associated with the creek. The year 1997 saw a major chemical spill (a pesticide called "Dursban") in central Birmingham that resulted in one of the largest fish kills and environmental cleanups in state history and affected communities as far away as Bayview Lake. In 2008 workers taking out a dam at Village Creek's headwaters inadvertently killed thousands of endangered watercress darters, a small fish found only in Jefferson County springs. In 2012 the EPA designated a residential area of north Birmingham (where the neighborhoods of Collegeville, Harriman Park, and Fairmont Park come together) as a Superfund site. These neighborhoods—bordered by the airport, rock quarries, and plants that make coke, asphalt, pipes, and steel—are now eligible for federal funding to clean up the soil's toxic levels of arsenic, lead, and benzo[a]pyrene, the cancer-causing chemical found in coal tar, cigarette smoke, and automobile exhaust. But hundreds of local kids still have trouble breathing, and can't play in their yards or on their school grounds.

Incidents like these propelled efforts at drawing attention to the creek's pollution and flooding problems. Three organizations—the Village Creek Human and Environmental Justice Society (VCS for short), the Freshwater Land Trust, and the Black Water Riverkeeper—are working to protect the creek and its surrounding environments, both human and nonhuman. A plan is also under way to develop a series of public trails, called the Village Creek Greenway, mirroring the string of parks that landscape architect Frederick Law Olmsted envisioned in 1925 for an ideal Birmingham. Back then, civic leaders scrapped the plan to set aside land running along the creek for both stormwater drainage and recreation, privileging industrial profits over the safety of workers and their homes. Today, with the industrial economy no longer dominant, the city sees the wisdom of green spaces that lure tourist dollars—as well as the economic sense of avoiding federal fines for environmental crimes. From drinking water source to emblem of environmental racism, Village Creek is currently being recast as symbol of hope for a better Birmingham future. As I learned from following the creek's path, this work in progress remains imperfect.

*

An honest account of my Village Creek quest will admit two points.

First, I made multiple attempts over several years, solo and in company, and each time got lost. Because of Birmingham's weirdly angled street grid or its history of prioritizing industry over environment or perhaps both, Village Creek isn't always where one thinks it is. The water one seeks in person does not necessarily correspond to the blue line on a map. Asking locals rarely helps. As with my own childhood experience, many people have heard of Village Creek, but few can give directions. The inability to locate it occurs irrespective of race but not place. Anyone who's had their home flooded or relocated knows exactly where Village Creek lies. Others might live, work, or play in close proximity to the creek without realizing it's the same one mentioned so often in the news. A white friend of mine who has lived for more than twenty years near the Village Creek springhead told me, "I've heard of it, but I can't exactly pinpoint its location." Two African American golfers playing a course near that same springhead shrugged their shoulders when I asked them about the creek, even as we stood just yards away from it.

Second, I followed the creek by car and on foot but didn't actually get *into* the water. Although I'm an experienced canoer, there are too many places, like the airport, where the creek, channeled underground, remains unnavigable.

There are also too many places, especially between the airport and Ensley, where it's just . . . gross. That rotten-egg, asthma-inducing smell I remember from childhood comes from the multiple Birmingham industries that still dump their by-products into water and sky. I also couldn't shake the words of a 2006 Black Warrior Riverkeeper video that warns potential visitors away from what sounds like a colonial-era heart of darkness. Wear old clothes, gloves, and rubber boots, *44 Miles Down Village Creek* tells us; avoid the water, avoid anything near the water. Its toxins can cause "staph infections, strep infections, meningitis, pneumonia . . . cholera, amoebic dysentery, all these third world diseases." As a Birmingham daughter, I'm naturally suspicious when other white people use terms like "third world" or "dangerous" to describe nonwhite spaces. A big chunk of this book's research entailed going to such places in order to parse out reality from myth, a process that continues even as the book nears its end.

So for this visit to Village Creek, one of my final research pilgrimages, I felt the need to bring in my intellectual "big guns."

My spouse, Thomas Hallock, is an environmental writer and educator, focusing on urban waterways. A modern-day Henry David Thoreau sporting Malcolm X glasses, Tom is undeterred by a creek's disappearance into concrete, the rhetoric of "third world diseases," and nature that creeps or crawls. With him I have canoed under a bridge roiling with fiddler crabs, through a swamp bellowing with alligators ready to mate, and alongside a downed tree branch where wolf spiders the size of my hand dropped into our boat. Frankly, after the gators and the spiders, Tom *owes* me. But I also needed him to keep me from quitting in frustration every time the map led not to the creek but to roads that curved around to double back on themselves.

We set out, on two hot, cloudless days in April 2021—dividing our journey by sections as described on the VCS website. Day 1 would take us to the primarily recreational Headwaters, Roebuck Springs to East Lake, then partially through the industrialized Mid-Section, from North Birmingham through Ensley/South Pratt to Mulga. I promised Tom that, as compensation for his expertise, we could pause midday to grab lunch from Niki's West, the kind of southern home-cooking institution that packs so much food into a Styrofoam takeout container that it won't close without also being sheathed in plastic wrap. On Day 2, we would pick up where the previous day's Mid-Section trip ended and continue to the Lower, again recreational, segment— from Bayview Lake to where Village Creek meets the Black Warrior River's Locust Fork. That day's payment would involve closing out our journey with a well-deserved beer at a brew pub that we had seen earlier near Railroad Park, a Birmingham greenway project that has transformed an old railbed into an urban oasis of bike paths, a baseball field, and park land.

I considered the home cooking and beer rewards to be worth any extra inches on our waistlines. To really understand Birmingham, I speculated, I needed to see, up close, how Village Creek has been treated, why so many locals fear it, why so few can find it, and how these factors are related. The result was a story as wonky as the city map.

Segment 1: Headwaters: Roebuck Springs to East Lake

Our journey began where a golf course meets a tennis court. Village Creek's headwaters are located at a pond tucked between Roebuck Springs' Don Hawkins Recreation Center and the grounds of an old reformatory, the Alabama Boys Industrial School. The pond was created as a water source for the school around 1900 by damming a spring on the site of the former George Roebuck plantation—hence, Roebuck Springs. The creek, flowing southwest from the pond, serves today as the recreation center's southern border. Farther down, the creek edges East Lake Park then moves toward a concrete culvert that runs it underneath the Birmingham-Shuttlesworth International Airport. All told, a short, five-mile segment. One can learn a lot in five miles, however. One can also learn a lot just from looking at one spot: the pond.

It's an unassuming body of water—about 150 x 400 feet, surrounded by vegetation and trees, including a large weeping willow, with an old pump house made of fieldstone—not easily seen from parking lot or road. Reaching the pond means walking across, or around, the rec center's tennis courts, squeezing through a gap in some chain-link fencing, and slogging through stinky, weedy muck. On earlier trips, the effort was worth it, providing glimpses of an otter and two kinds of heron, a great blue and a tri-color. On this trip Tom and I saw only "No Trespassing" signs and one species of bird, the large metal one cruising low on the flight path above our heads.

The area is closed off for two reasons. The first is that, historically, the pond served as a buffer zone between the Industrial School and the Roebuck Springs Country Club. Each has been superseded by other entities, but the physical buffer still exists. The reform school was founded in 1899 as an alternative for troubled boys who otherwise would be sent, or leased out as convict labor, to work in Alabama's coal mines. In 1975 the Department of Youth Services took over the school, which has now relocated next door to a newer facility, still housing juvenile offenders and offering substance-abuse rehabilitation. The Roebuck Springs Country Club opened in 1911, enjoying success as a private eighteen-hole course (and hosting two Southern Golf Association tournaments) until the 1929 stock market crash. The city bought the land in 1930, operating it today as the Roebuck Municipal Golf Course, open to the public. Still, the recreation center and its waters function as a partial border between the predominantly white Roebuck Springs neighborhood, with its bungalows and Tudors tucked into the hills near Ruffner Mountain, and the predominantly Black Zion City, near the airport. Here, and across the city, Village Creek exists as a natural boundary put to use as a racial and economic divide.

Tom noted how geographic features like waterways—and in Birmingham, mountains—often function this way, making such divides appear inherent in nature rather than part of a constructed order.

But make no mistake: Village Creek is managed—in different places for different reasons, and not always to benefit the humans that live alongside it or the flora and fauna that live in it. Another reason that the pond is closed off is to protect an endangered species habitat that the city had destroyed. The watercress darter—a tiny fish about two and half inches long, with blue fins dotted orange—lives in only a handful of spots along the Black Warrior River drainage basin, keeping to the vegetation (hence the name "watercress") inside springheads and spring runs. Farther west, Bessemer's Thomas Spring—connected to Valley Creek, another large, local waterway—was set up in 1980 as a National Watercress Darter Wildlife Refuge. In 2008 the City of Birmingham, even though it knew that the Hawkins Recreation Center pond contained a population of this protected species, ordered workers to take out a beaver dam, because it was flooding the tennis courts. As the dam was being bulldozed, the frightened darters didn't follow the water's outward flow; instead, they hid in the aquatic grasses, where they slowly suffocated. An estimated twelve thousand fish, more than half the pond's population, died. The federal government, describing the incident as one of the largest fish kills ever reported under the Endangered Species Act, fined the city $3 million. The pond has since been put back to right, with the city working with the Freshwater Land Trust and US Fish and Wildlife to construct retention areas and add native plants to protect the fish—to some extent.

Tom and I walked the path that led from the tennis court past the golf course, crossing a small cart-path bridge and watching the waters closely, hoping to glimpse the shy darter. That didn't happen. What did happen is that we noticed the difference between the water on one side of the bridge and that on the other. (This is why I brought an expert: to help me see what I otherwise wouldn't notice.) On the pond and tennis center side of the bridge, the creek is clear, like the beautiful stream of John Milner's 1858 description. Water glistens, grasses dance. On the other side of the bridge, which catches golf course runoff, the creek is overrun with algae—a by-product of the nitrogen in the heavily fertilized greens—making it look more like fluorescent green sludge.

"They're not taking care of the native plants either," Tom said. He was right. The area was covered in weeds.

Such became the story for most of our journey along the creek: environmental remediation signage within a landscape that was poorly maintained. In retrospect, I took these headwaters as Village Creek synecdoche. If people perceive the creek and its surrounding areas as a dangerous, liminal space—where delinquents lurk and the other half lives, or as a space set aside for play—where one can duck in and out for golf or tennis but not make a home, then they don't feel the need to respect it or treat it with care.

Segment 2. North Birmingham to Mulga

Despite the sad fate of the tiny watercress darter, the creek's short segment from Roebuck Springs to East Lake is the easiest, intellectually and emotionally, to understand. Much more complicated, and longer (at roughly fifteen miles), is the portion that runs from North Birmingham, near the airport, to Mulga, a small town near the eastern edge of Bayview Lake. Here lies the city's industrial heart and some of its more insidious environmental history. Here, too, is where one is most likely to wind up lost and frustrated trying to follow Village Creek.

That's definitely what happened to Tom and me. We started out early, so it was still morning when we moved from the first to the second segment of our trip. We hoped to follow the creek from the airport to Enon Ridge, near Center Street and Dynamite Hill, before lunch and then enjoy our Niki's takeout at one of the many parks we saw on the map. After lunch we would close out the day going to Ensley. This steel town just west of Birmingham was made famous, during the mid-twentieth century, for the jazz standard "Tuxedo Junction" (a streetcar crossing and a nightlife hub) and, during that century's latter half, for the flooding that plagued residents along Village Creek.

But my ideal plan assumed that map and reality would line up. I should have known from following the water's path on previous occasions that such alignment does not exist in reality.

Another ideal plan got thwarted later in trying to reproduce, for readers, this leg of our Village Creek journey. There were simply too many examples of driving around Birmingham hoping to find what we believed *should* exist but did not—like, say, a road, a park, or environmental justice. There were also so many stories of ecological disaster, especially in the African American communities along this route, that I could barely keep track of them. The Superfund sites blurred into the chemical spills that blurred into the floods of toxic sludge. I worried that, by recounting each story, they would stop seeming extraordinary and instead seem mundane. A litany of tragedy can have an effect opposite from the one intended: distancing audiences rather than bringing them in closer to see. Kind of like the roads around Village Creek.

Here, then, in lieu of coherence, a refrain and two snapshots.

First, the refrain: the white bespectacled academic couple in the white Subaru grows increasingly hot, hungry, lost, and snappish. A handful of major roads run north-south along this stretch of Village Creek (Oporto-Madrid Boulevard, Messer-Airport Highway, Vanderbilt Road, Highway 31, Arkadelphia Road/Highway 78, and Ensley's Avenue V). But following the creek means heading east-west, traversing a grid that seems orderly but repeatedly hits a dead end: interstate, airport, rail yard, or plant yard (not the green kind, but iron, steel, coke, or other manufacturing). Sometimes the creek itself is the dead end. Although the couple rarely sees it, they know it is there—just beyond that tree line, past that chain-link fence, or over that ridge. They devour snack bars as they circle the airport once, then twice, and run out of water as they drive up and down the intersection of Arkadelphia Road and Finley Boulevard, just west of the city—once, twice, and again. "Stop staring at the map!" the wife barks at the husband, and then vice versa. "Focus on what the road actually does!"

Next, a snapshot: the couple stands in a park. It could be any park near the creek: Greenwood, Spears, Tuxedo. The park has a nature trail, unused, and environmental signage, unread—except by the white guy in Malcolm X glasses. He tries explaining to his wife, whose glasses look more like Flannery O'Connor's cat-eyes, how bio-swales work. She hears "something, something, vegetation that catches and filters storm water runoff, something something." Instead of paying attention, she's thinking that she needs to pee, but, depending on the park, the bathroom is either locked or too filthy to use. She'd like to put her snack-bar wrapper in the trash—not the trash lying all over the ground, but an actual garbage can that does not seem to exist in this, or any, Village Creek park. She'd like to sit, but there are no picnic tables, pavilions, or benches. Instead of grass, there is concrete, interspersed with weedy, rangy, unkempt spots of dirt. "Something, something got government money to put in a park and then left it alone," the husband explains and the wife records, partially, in a notebook. After a few minutes of walking around the park, both husband and wife realize that it's the air, not just their hunger, making them edgy. The rotten-egg smell sticks in their nose hairs. A metallic taste runs down the backs of their throats. They take off their glasses to rub their irritated eyes.

Later, the wife will learn two important facts. First, in Greenwood Park that edgy air came from the Collegeville/Harriman/Fairmont Superfund site just up the road. Cleanup, which involves digging out and replacing the topsoil from area schools, churches, businesses, and roughly six hundred homes, began in 2012 and will continue until at least 2023. Second, the husband really knows how to size up urban nature. What wound up in her notebook as "blah blah" and "_____" were stories that she heard repeated in interviews with representatives from the Freshwater Land Trust, the Village Creek Society, and the Black Warrior Riverkeeper. Funding for Greenwood came from a $4 million fine that plumbing products manufacturer McWane, Inc., paid for allowing pollutant-filled stormwater to run off into Village Creek. Parks like Tuxedo, in Ensley, were funded through federal grants after FEMA relocated homes away from the creek. Once the fine is paid or the grant money runs out, the upkeep slows or stops.

To end this leg of the journey, a second snapshot: the couple sits on steps leading down to a trail that runs along Enon Ridge, at the north end of Center Street/Dynamite Hill. Balanced precariously on their laps, because they couldn't find a decent park, is the dinner that was supposed to be lunch: Styrofoam containers overflowing with fried chicken, green tomatoes, okra, field peas, turnip greens, and cornbread. They're both thinking that what they really want to do is go back to their hotel and sleep. They're also thinking what they want to say about the creek that they cannot see from their concrete perch but know exists, per the refrain, somewhere past the trail, over the ridge, beyond the tree line, across a chain-link fence.

The husband, who's been writing about similar waterways off and on for two decades, pegs Village Creek with a tweet:

How to write about urban nature in 3 easy steps: Frederick Law Olmsted [or equivalent famous planner] laid out a design in 19__. Voters rejected this plan, however, developing areas that had been set aside as greenspace. Today this same area experiences major problems with _____.

He's seen stories like this play out across the country, from New York to Los Angeles and many points in between.

The wife, who's been writing about Birmingham off and on for two decades, sees the wisdom in this tweet. She also thinks that the creek needs more than 280 characters, and even more than the chapter she will devote to it. The book that Village Creek deserves would show how the physical distance engineered around the creek creates a psychic one that allows all kinds of bad things to happen.

But solutions to those many problems can create their own difficult-to-bridge physical and psychic distances.

In Ensley the neighborhoods close to Village Creek are slowly disappearing. What's left after FEMA relocated homes looks more like a ghost town. The angled street grid remains intact, cross-hatching through mostly empty blocks full of weeds and broken-up concrete that used to be sidewalks and driveways. Dotting the denuded landscape are a few abandoned houses—shotguns and wood-frame cottages, either falling in or burned out—and even fewer holdouts in the process of rebuilding. These properties look poor but maintained. Lawns are mowed, flowers are planted.

A few blocks from the flood zone and across from an abandoned school, the wife meets an African American woman named Kay, about her age, also married to a man named Thomas. Kay is putting pepper plants into the dirt. Kay says that she went to the school across the street and a church that moved out of the flood zone. She says that most people took their FEMA money and moved on. Others don't want to leave the homes where they, their parents, and their grandparents grew up. But the area is not replenishing. Older residents are aging, dying off, and new ones aren't moving in. Flooding remains a problem, as does economic downturn in this community founded on iron and steel. Kay plans to stay on; she has her sister nearby, and her garden.

Later, as the white couple sits on their concrete perch looking toward, not at, a Village Creek rendered invisible, the wife recalls how places like Kay's neighborhood existed outside her childhood's mental map—a function of race and location. She wonders, as weeds overtake what used to be homes, whether future writers will describe this creek story in terms of violence or resilience.

And how many stories will simply be erased.

Segment 3. Ensley to Locust Fork

The final segment of Village Creek, from Ensley to Bayview Lake to the Black Warrior River's Locust Fork, is about twenty miles as the roads go, but much longer on the water, which snakes around through the green rolling hills of western Jefferson County's old coal mining country. Riverkeeper Nelson Brooke told me that canoeing the stretch from Bayview Lake to the Locust Fork is "magical," showcasing Village Creek in its wild, untamed, natural glory. A *Birmingham News* article echoes his sentiments. Writer Thomas Spencer explains that the lake catches "the flotsam and jetsam" spit out from the industrial areas upstream. Downstream, the "relatively undisturbed plant communities along the banks" provide an idea of what "the county looked like prior to settlement." Here one finds canyons, "relics of the last Ice Age," and one of the "southernmost naturally occurring stands of hemlock trees in the Eastern U.S." The area has been strip-mined, but one can't see that from the water. For most of the daylong paddle, humans and the marks they leave on nature remain invisible.

In retrospect, I'm glad that Tom and I didn't canoe this part of Village Creek. The whole point of the trip was to find what gets hidden. This far into

16. Shorpy Higginbotham, center, with other workers from the Bessie Mine, 1910. Photograph by Lewis Wickes Hine, courtesy of the Library of Congress.

a book on Birmingham, I know how well the "Magic City" pulls off tricks with smoke and mirrors.

It's easy to drive these back roads and see why the state is referred to as "Alabama the Beautiful." But that slogan obscures a whole lot of ugly.

Take, for example, an old coal mine nicknamed "Bessie," tucked into these hills just north of Village Creek. Bessie, belonging to the Sloss-Sheffield Steel and Iron Company, was one of many mines that employed child and convict labor. Photographer Lewis Wickes Hine came through here in 1910, snapping some of the shots that would become instrumental in passing the 1938 Fair Labor Standards Act, which, among other social reforms, ended the use of minors in oppressive labor conditions. One of Hine's subjects, Shorpy Higginbotham, later developed somewhat of a cult following online.

Shorpy, who claimed to be fourteen, worked twelve to fourteen hours a day as a greaser, lubricating the axles of trams that carried coal aboveground from inside the mine. Shorpy would be crushed by a rock in his early thirties during one of the state's hundreds of mining accidents—a litany as difficult to wrap one's mind around as the number of Village Creek environmental disasters.

17. James H. Miller Electric Generating Plant, near Village Creek's Warrior River terminus. Image courtesy of the Library of Congress.

Also hard to reconcile is the persistence of environmental threats along the creek. As Tom and I spent a long afternoon following these lovely roads, we began to catch glimpses of what looked like a nuclear plant's cooling towers belching smoke. We didn't realize until we were parked and looking straight at them that the towers marked the end of our journey. Village Creek's confluence with the Black Warrior River's Locust Fork is also the site of the James H. Miller Electric Generating Plant (Miller Steam Plant), named in 2017 by the EPA as the largest emitter of greenhouse gases in the United States.

As we began to feel the kind of edginess in the air that we'd experienced at Greenwood Park, my environmentalist husband—typically undeterred by nature that creeps, crawls, or makes the eyes itch—turned to me and said, "Let's get outta here."

I agreed. After two days of Village Creek, I was ready to heed my grandmother's warnings to stay away, and sure as heck ready for a beer.

13 / BEAUTY IN BIRMINGHAM?

The Art Gardens of Lonnie Holley and Joe Minter

Birmingham visitors arriving by airplane land northeast of downtown at Shuttlesworth International. The airport, originally Birmingham Municipal, was renamed in 2008 for the Reverend Fred Shuttlesworth (1922–2011), the local activist who founded the Alabama Christian Movement for Human Rights (ACMHR) and played a significant role in the 1963 Birmingham Campaign. As a civil rights educator, I feel great pride with each Shuttlesworth landing. Flying into my hometown from Florida, where I live now, planes typically approach Birmingham from the southeast, bank left south of Red Mountain and then right before downtown, hitting the runway from the west. I like sitting on the plane's starboard side to better see the spots that, for me, mark home: atop the mountain, Vulcan, the city's beloved god-of-the-forge statue; Kelly Ingram Park, the site (just west of downtown) of the city's infamous civil rights showdown; and, before the plane touches down, East Lake, where I grew up. The bird's-eye view reminds me that no matter how far I travel, I am rooted to this place and its history, part of something much larger than myself.

Then the plane bumps to the ground. As it skips, slides, and slows to the gate, I remember that we travel over blood and bone.

Technically, the airport sits next to, not atop, two burial grounds: Forest Hill Cemetery, where as children my cousins and I walked among the headstones looking for ghosts, and Greenwood Cemetery, which houses spirits that the city still struggles to put to rest. Three girls killed in the 1963 Sixteenth Street Baptist Church bombing—Addie Mae Collins, Carole Robertson, and Cynthia Wesley—are buried at Greenwood. A fourth, Denise McNair, is buried at Elmwood Cemetery, to the city's southwest.

Even though the blood and bones are not literal, the metaphor contains a truth. Underneath the Shuttlesworth International Airport lies part of Village Creek, the city's dammed and tunneled pulse. The airport's primary runways point directly at Roebuck Springs, Village Creek's headwaters. In the late 1990s, when a key runway was extended by seven thousand feet to accommodate bigger jets, the airport expansion took out a section of the Airport Hills neighborhood. Among the residents displaced was the celebrated visionary artist Lonnie Holley, whose site-specific sculpture garden fell to a bulldozer.

The broader context of Holley's displacement sheds light on a question that has concerned me since *Learning from Birmingham*'s early stages. During one of my first research trips to the Birmingham Civil Rights Institute, I came across a 2010 oral history interview with writer-activist Alice Walker. Visiting Birmingham to accept the Estelle Witherspoon Lifetime Achievement Award from the Federation of Southern Cooperatives, Walker spoke to the institute's then-archivist, Laura Anderson, about her impressions of the city. Walker confessed that she, like many, knew Birmingham only as a "poster of violence," but she was eager to learn something beyond what she had seen on television during the 1963 civil rights protests. "What grows here?" Walker asked Anderson. "Do the people love the environment? . . . How do they show that? Is there beauty in Birmingham?" My thinking about Walker's questions shifted as I wrote this book. I left my hometown in the 1980s with its steady thrum of ugliness buzzing through my body and soul. Not until the early 2000s, as I began immersing myself in the city's history, bad and good, did I begin to feel the connection to place that comes, today, with landing at Shuttlesworth. Even now, however, my answer to a question about beauty in Birmingham remains vexed. Yes, I would say to Walker, but separating the beauty from the ugliness is next to impossible. To make that case, I would point to Birmingham's visionary artists. This dirty, polluted, gritty industrial town has produced a striking number of them, including painter Thornton Dial, quilter Chris Clark, and Joe Minter, who, like Holley, transforms found-object detritus into sculptural wonderlands of history and humanity. These artists' off-kilter ways of creating beauty give us a truth we need to see.

The trouble is that many Birmingham residents do not understand the value of what lies in their backyard. Both Holley's and Minter's works can be found in the Smithsonian American Art Museum, the Metropolitan Museum of Art, and other major collections. Just one Holley sculpture can sell for thousands of dollars. When the city wanted to expand the airport, it offered Holley $14,000 for his entire property, including all its site-specific installations. He took the price to court, ultimately getting $165,000 to relocate, but was unable to remove much of his work before it was destroyed. In 1997, while his case pended in probate, local debates raged over whether Holley's sculpture garden was "junk" or "art." Similarly, Minter, represented like Holley and many other southern self-taught artists by the Souls Grown Deep Foundation, finds himself an outsider even to local celebrations of "outsider art." Prior to the COVID-19 pandemic, Minter maintained a vigil with elaborate signage and ringing bells outside Birmingham's city hall, demonstrating about a variety of issues, from waterworks board corruption to world peace. Out of curiosity during a 2016 visit, I asked several people in front of the art museum (a block away) if they knew local artist Joe Minter. No one did. When I shifted the question to ask about "the guy with the bells," most everyone pointed me in his direction. The irony here is that Birmingham so often looks outward, holding a grudging, one-sided competition between itself and Atlanta, the larger city 150 miles east. The airport expansion emerged from that civic desire to keep up, to make Birmingham competitive for business travelers and tourist dollars. Such outward looking prevents the city from recognizing what is special inside, artists such as Holley and Minter.

It was Walker herself who taught me how to find the unexpected beauty in those yards seemingly filled with junk. Her essay "In Search of Our Mothers' Gardens" describes how everyday people use the tools at hand to keep alive an artistic spirit, often amid the most challenging conditions. Walker writes of wondering how her ancestors, including her mother, nurtured the seeds of creative genius through soul-killing centuries of race, gender, and economic oppression. Seeing in the Smithsonian a beautifully crafted quilt made by an anonymous enslaved woman shifted Walker's notions of art. The question became not whether women like her mother and the quilter produced works conventionally perceived as artistic but how they developed complex aesthetic practices within the ordinary, domestic realm of quilts and gardens. "But when, you will ask, did my overworked mother find time to know or care about feeding the creative spirit?" Walker asks. "The answer is so simple that many of us have spent years discovering it. We have constantly looked high, when we should have looked high—and low."

A similar statement can be made about artists such as Holley and Minter, and of the city itself. Is there beauty in Birmingham? Yes, if one learns how to look. Why Walker described the city as a "poster of violence" is obvious. Interwoven within that often horrific story is also one about the courage and resilience of freedom fighters such as Shuttlesworth. The art gardens of Holley and Minter likewise tell a story about fighting back, about daring to make beauty from the cast-offs of an ugly world. Like Village Creek, which offers a lens into Birmingham past and present, Holley and Minter lead us through where the city has been and where it is today. Buried beneath an airport or tucked behind the fence of a working-class neighborhood, these gardens provide a place apart that is also a road inside.

*

To understand Holley and Minter, one must first understand the concept of visionary art gardens. Such spaces are found often in the US South, in working-class yards of different races, in rural and urban areas. Some are more decorative: the hodgepodge of whirligigs, flamingos, and statuettes familiar to almost anyone who has ever traveled a southern back road. Others contain site-specific installations with spiritual and political messages, created by people (like Holley and Minter) who are described variously as "vernacular," "folk," or "self-taught" artists. Readers who know 1980s popular music might remember Howard Finster, the Georgia artist/minister who developed Paradise Garden and whose work is featured on album covers for bands R.E.M. (*Reckoning*, 1984) and Talking Heads (*Little Creatures*, 1985). Visitors to the Smithsonian might recall seeing James Hampton's large, striking *Throne of the Third Heaven of the Nations' Millennium General Assembly*, put together from found objects and foil over a period of years in a Washington, DC, garage. For Lonnie Holley, who endows the detritus of industrialization with spirit and humanity, abstract art—including his yard installations, sculpture, painting, and music—acts as a fortress of dignity. For Joe Minter, who comments more concretely on civil rights and related historical events, found objects channel ancestors who keep watch, educate, and speak truth to power. Both men's art draws from African and diasporic practices in a form of aesthetic defiance that stands in direct contrast to traditional, Eurocentric modes of creative expression and landscape cultivation. Their art yards bring Africa to an epicenter of Jim Crow, in an act that, to paraphrase feminist theorist bell hooks, transforms gardens into sites of radical resistance.

Minter lives with his wife, Hilda, about two miles southwest of downtown Birmingham. A Vietnam veteran, Minter held a series of jobs after his army service, including road crew, construction, and auto-body repair. Like many Birmingham men his age, he found himself out of work during the late 1970s when his shop closed down. His pension ran out soon after, and Minter asked God for help. He calls the vision he received his "African Village in America." It's a half acre of materials that he finds in "streets . . . in flea markets, outlet stores, Goodwill [and the] Salvation Army"—"what other people throw away as junk"—repurposed into sculptures, memorials, signs, and other markers of what Minter says is his divinely inspired mission as "Peacemaker."

Minter's property borders a historically Black cemetery, Grace Hill, which is just down the road from Elmwood, the city's largest and oldest burial ground—a holdover from the days when segregation persisted into death. I first encountered his art yard when searching Grace Hill for the grave of my former babysitter Ceola. As I followed the caretaker, Charles, through winding cemetery roads, I noticed off to my right a series of large sculptures made of used auto parts, with faces that looked like African masks. Needless

18. Artist Joe Minter, 2018. Photograph courtesy of Colby Rabon.

to say, I had to check them out. "We are in the presence of about 100,000 African ancestors," Minter tells visitors. "These are the emancipated slaves and farmers and steelworkers who made Birmingham: the muscle that built the 'Magic City.'" Walking through Minter's African Village, one sees evidence of this ancestral presence around every corner. Hubcaps and lug nuts, or a bowling ball, become a face. Put the face atop a wheel and a strut, and the figure becomes a body. Add a garden tool, such as a shovel or a hoe, and the piece becomes a warrior. Stick a Statue of Liberty head on a rotting two-by-four to create the "*Slave Ship America.*" Add brown dolls, chains, and toy sharks to create a visceral reminder of the Middle Passage. No matter where one turns in the garden, one bumps into history made tangible.

Holley's story begins similarly, but it has a more complicated trajectory, because his original space no longer exists. Holley also found himself unemployed in the late 1970s, when Birmingham's iron and steel economy flatlined. His first artworks were deeply personal memorials to two nieces that died in a fire: African-masklike carvings from the sandstone by-products of industrial pipe casting. Soon he began making more and more of these sculptures, earning a local nickname, "Sandman." Then his art turned, like Minter's, to materials scavenged from dumpsters, alleys, and thrift stores and transformed into installations that he kept in his one-acre yard near the (then) Birmingham International Airport. Later, Holley expanded his repertoire to include painting: mostly abstract pieces in earth tones with craft-store materials like glitter added for visual depth and texture. The difference between Holley and Minter is that, early on, Holley marketed himself to art-world powers that be, taking selections to Richard Murray, then-director of the Birmingham Museum of Art. Murray, in turn, brought Holley's work to curators at the Smithsonian, where it wound up in a 1979 exhibit, *More than Land or Sky: Art from Appalachia.* From there Holley gained notoriety as interest in self-taught artists expanded during the 1980s and 1990s. But a national reputation did not translate into local respect, as the Birmingham Airport Authority's eminent-domain claim over his yard demonstrates.

After the 1997 bulldozing of his property (originally purchased by his grandfather), Holley moved his family to a foreclosed homestead in Shelby County, south of Birmingham. His new neighbors, relatives of the woman who lost her land in the foreclosure deal, tried to drive him out by slashing his tires and shooting into his home. At one point, they shot him. Finally, in 2010, he moved to Atlanta. In a *New York Times* article, Holley said, "What I'm doing here, I think Malcolm said it best: by any means necessary. . . . We

19. Artist Lonnie Holley with work, circa 1980s–90s, Slide 1260 in the Souls Grown Deep Foundation Collection #20491, Southern Folklife Collection, The Wilson Library, University of North Carolina at Chapel Hill.

can make art where we have to." His current medium of choice is music: experimental, structure-defying, improvisational pieces offering the aural equivalent of his visual art's raw power

One reason that some audiences might struggle to see the beauty in what Holley and Minter create lies in how to categorize these artists. Both make art "by any means necessary," where they have to, how they have to. They employ nontraditional materials and practices, and transcend familiar boundaries of genre. Holley, moving from sand sculpture to music, seems particularly fluid, but one might also view Minter, who takes time away from his yard for protests that verge on performance, as a transmedia artist. From a critical perspective, however, neither man fits easily into a definitional box.

A telling story about Holley can be found in the liner notes to his 2018 recording *Mith*. There, Matt Arnett (son of William Arnett, who helped to collect and preserve a substantial amount of self-taught art) recounts how he and the artist attended a music festival in Rennes, France, where they were met by a large Venn diagram of how the festival's musicians and genres overlapped. They searched, unsuccessfully, for Holley's name among the circles of folk, jazz, blues, traditional, and electronica, only to find him listed alone and apart, in "the blank space between the diagram's circles and the bold title of the festival."

A catalog from a Birmingham Museum of Art exhibit on Holley, *Do We Think Too Much? I Don't Think We Can Ever Stop*, similarly struggles to pin down the artist. For Thomas W. Southall, former curator of photography at Atlanta's High Museum of Art, Holley's work appears sui generis, Birmingham-strange: emerging "from the debris haphazardly, yet at the same time seeming to be in a process of returning to earth." David Moos, former curator of modern and contemporary works at the Birmingham Museum of Art, sees Holley as akin to international figures such as Joseph Beuys, Sigmar Polke, and Robert Rauschenberg—an artist whose "Combines" famously incorporated found-object and natural materials. Holley, Moos explains, is from Birmingham but "liberated" from "vernacular encumbrance." It's a condescending statement, at best.

Minter—who has not received the same amount of critical attention as Holley and has just recently begun to see his work appear in galleries and museums—also defies labels and receives his share of condescension. Is he the visionary maker of "one of the last great 'yard shows' in Alabama," or is he the crazy guy who protests in front of city hall ringing bells?

For either man, how does one draw the line between art and junk?

Consistencies of form and theme do exist for each artist, and between them as well. When I visited Minter's home in September 2019, he described the foundation of his work to me as "ARTS: Aesthetics, Rhythm, Truth, and Soul." A similar statement might be made of Holley. Their works do not line up to traditional ways of framing beauty, but they do follow an internal aesthetic compass, a rhythm of their own in search of truth, one that is rooted, deeply, in soil and soul. Poet and cultural critic Amiri Baraka, speaking of self-taught southern artists, perhaps said it best: "Powerful art is not the expression of lifeless social convention" (what he calls earlier 'the formal mediocrity of bourgeois . . . culture'). Instead, "powerful art is . . . the recreated emotional and intellectual life of the artist and of the time, place, and condition of the artist's world."

Holley's and Minter's art gardens draw their power from time and place: Birmingham's industrial castoffs offer a medium, while the city's history provides a theme. Yet these spaces also exist within a context. The question, as Walker might put it, is where to look. If a European music festival could not find a place for Holley within its Venn diagram, perhaps the problem lies with the diagram rather than with the artist. That each employs language ("by any means necessary," "soul") of the late 1960s and early 1970s Black Arts/Black Power Movements seems key. These art gardens, products of the US South, embrace practices that are specifically Black diasporic, Afro-Atlantic. In doing so they more closely resemble works by writers like Walker and Baraka than they do the visions of someone like Howard Finster or the "Combines" of a Robert Rauschenberg. They provide not only beauty *in* Birmingham but also beauty *of* a Birmingham that is Afrocentric, with overlapping circles of past, present, and future.

Seeing the beauty in Holley's and Minter's art was not something that came naturally to me, schooled like so many in white, Eurocentric aesthetic norms. Instead, I came to that knowledge through researching Civil Rights Movement literature and related cultural productions. Two studies in particular helped alter my field of vision: Grey Gundaker and Judith McWillie's *No Space Hidden: The Spirit of African American Yard Work*, and Brian Norman and Piper Kendrix Williams's edited volume on the literature of segregation. First, Norman and Williams prompted me to look at these art gardens as physical locations that attempt to question and transcend an equally tangible racism. In the introduction to *Representing Segregation*, they outline how authors spatialize race, marking boundaries and delineating ways in which lines get crossed. More recently, in the *Cambridge Companion to American Civil Rights Literature*, Norman (writing solo) describes how authors move beyond those boundaries by imagining other racial configurations in, for example, speculative and transnational settings. This latter point connects Norman/Williams to Gundaker/McWillie, who detail the ways in which self-taught artists such as Minter and Holley, and vernacular gardeners more generally, engage in practices that are specifically Afro-Atlantic. Gundaker and McWillie documented approximately two hundred yards over twenty years and found in them striking consistencies of materials, strategies, and themes that evoke a "creole way of doing things." Linking these different perspectives are three terms that seem particularly appropriate to Minter and Holley: "wildness," "transformation," and "elsewhere."

Wildness. The word carries specific meaning with regard to these artists. Their yards, like other art gardens, blur distinctions between "cultivated" and "wild," as Gundaker and McWillie demonstrate through historical African American and West African practices. The basic binary is familiar and shows up in segregation literature as well. Cultivated space has a distinct purpose, symmetry, and clean lines; it is the site of safety and social order, often coded as white (think: suburban lawn). The wild appears haphazard and

190 / CHAPTER 13

unpredictable; it is the dangerous space of wilderness where the usual rules do not apply, often coded as black (think: dark forest). For Gundaker and McWillie, Lonnie Holley's yard epitomized "a wilderness zone in which the 'natural' and 'human-made' were so densely layered that they were barely distinguishable." The same is true of Minter's yard. At what point does wild nature stop and cultivated art begin? Lines can be hard to distinguish when the grass, rocks, and trees flow seamlessly into artworks derived from an Afro-Atlantic lexicon. Gundaker and McWillie detail the signs and symbols:

- Glass, mirrors, and other reflective surfaces to honor ancestors and ward off evil
- Automobile wheels, tires, and similar circular objects to signal progressive action
- Animals, mannequins, or other statues placed at boundaries as figures of judgment and authority
- Tying and wrapping fences to hold in protective powers.
- Repurposing objects because they are "experienced, not used."

Both Norman/Williams and Gundaker/McWillie blur the categories of cultivated and wild even further, specifically considering how words such as "safe" and "dangerous" are coded differently by race. During Jim Crow the white social order used violence and the fear of violence to police its supposedly safe "cultivated spaces." In turn, swamps, woods, and other purportedly wild places became good hideouts. Many art gardens cultivate (pun intended) an intentionally wild look to keep out potential threats, whether vandals or visitors.

I admit that Minter's towering ancestor sculptures, placed on the edge of his yard to watch over the cemetery, initially frightened me. Before knocking on his door for the first time, in 2013, I brought Tom, and we checked with Minter's neighbors to see if he was friendly. Turns out that Minter seems to enjoy sharing his vision, especially with those who make purchases. (A four-foot-high *Zulu Warrior* made of car parts sits in my home office.) We've been back to visit several times over the years, and I've joined Minter on a bell-ringing protest.

Holley is much more guarded. Tom attempted a visit during the late 1990s, as the airport extension loomed. "Mind the signage," warned the art museum employee who gave him directions to Holley's house. Tom turned back after finding the front gated closed, wrapped in crime scene tape (holding in protective powers?), with a gun illustrating a "No Trespassing" sign. (We wound up purchasing one of Holley's paintings a few years later, from a gallery, and I've never managed to talk to the artist himself.) After Holley's move to Shelby County, when he reported that his neighbors watched him "like a hawk watches a chicken" and shot out his windows, he replaced the broken glass with mirrors to keep out their evil. Gundaker and McWillie explain that a mixture of conjure, Christian, and secular signs is common in such yards. One must honor the spirit that exists in wildness; one must approach the sacred grove with respect. For Minter, this is where the ancestors abide. For Holley, this is where transformation takes place.

Transformation. Both artists see their work as transformational, life changing. Holley, who led a chaotic childhood, bouncing around different families and serving time at what was then called the Alabama Industrial School for Negro Children, uses art to keep the demons, external and internal, at bay. He states: "To deal with me as an artist, and see all of my art as art and not just as garbage or junk, is to see that I went to the depths of where no one else would even go to speak for life. God said, 'I made enough in your yard that I could show my people how to change.' . . . And that's what keeps me from going insane." Holley's words also speak to Minter's process. The latter's vision was not just to make art but to heal others as well as himself. Minter's adult life, like Holley's childhood, was chaotic, moving from one low-wage job to another. When an employer shut down in 1979, he found himself profoundly alienated: a working man with no work. He also felt lost in a world fragmented by race. "I asked God to help me bring people together as one," he says. And God spoke back. "The whole idea handed down to me by God is to use that which has been discarded, just as we as a people have been discarded, and make it visible. . . . I wanted *The African Village in America* to demonstrate that even what gets thrown away, has a spirit and could survive and continue to grow." Minter believed his art "could heal wounds everywhere." He adopted the moniker "Peacemaker." Each artist cultivates wildness as a balm against the wilderness inside. For Holly and Minter, becoming an artist was a form of economic, existential, and spiritual salvation.

By extension, both see their work as a form of salvation for the broken world they inhabit. Minter's work is distinctly political. His *African Village in America* memorializes a variety of historical events, from the Middle Passage, to Birmingham's Sixteenth Street Church bombing, to Hurricane Katrina and the shootings at Sandy Hook Elementary School. Holley's visual art occasionally references specific people and events, such as Martin Luther King Jr. and the church bombing, but more often he operates by "animating" inanimate objects, finding the spirit within them. The 2004 retrospective *Do We Think Too Much? I Don't Think We Can Ever Stop* featured items that looked like old bicycles, electronics, and telephone wires, until closer inspection revealed the human forms and faces. Minter, speaking to the process of becoming an artist, says, "I was living in a place that looked upon Africans as less than human beings." His work bears witness to that ugly history of dehumanization. Holley's work, conversely, uncovers humanity in the most unexpected places.

Encountering a Minter or Holley work, entering into its space, accommodating its vision of the world, transforms perceptions of art, place, and history. Gundaker and McWillie put it this way: "Many of the people we have met are motivated to work in their yards . . . in the hope of making things better, starting at home and then turning outward. For many of them . . . this has meant coming to terms with oppression and seeking a positive outlook even in the most soul-daunting circumstances." As both Norman/Williams and Gundaker/McWillie note, the process of transformation involves naming and renaming. "Junk" becomes "art"; a yard becomes a gallery; dangers are made known, dismantled, and repurposed into spiritual spaces.

Elsewhere. Sometimes one must transcend rather than transform those "soul-daunting circumstances." A key word that Norman uses (in his solo essay) is "elsewhere," a concept that he takes from the poet Kevin Young. "However we conceive it," Young states, "Elsewhere is central to the African American tradition." For Young, "elsewhere" is a figurative—and sometimes literal—space of freedom, where one can rename or reclaim the self, imagine new possibilities. Under slavery, African Americans dreamed of Canaan and Canada. No one, perhaps, embodies "elsewhere" like the musician Sun Ra, whose abstract, improvisational, futuristic recordings link him specifically to artists like Holley and Minter. A Birmingham native, Ra (1914–93), rechristened himself twice (born Herman Poole Blount, he first changed his name to Le Son'y Ra) and relocated his birthplace out of the Jim Crow South, to Saturn. Such a move—to other locations, other worlds—occurs in segregation literature as well. Norman connects "elsewhere" to writers who respond to Jim Crow by imagining configurations beyond the color line. Think James Weldon Johnson's Ex-Colored Man in Latin America, the Pan-African Richard Wright, James Baldwin in Paris, or Octavia Butler in the speculative realm. In his 1931 novel *Black No More*, George Schuyler explains that the

US offers three options, "Either get out, get white, or move along." For some, Norman states, "get out is the most appealing option."

For Minter and Holley, getting out entails going in. Their Afro-Atlantic yards take them, and their visitors, elsewhere. Minter made an African Village in America that navigates past and present traumas via the protective presence of ancestors. Holley picked through Birmingham's scrap heaps hoping to find enough beauty to keep himself sane and to help his city heal. Does it matter that the airport ran him off, and so did his neighbors south of town? Yes and no. Gundaker and McWillie point out that art gardens are ephemeral, rarely preserved. Thinking about them as process rather than product is helpful. They are spirit-work, liturgical, performance, prayer. One important lesson I learned from Holley and Minter is that their creative ways of doing things act as powerful mojo for resisting the forces of hate and dehumanization.

The question, it seems, is not whether there is beauty in Birmingham but whether Birmingham can nurture and sustain the unconventional beauty that its considerable ugliness has generated.

14 / HUSTLING HISTORY

It's 2015: standing in line for the flight from Tampa to Birmingham, I overhear a golf-shirted business man snort, "There's no reason to go except for work."

Flashback to 1997: An aging flower child standing behind me for tickets to see Spike Lee's *4 Little Girls* at Manhattan's Film Forum hears where I am from and asks wide-eyed, "What's it like there?"

Flash-forward to 2010: "I felt chills the moment I saw the city limits sign," an earnest graduate student tells me after going on a colleague's Civil Rights Movement bus tour.

And back again to 2015: I meet the department chair from my PhD alma mater, New York University, at a conference. He doesn't bother finding out what I teach or write about. Instead, the conversation stops cold when he hears I am from Birmingham. "I wouldn't even drive through a place like that," he says with a shudder.

In the popular imagination, Birmingham represents a racial heart of darkness, where Black Americans got beaten up, locked up, blown up: Bull Connor's police dogs and fire hoses, Martin Luther King's letter from jail, Bombingham's four little girls.

The city has worked hard to redeem itself from the wrong side of history. The process began with a series of long-overdue murder convictions in the Sixteenth Street Baptist Church bombing: Robert Chambliss, in 1997; Thomas Blanton, in 2001; and Bobby Frank Cherry, in 2002. Next came the transformation of Sixteenth Street and Sixth Avenue North. Once the scene of devastating Jim Crow violence, the intersection now centers a large memorial complex that includes the church, the Birmingham Civil Rights Institute, the Civil Rights Heritage Trail's multiple walking tours, and Kelly Ingram Park's public art. The complex attracts thousands of visitors each year, from local school groups to international tourists, to see what a historical marker at the park's southern edge calls "Ground Zero," a movement epicenter that radiated across the nation. A culminating effort in this process of redemption came in 2013, when the city marked Fifty Years Forward, a commemoration of lives lost and a celebration of progress made.

Since starting the research for this book, I make sure once a year or so to visit my hometown's historic Civil Rights Movement intersection, and especially Kelly Ingram Park. Billing itself as "A Place of Revolution and Reconciliation," the park offers the perfect space for reflecting on changes past, present, and future.

*

Sometimes I take Tom and Zack.

In 2013 Zack, then twelve, went with his parents to the unveiling of *Four Spirits*—a monument dedicated, on the anniversary of their deaths, to the girls lost in the church bombing. Zack paid attention for some of the time we spent standing under a blinding September sun, then sat with other children, dragged by their parents to the historic event, under the shade of a historical marker on Kelly Ingram Park's northwest corner. "Jim Crow on the Books" quotes one of the more ridiculous segregation laws that the 1963 movement worked to overturn: "It shall be unlawful for a Negro and a white person to play together or in company of each other," games including cards, checkers, baseball, and football. At one point in the ceremony, I looked down to see, reflected in the marker's shiny surface, our white son with an African American boy about his same age digging sticks into the dirt. I thought to myself that the city, and the nation, had indeed spent the past fifty years moving forward.

Then we went back a year later.

Zack was thirteen and a bit less willing to accompany his parents anywhere, much less to Birmingham (*Again? Really, Mom? Ugh*). For a bribe of his favorite Dreamland Barbeque, however, our son summoned the will to endure one more of his mother's earnest lectures about people his age risking their lives against segregation's police dogs and fire hoses.

And so Zack marched through Kelly Ingram Park, a skinny blond in skater garb, eyes on the rib-prize. His bespectacled middle-aged parents toddled ten feet behind, theorizing public space and historical memory in the language of white academics.

Our first stop was artist James Drake's two bronze parallel walls of lunging, fang-baring German shepherds. In 2013 a younger Zack was terrified of the dogs towering over him, so he ran behind them. A year later, Tom pointed out that they were beginning to rust. Zack swiped a few flecks off their paws and jogged across the park.

We caught up to him as he poked his head through the metal bars of a sculpture meant to invoke a cell.

"I ain't afraid of your jail," he yelled out words from the freedom song inscribed on the pedestal. The piece, also by Drake, honors the thousands of school children—and some adults, including Martin Luther King Jr.—arrested during April and May of 1963 for protesting segregation. Zack had no time for quotes from King's famous letter. Ten seconds in mock jail, and he moved on to the park's northern edge so he could aim water cannons at the backs of bronze teenagers.

His dad and I huffed across the park to Drake's third monument. Our son's brow was furrowed.

"Mom, tell me why people were shooting kids," he said. "That's just stupid."

"You know the reason," I reminded him. "You've been here before."

Instead of taking my bait to answer the question for himself, Zack zipped away. By the time his parents took twenty steps, he was across the street, milling with some middle-schoolers next to a statue of local leader Fred Shuttlesworth.

The truth was that I evaded Zack's question because I struggled for words.

This particular visit to Kelly Ingram Park, in December 2014, coincided with unrest in Ferguson, Missouri, over a grand jury's decision not to indict white police officer Darren Wilson for shooting an unarmed black teen named Michael Brown. A few weeks earlier, police shot twelve-year-old Tamir Rice in Cleveland, Ohio, after mistaking his toy gun for the real thing.

I wanted my son to see paradox, but I had little to offer beyond his own assessment, "That's just stupid."

So much, and yet so little, had changed since Bull Connor turned segregation's might against teenagers dressed up in their Sunday best, toothbrushes in their pockets, jail-ready to change their world. Not much, and yet everything, separated Zack from a boy about his age walking through a Florida neighborhood, hoodie on, texting friends, eating Skittles.

A man like George Zimmerman would not follow a boy like Zack. If Trayvon Martin had been white, he would still be alive.

How does Birmingham's white daughter respond to her son's Civil Rights Movement questions in a Black Lives Matter era? She treats him to his favorite restaurant when he walks with her through Ground Zero.

Dreamland fills the empty spaces where the answers should be.

*

When I have my own civil rights questions, I ask my aunt, Martha Wynell Hughes. Aunt Nell has lived in Birmingham most of her life but did not go to the memorial complex until she was old enough that she needed a walker to navigate it.

We visited in December 2013, near the close of the Fifty Years Forward anniversary. Aunt Nell and I started our tour in the Sixteenth Street Baptist Church basement, a place she had seen only in evidence photos from her time as a juror in the 1977 Robert Chambliss trial. I wanted to jog Aunt Nell's memory of events before interviewing her for this book. Before going inside the church, I steeled myself to be strong for my elderly aunt. I have written about the literature of Jim Crow and civil rights for two decades. I once wrote a book about a lynching. Surrounding myself with a protective shield of academic objectivity has become second nature.

Almost.

The basement, close to where the dynamite exploded in September 1963, has a small display on the incident, which includes artifacts related to the church's role in the movement and to the spring 1963 Birmingham campaign. Aunt Nell and I weren't in the room two minutes before we came across a well-known civil rights movement image: two white police officers wielding German shepherds against a young Black man. Standing before it, I started shaking and crying.

The reaction made me feel stupid. Aunt Nell stared down Dynamite Bob. And I steeled myself to help *her*?

The reaction also felt inappropriate. I couldn't help but think about a line from the Sena Jeter Naslund novel *Four Spirits*, which gave its name to the memorial in the park across the street. The character Gloria, who survived the bombing, questions her white friends' motivations for being involved in local protests. "Could white women know anything beyond personal tragedy?" she asks. Gloria was right. Here I was, at Birmingham's Ground Zero of racist violence, acting as if I were the victim. I might as well have snapped a selfie and made myself into a meme: white fragility, maybe, or white woman tears.

Aunt Nell, who has soothed my tears many times since childhood, reached over to pat me on the arm, saying, "That right there is the very image we need to work through to make any progress."

What I heard at the time: this is the image that Birmingham needs to work through.

Later, I would come back to those words, but for the moment Aunt Nell and I kept walking. We had a full civil rights memorial complex to see, and I promised to take Aunt Nell out for dinner.

A little Dreamland after a long day comforts the soul.

*

I have come back to that photograph from many angles during the past few years. I reviewed history, literature, and video footage. I circled the Sixteenth Street-Sixth Avenue intersection, where the photo was taken, snapping my own images. I read the Birmingham Civil Rights Institute's interviews with people who were there. I visited the park to ponder sculptor Ronald McDowell's *The Foot Soldier*, a bronze replica of the scene. With each examination, the photograph's story grew more complicated.

Let's begin with what exists inside the frame. The shot captures a white police officer grabbing a young Black man, whose knees appear bent as if caught mid-sprint, while the officer's German shepherd lunges, about to bite the man's midsection. Another white police officer stands with his back to the camera, dog at bay. The action occurs at an intersection full of people,

20. An African American high school student, Walter Gadsden (15) is attacked by a police dog during a 1963 civil rights demonstration. Photograph by Bill Hudson courtesy of the Associated Press.

with a restaurant, Jockey Boy, visible in the background. Some of the people watch the incident; others move hastily away. The emotions discernible on their faces indicate that most are upset. The police officer facing forward wears sunglasses, but his gritted teeth reveal tension. The man he grabs looks determined rather than frightened, as one might think he would be when facing a dog attack. The scowling woman over the police officer's left shoulder appears angry, as do the people behind her. The man to her left seems concerned.

Who are these people, who took this photo, and what brought each person to this moment?

The Black teenager's name is Walter Gadsden. The white police officer facing the camera is Richard "Dick" Middleton, and his dog is Leo. After the photograph, a policeman named Wallace Chilcoat arrested Gadsden for parading without a permit, so it's possible that Chilcoat is the officer whose back is to the camera. Associated Press photographer Bill Hudson took the shot on Friday, May 3, 1963. It ran on the *New York Times*' front page the following day, above another photograph that would also become iconic and get replicated in Kelly Ingram Park's bronzes: Charles Moore's image of three teens protecting themselves from a fire hose blast. The caption for both read, "Violence Explodes at Racial Protests in Alabama."

The best way to explain how Gadsden, Middleton, Chilcoat, and Hudson came to the intersection of Sixteenth Street and Sixth Avenue North on May 3 is to begin with May 2, what movement historians call "D-Day." Thousands of teens and children skipped school to join the demonstrations that had been going on downtown for several weeks, where they faced the brunt of Birmingham's institutional violence: Bull Connor ordering dogs and hoses turned on them in an attempt to stop the protests. Connor's bullying show of force played directly into movement organizers' hands. As King noted in his "Letter from Birmingham Jail," written just two weeks earlier, "The purpose of our direct action program is to create a situation so crisis-packed that it will inevitably open the door to negotiation." King was right, and photographers were ready.

Men like Moore and Hudson risked their lives to capture images that would define the Birmingham movement. When Freedom Riders got off the bus in Montgomery two years earlier, the angry mob first attacked reporters and photographers, ripping film from cameras; anyone going into Birmingham in 1963 must have known the potential dangers in store. Moore, a Marine combat photography veteran, sustained injuries from a chunk of flying concrete. Hudson set his sights on "making pictures and staying alive" and "not getting bit by a dog." He kept his 35mm Nikon hidden in his coat. When a tall Black teen and two white police officers with K-9s crossed his path, he snapped pictures at random, not knowing that he captured history until he developed the film.

I see how that happened. On one trip to Birmingham in 2016, I walked different paths of the Civil Rights Heritage Trail, photographing its historical markers. On the March Route to Retail, which details protests against segregated downtown stores and businesses, I took several pictures of markers, one focusing on Bull Connor. (A corresponding path, the March Route to Government, traces protests against the city's seats of power.) Later, when pulling up the images on my computer, I chuckled at how the marker labeled Connor

21. Historical marker describing former Birmingham commissioner of public safety Eugene "Bull" Connor as the "Bad Guy." Photo courtesy of the author, whose image is reflected behind the cutout.

"The Bad Guy." He might have directed some of the action, I thought, but he was hardly the only player. Then my laughter got cut short. Reflected in the marker's text was my own image, just above the "The Bad Guy" heading, and Connor's finger pointing at me.

I realized then that looking at the Hudson photograph as a white person from Birmingham—*really* looking—means recognizing oneself within it. The police officers holding the dogs embody the racism that each of us begins learning in our cradles, and some of us will take to our graves.

Most of us do what we can to avoid confronting this version of Birmingham in ourselves, in the same way that many white outsiders hold the city at arm's length "What's it like there?" they say to me, or "I wouldn't even drive through a place like Birmingham." James Baldwin captured it best, in a statement that serves as one of this book's epigraphs: white people want to believe that Birmingham is on Mars—alien, distant. One reason I became a Civil Rights Movement scholar and educator was to prove to myself, over and over again, that this photograph is *not me*. The city of Birmingham worked for fifty years to prove that the photograph is *not us*.

Even the people in the photograph tried to distance themselves from it. In an oral history from 1996, Chilcoat, the officer who arrested Gadsden and might be the one with his back to the camera, denies having a dog. Not long after the incident, Middleton, the officer wearing the sunglasses, left the police force to spend the rest of his life as a baker. When Diane McWhorter was researching *Carry Me Home*, Middleton refused to talk with her about the photograph, saying it "didn't bother me." When she called Walter Gadsden, he likewise told her that he didn't want to "get involved" and hung up.

A significant amount of revisionist history now surrounds the Hudson image. In a 1996 oral history interview, Gadsden reports that he was not a protestor, just a teenager curious about events happening downtown and eager to skip school. Trying to get closer to the action, he ducked behind the park's police barricade and found himself face-to-face with Leo the dog. As McWhorter notes, if we look closer at the Hudson photograph, we can see that Gadsden does not practice nonviolence but self-defense. His hand grips Middleton's wrist; his knees bend, not in a sprint, but to stop Leo's lunge. Legend has it that Gadsden broke Leo's jaw.

The McDowell sculpture, the first piece of public art unveiled after Kelly Ingram Park's 1992 renovation, offers its own revision. Paying homage to the "Foot Soldiers of the Birmingham Civil Rights Movement" (as do most of the park's monuments), the work stands about thirteen feet high, across the street from the Civil Rights Institute. *The Foot Soldier* features, atop a granite pedestal, a bronze police officer and dog confronting a teenage boy, but there the resemblance to Hudson's photograph ends. The boy is smaller, unlike Gadsden, who was about Middleton's height. He holds his arms back from his body, as if he is falling backward rather than defending himself. The police officer stares past the boy, as if he does not see him. The boy looks scared. The dog looks more like a snarling wolf, ready to devour. In their oral histories, Gadsden and Chilcoat comment on the differences between the photograph and the sculpture, which they both describe as exaggerated. In 2017 Malcolm Gladwell did an episode of his *Revisionist History* podcast on the statue and its maker. McDowell admits to taking significant artistic license.

As a work of art, *The Foot Soldier* does not necessarily owe allegiance to historical facts. Instead, McDowell captures a truth about perceptions of the Hudson image. His larger-than-life sculpture depicts an event that now seems itself to be larger than life. In the national imagination of the Birmingham Civil Rights Movement, Hudson's photograph captured a clear instance of the battle between good and evil, resistance and power, black and white. The image embodies the ways that many people prefer to see the past: tidy, with clean lines, a space apart, frozen down there and back then inside a photograph's frame.

*

Just before I finished this book, my spouse published his own, *A Road Course in Early American Literature: Travel and Teaching from Aztlán to Amherst*. In it Tom references a talk he attended by literary scholar John Elder, who described the two opposing meanings of the word "cleave." In one sense "to cleave" means "to split apart"; in another, it means "to adhere." "Literature professors," Tom explains, "assign texts that break down beliefs, but we rarely discuss how to help undergraduates put things together." When I first read his words, I realized that I had been trying to understand Birmingham by dissecting it, separating myself from my hometown through academic objectivity. What I needed to do instead, as I learned from my photograph of the Bull Connor marker, was learn to see where I fit into the city's complex history. Rather than take apart, I needed to repair the breach.

I went back to the city again in 2016, this time alone. If I couldn't avoid the intersection, I thought, I'll walk directly into it. That year marked fifty since Shuttlesworth's Alabama Christian Movement for Human Rights initiated its work in Alabama. The anniversary seemed auspicious. I wanted to walk mindfully through Kelly Ingram Park, follow the Civil Rights Movement Heritage Trail, go through the Civil Rights Institute once more, wander up Dynamite Hill.

I planned my walk for April and May, to coincide with events of spring 1963. In Kelly Ingram Park, I couldn't help but think about how beautiful the city would have been during the protests. I was struck by the juxtaposition between the viciousness of police dogs and fire hoses turned on protestors and the park's pink azaleas, red roses, green grass, and white baby's breath. Iconic photographs of that spring's events, most in black-and-white, don't capture the irony. This time I had a new camera—a new way of seeing. The Canon T3i is a hand-me-down from my late father-in-law, who bought it when he went on safari. This irony did not escape me either. Reviews on sites such as TripAdvisor sometimes describe the park as dangerous, full of vagrants and panhandlers. Birmingham's heart of Civil Rights Movement darkness has become, for some of today's tourists, a voyage into a frightening world of economic and mental-health untouchables.

I was trying to snap a photograph of "I ain't afraid of your jail" when a man approached me, asking if I wanted him to take my picture. From my many visits to the park, I'm used to encountering its homeless, typically men, who come up offering historical facts, some truthful, some fanciful. A particularly hyperactive potential tour guide once offered his expertise, volunteering that Rosa Parks (in Montgomery, ninety miles away) had gotten on the bus right at the spot where I was standing. I see, and avoid him, each time I go the park. I want his lectures about as much as my son wants mine. I decided, however, to talk to this other man asking about the picture. I was here to interact with Ground Zero, spend all day if necessary, not hurry through on a Dreamland promise.

The man's name was Lewis. He was born a couple of blocks away. He said he was bipolar and did not take medication. Sometimes he had what he called "episodes" that kept him from working regular jobs. He just had an "episode" and hurt his head. He showed me the gash.

I asked him why he stayed in this park and not other downtown parks. Was it the history?

No, he said, it was the safety. Because Kelly Ingram Park got so many tourists, the police, once dispatched to close off the park with K-9 forces, watched over it. Lewis said that Linn (formerly Woodrow Wilson) Park, by City Hall and the Public Library, was nice, but too many people hanging out there were drunk and on drugs. He told me to stay out. He was concerned that someone might knock me on the head.

I asked him how much money he made from showing tourists around the park. On nice days, he said, enough to pay for a daily room in a house up the street. Winter was different. At 11:00 a.m., the old firehouse down the street—from which, in 1963, firefighters were dispatched to turn hoses on children—handed out sandwiches.

We both looked around, 10:30. The other men in the park were making their way south. I fished $10 out of my pocket and thanked Lewis for his time.

I went back to the park a couple of days later, in the late afternoon after picking up an order of fried green tomatoes and sweet tea from Green Acres, a home-cooking place on Fourth Avenue. I saw Hyperactive Man talking to a family near the water cannons installation, so I drove around to the park's opposite corner, by the Ground Zero sign. I looked for Lewis, thinking about his episodes and the gash. I had a follow-up question about the neighborhood where he was born and where he stayed at night. During the 1960s a photographer named Jim Peppler did a series to draw attention to urban poverty. He referred to the area up the street as "Little Korea." No one else in Birmingham seemed to recall the name: no locals, not the Civil Rights Institute archivists, not the public librarians. (I'm still trying to solve this mystery: stay tuned.) I also wanted to report that I successfully avoided anyone in Linn Park who might be a drunk or a drug addict, and I did not get knocked in the head.

No Lewis. But I did meet Tony. He was also a Birmingham native, who moved to Detroit to work in the automotive industry, got laid off during the most recent economic downturn, and came back home to live outside. He said it was hard for people our age—middle fifties—to find jobs. He said that Birmingham got cold but not like Detroit.

I asked Tony the same questions I asked Lewis and got almost the same answers. Stay out of Linn Park. Kelly Ingram is better. The fire station has sandwiches. The police keep trouble at bay.

White people give you money because they feel guilty.

I gave money, fried green tomatoes, and sweet tea.

But I did have just one more question: did he know anything about the neighborhood that used to be underneath the interstate?

Tony had never heard the name "Little Korea," but he was adamant that I not walk north to investigate. "Lady, they sell a lot of drugs up there. Someone is going to knock you in the head and take that nice camera."

He would not part with me until I promised not to venture off of the Civil Rights Heritage Trail's beaten path.

*

The memorial complex, especially the Birmingham Civil Rights Institute, has gotten criticism for catering to corporate interests and tourist dollars, for reinforcing status quo, "feel-good" movement stories. The stories themselves—about segregation, oppression, and violence—might be horrific, but the history lesson visitors get there confines that horror safely to the past. Institute exhibits, moreover, subtly recenter Birmingham's place in the movement: a bastion of Jim Crow, yes, but also where everyday people, foot soldiers, created lasting social change.

Visitors flock to the intersection to see the city's civil rights heritage, but not much has really changed, structurally, in Birmingham. Instead of wielding dogs, local police make people in the park feel safe. The fire station that used to dispatch hoses for shooting at teenage protestors now feeds the homeless. But economic disparities, and their accompanying social ills, remain the order of the day. Get two blocks off the beaten track, and get your head knocked in.

Birmingham has worked so hard to distance itself from the image of negative history that it sometimes forgets about the substance of civil rights progress.

Many critiques about the memorial complex make a valid point. Neighborhoods near Dynamite Hill/Elyton Village and where I grew up have been devastated by urban blight. Driving back to Aunt Nell's house after our 2013 visit to the park, she remarked that the "Magic City" looked as if someone had tried to perform the old pull-out-the-tablecloth trick but broke all the dishes. Meanwhile, in the suburbs, the glasses and plates not only remain intact; they sparkle.

The memorial complex, like much of downtown Birmingham, also shines, but both areas are designed primarily for people who commute to work from the suburbs or visit from out of town. Tourists often come to Birmingham expecting Mars, as Baldwin said. Instead, if they stick to that beaten track, they find a pretty city. But what of the people who live on the margins of that beauty? While I do not know the specifics of Lewis's and Tony's histories, it did seem a shame that two obviously smart, capable men did not have access to the employment and mental health resources they needed, so they made their way in the world hustling history.

And yet Birmingham has done a far better job than other cities in facing up to its difficult past. In a country where thousands of African Americans were lynched, very few cities dedicate monuments to racial violence. Most pretend it never happened. Despite nationwide issues such as police violence that continues to claim Black lives, public schools resegregating, or recent attacks on voting rights, the civil rights consensus narrative speaks of progress, of distance from the past and from the retrograde "bad guys" on history's wrong side.

It was a lot easier to photograph the Old Jim Crow. The images were so much clearer, so black-and-white. Yet their clarity allows those of us in the present, especially if we are white, to do our own version of hustling history, playing a shell game with the past. We pretend that connections to the movement and its legacies lie somewhere else. Down there. Back then. But never with us.

I have certainly been guilty of doing this, despite decades of experience teaching and writing about the topic. That is why I had trouble answering my son's questions in Kelly Ingram Park. It's why I broke down in the Sixteenth Street Baptist Church basement. I did not want to look at the Bill Hudson photograph for fear of seeing what Aunt Nell really meant: that the "we" who need to work through that image means people like "me," who need to confront the racist in ourselves. I realize now how Aunt Nell's words mark the distance between "cleave" and "cleave." The photograph points to a Birmingham that white people want to split off from themselves, but it is instead an image we should adhere to, that we must grapple with as a mirror of our collective, ongoing participation in a broad Civil Rights Movement story.

This point seems relevant to everyone, no matter what their background. The same power lines that run through Ground Zero run through where I live in St. Petersburg, Florida—and also through most of the United States. That's why it's important for everyone to imagine themselves in the civil rights intersection, not to see it as a space apart.

If I had the opportunity to go back in time and respond to Mr. Golf Shirt in the airport line, I would say, yes, the reason to go here is for work. Each one of us needs to put our shoulder to the wheel to keep that movement moving.

ACKNOWLEDGMENTS

When our son, Zackary, was young, Tom and I had a nightly ritual for settling his mind before bedtime. We'd ask him three questions: What was the best part of your day? What are you thankful for? Who needs a blessing? Then Tom would tell a story. Whether Zack drifted off into sleep or remained awake, we finished with reminding him, "You are the best son in the whole world." As I send *Learning from Birmingham* to press, it occurs to me that the ritual has other uses—namely, for writing acknowledgments.

The best part of writing any book, even more than seeing it for the first time in print, is feeling profound gratitude for those who helped along the way. I have so many people to thank.

First, family. My immediate family members—Tom and Zack—have been my most consistent helpers and cheerleaders. They traveled to and around Birmingham with me on multiple occasions. They gave me space (physical and emotional) to write. They listened patiently to my stories. Zack generously permitted me to write about his own, sometimes difficult, past. Tom has been my in-house editor for the nearly thirty years we have known each other, reading more than once every word of this manuscript. We have both published with the University of Alabama Press and appear as characters in each other's books. The subtext of both books is the story of a strong, ongoing intellectual collaboration. I could not ask for a better life partner, colleague, and friend.

My Buckner-Armstrong families have assisted me in multiple ways, from helping me get facts straight to putting me up during visits homes and, more accurately, putting up *with me*—hardly an easy task. Shout-outs go to the following aunts, uncles, and cousins: Ann Kreitlein, Reba Coe, Rebecca Postell, Janis Armstrong, Joyce Armstrong, Vicki Hubbard, Patti Armstrong, Cindi James, Rachel Drake, Brann Armstrong, Mary Sue Harris, Susie Pruitt, and Donald Armstrong. I am especially grateful for the open hearts and open homes of Martha Wynell (Armstrong) Hughes, the late Bobby Hughes, their daughter Tracy, and her Taylor crew: Jamie, Zac, Miranda, Colby, Mariah, Sydney, and Macy. I can't thank them enough for making this book possible.

In addition to family, I am blessed with many friends who have helped me with this project in ways large and small. From Birmingham: Mary Preston (my bestie of forty-plus years), Scott Adamson, Tracy Ormond Kerley, Owen Kerley, Jennifer James, Kay Misenhimer Murphy, Carolyn Kingsley, Shawn Maddox, Cathy Dickerson Kerrigan, Mabel Dickerson MacMillan, Woni Lawrence, Cathy Bowen Phares, Sonya Gravlee, Laurette Orum Hall, Connie Norton Scott, and Lauri Owens. My NYU crew: Molly Sackler, Brian Saltzman, Michael Schiavi, and their fabulous families. And, finally, Team St. Petersburg: Heather Jones, Anda Peterson, Gianmarc Manzione, Eric Deggans, Jonathan Tallon, the late Russell Crumley, George Spence, Jay Wood, Dawn Cecil, Edie Daley, Jackie Mirkin, Donna McRae, Andrew Walker, and Jacqueline Hubbard.

Multiple writers, activists, and colleagues have invited me to their campuses, hosted me for podcasts, answered my often-dumb questions, or taken the time to read and talk to me about drafts: Kari Winter, David Davis, Barbara McCaskill, Susanne Knittel, Christopher Metress, Michael Bibler, Matthew Teutsch, Koritha Mitchell, Brian Norman, Hasan Jeffries, Charles McKinney, Christopher Strain, Kathryn Holland Braund, Anthony Grooms, Susan Glisson, April Grayson, Thomas DeWolfe, Sharon Morgan, Max Houck, David Watts, John Archibald, Roy Johnson, Nick Patterson, and especially Jesse Chambers.

I am grateful to *Weld*, Birmingham's former alternative weekly, for publishing a previous version of chapter 6 and for posting my queries about Jody Ford and David Armstrong. I am similarly thankful to *Chattahoochee Review* and *Narratively* for publishing previous versions of chapter 7, to *Evansville Review* for publishing a version of chapter 3, to Martha J. Cutter and Cathy J. Schlund-Vials, whose edited volume *Redrawing the Historical Past: History, Memory, and Multiethnic Graphic Novels* (Athens: University of Georgia Press, 2018), includes material that I reworked into chapters 3 and 6; and to Vicki Breitbart and Nan Bauer-Maglin, whose volume on parenting after 40, *Tick Tock* (New York: Dottir Press, 2021) contains material from chapter 11.

This book has benefited in major ways from the assistance of staff members at several libraries, archives, and artist retreats: the Lillian E. Smith Center, Wildacres, the University of Texas at Austin's Harry Ransom Center, the New York Public Library's Schomburg Center for Research in Black Culture, the Alabama Department of Archives and Manuscripts, the University of Alabama's Summersell Center for the Study of the South and W. S. Hoole Special Collections, the Birmingham Civil Rights Institute (especially Laura

Anderson and Ahmad Ward), and the Birmingham Public Library's Departments of Archives and Manuscripts, Southern History, Microforms, and Government Documents (especially Jim Baggett, Don Veasey, Mary Beth Newbill, Laura Gentry, Mary Anne Ellis, Paul Boncella, Elizabeth Winn, Elizabeth Willauer, and Jason Burks). Research support was funded by a University of South Florida Creative Scholarship Grant.

And, finally, I give thanks to the University of Alabama Press. I first talked about *Learning from Birmingham* with Daniel Waterman and Beth Motherwell in 2017, when Tom and I evacuated from St. Petersburg to Birmingham during Hurricane Irma. Tom came away from our Tuscaloosa side trip with a contract for his *Road Course in Early American Literature*, and I came away thinking that my quirky project-in-process had found its heart-home. Since 2019, I have worked with Senior Acquisitions Editor Claire Lewis Evans, whose patience, grace, and vision have transformed that quirky project into an actual book.

As I learned with Tom and Zack, the ritual is not complete until one sends out blessings. Here, I have two very different, but important, groups.

One includes the family, friends, acquaintances, classmates, and coworkers whose names or voices do not appear in this book. Some didn't respond to phone calls, emails, or social media messages. Some spoke to me but didn't want me to use their name or experiences. Some died young—from violence, overdoses, or pollution-exacerbated "natural causes." Some people simply fell off the map. As the Quakers say, I hold in the light each of the missing ones. The erasures and the silences say as much about Birmingham as any words I could write.

Another set of blessings goes out to my former students—especially Jay Boda, Juan Diaz, Billy Huff, Angie Furney Chambliss, Eric Vaughan, Martha Canter, Veronica Matthews, Albert Moreno, Jesse Nevel, Sarah Edwards, James Simpson, Akilé Anai, Joe McCue, Jeffrey and Christina Skatzka, Maggie Lyons, Summer Carnley, Chloe McRea, Ariel Ringo, Grace Thompson, Amy Fusco, LeQuina Knox, Jan Lowe, and the late Paula Witthaus. These beautiful spirits have taught me more than I could ever teach them about equity, justice, basic human decency, and, in the words of the late civil rights warrior John Lewis, "Good Trouble."

NOTES

Epigraphs. Adrienne Rich, "Diving into the Wreck," *Adrienne Rich's Poetry*, edited by Barbara Charlesworth Gelpi and Albert Gelpi (New York: Norton, 1975), 65–68; James Baldwin and Raoul Peck, *I Am Not Your Negro* (New York: Vintage, 2017), 34.

Chapter One

24   Below that lies a third plantation: Elizabeth Anne Brown, "The Birmingham Belles Celebrate the Old South in Hoop Skirts. Some Former Belles Say It's Time to Stop," *Washington Post*, August 17, 2020, accessed May 17, 2022, https://washingtonpost.com.

24   Center Street ends: Jimmie Tarlton and his partner Tom Darby recorded "Down in the Valley (The Birmingham Jail Song)" in 1927. Many others, from Lead Belly to the Andrews Sisters to Slim Whitman, have also performed the song. See Charles K. Wolfe, *Classic Country: Legends of Country Music* (New York: Routledge, 2002), 90; Martin Luther King, Jr., "Letter from Birmingham Jail," in *Why We Can't Wait* (Boston: Beacon Press, 1963), 85–110.

24   Long before King wrote: Marjorie Longenecker White, *The Birmingham District: An Industrial History and Guide* (Birmingham: Birmingham Historical Society, 1981), 25–30. Arlington was spared during the Civil War because it served as General James Wilson's headquarters. See "History," Arlington Antebellum Home and Gardens, accessed April 16, 2020, https://www.arlingtonantebellumhomeandgardens.com.

25   The first Birmingham census: U.S. Decennial Census, accessed April 13, 2020, http://census.gov.

25   In an 1892 report: H. M. Caldwell, *History of the Elyton Land Company and Birmingham, Ala.* (1892; rpt., Birmingham Publishing, 1972). The term "Magic City" has been traced back as far as an 1872 editorial by W. M. McMath, "Birmingham, Ala.," May 29, 1873, *The Shelby Guide* (Columbiana, AL), 3.

25   During the early 1900s: "The Heaviest Corner on Earth," National Registry of Historic Places, accessed April 13, 2020, https://npgallery.nps.gov.

25   By the mid-1920s: "Then and Now: Magic City Rotary Trail Sign," *Birmingham Magazine*, November 29, 2018, accessed April 13, 2020, https://www.al.com.

26   The arrangement was lucrative: Bobby M. Wilson, *America's Johannesburg: Industrialization and Racial Transformation in Birmingham* (New York: Rowman and Littlefield, 2000), 107–21.

26   In 1898 Alabama's convict labor: Robert Perkinson, *Texas Tough: The Rise of America's Prison Empire* (New York: Henry Holt and Company, 2010), 105. On working and housing conditions for Birmingham's mill and mine laborers , see Charles Connerly, *"The Most Segregated City in America": City Planning and Civil Rights in Birmingham, 1920–1980* (Charlottesville: University of Virginia Press, 2005), 20–35, 60–68.

29   When Elyton Village opened: "860 White Families Will Move into Virtual Fairy-
      land—Elyton Village," *Birmingham Post*, n.d., n.p., Vertical File, Birmingham Hous-
      ing—Elyton Village, Southern History Department, Birmingham Public Library.

30   The city's first zoning laws: Connerly, *Most Segregated City*, 47–48.

30   The city's General Code: *The General Code of the City of Birmingham, Alabama* (Char-
      lottesville, VA: Michie, 1944). The laws against interracial play were found in chapter
      23, article 1, section 597.

30   From the late 1940s through the early 1960s: Glenn T. Eskew, *But for Birmingham:
      The Local and National Movements in the Civil Rights Struggle* (Chapel Hill: University
      of North Carolina Press, 1997), 53.

31   The first home to fall: Eskew, *But for Birmingham*, 56–57.

31   Dynamite attacks continued: Jeremy Gray, "Horrific Years of 'Bombingham' Cap-
      tured in Vintage Photos," *Birmingham News*, June 26, 2016, accessed April 21, 2020,
      https://www.al.com; see also Arthur Shores, Oral History Interview A-0021. 17 July
      1974. Southern Oral History Program Collection (#4007), Southern Historical Col-
      lection, Wilson Library, University of North Carolina at Chapel Hill.

31   Another prominent civil rights activist: Andrew Manis, *A Fire You Can't Put Out: The
      Civil Rights Life of Birmingham's Fred Shuttlesworth* (Tuscaloosa: University of Ala-
      bama Press, 1999), 108–12, 168–70, 328–29.

31   Although Matthews filed a crime report: Eskew, *But for Birmingham*, 57.

32   Responsibility for the bombings: Eskew, *But for Birmingham*, 60; and Diane McWhorter,
      *Carry Me Home: Birmingham, Alabama: The Climactic Battle of the Civil Rights Revolu-
      tion* (New York: Simon and Schuster, 2001), 72–73, 97–99.

32   The Selma lawyer: McWhorter, *Carry Me Home*, 98.

32   When Center Street's houses blew: Debbie Elliott, "Remembering Birmingham's Dy-
      namite Hill," NPR, July 6, 2013, accessed April 21, 2020, https://www.npr.org.

33   Angela Davis: Angela Davis, *An Autobiography* (New York: Random House, 1974), 95.

33   In a letter to Birmingham's city attorney: Eskew, *But for Birmingham*, 62.

33   In a 1974 interview: Arthur Shores, Oral History Interview.

33   In other parts of town: Lloyd Harper, Oral History Interview, in Horace Huntley and
      David Montgomery, eds., *Black Workers' Struggle for Equality in Birmingham* (Urbana:
      University of Illinois Press, 2007), 61.

33   In her autobiography: Davis, *Autobiography*, 80, 95–96.

35   In order to qualify: "Income Rent Schedule Explained as Applied to Elyton Tenants,"
      Birmingham News August 24, 1941, n.p., Vertical File, Birmingham Housing—Elyton
      Village, Southern History Department, Birmingham Public Library.

35   Also at work: Carol Anderson, *White Rage: The Unspoken Truth of Our Racial Divide*
      (New York: Bloomsbury, 2016), 3.

Chapter Two

37   Little did I know at the time: Kathryn Stockett, *The Help* (New York: Penguin, 2009),
      398–99.

38   Indeed, at $4,500 a year: The amount reflects my grandmother's salary as found on
      income tax records, some of which she kept (along with dates of family births, mar-
      riages, and deaths) in a large family Bible.

39   They hired her: For the typical pay rate for Black female domestics at the time, see
      oral history interviews at the Birmingham Civil Rights Institute, especially Mary

Betts Rutledge, interviewed by Horace Huntley, August 2, 1996, and Mattie C. Haywood, interviewed by Binnie Myles, March 1, 1996. Advertisements for domestics in the *Birmingham News* for April 1963, during the Birmingham campaign's height and around the time Ceola came to work for us, put pay for "colored girls" at $4–$5 a day and $20–$30 per week; pay for "white ladies" doing the same jobs averaged around $30–$40 per week.

40   After a mob burned: The Freedom Riders' Alabama experience is described in Raymond Arsenault, *Freedom Riders: 1961 and the Struggle for Racial Justice* (New York: Oxford University Press, 2006), 93–124.

40   My grandmother was born: Rayford Logan, *The Betrayal of the Negro, from Rutherford B. Hayes to Woodrow Wilson* (New York: Da Capo Press, 1997), xxi.

40   Violence peaked: Equal Justice Initiative, Lynching in America, accessed May 13, 2020. https://lynchinginamerica.eji.org.

40   Such places: See James W. Loewen, *Sundown Towns: A Hidden Dimension of American Racism* (New York: Touchstone Press, 2006); and Sundown Towns, Oneonta, accessed May 13, 2020, https://sundown.tougaloo.edu.

40   Blount County, where Oneonta was located: Robin Sterling, *Tales of Old Blount County* (self-published, 2018), 339–42.

40   East Lake, where our family lived: Glenn Feldman, *Politics, Society, and the Klan in Alabama, 1915–1949* (Tuscaloosa: University of Alabama Press, 1999), 25.

41   "They're 'just like family'": Stockett, *The Help*, 443; Faulkner, *The Sound and the Fury* (1929; rpt., New York: Vintage, 1990), 343.

41   Popular culture going back to the nineteenth century: Robin Bernstein, *Racial Innocence: Performing American Childhood from Slavery to Civil Rights* (New York: New York University Press, 2011), 19, 33.

42   Equally pervasive: See Tera W. Hunter, *To 'Joy My Freedom: Southern Black Women's Lives and Labors after the Civil War* (Cambridge: Harvard University Press, 1997), 187–218.

43   Some of these families lived: Lynne B. Feldman, *A Sense of Place: Birmingham's Black Middle-Class Community, 1890–1930* (Tuscaloosa: University of Alabama Press, 1999), 24–40.

43   They kept the same address: "Tornado Outbreak of April 1977," accessed April 30, 2020, https://en.wikipedia.org. This same tornado is discussed in this book's chapter on Jody Suzanne ("Ms. Sid") Ford. Birmingham's 1926 zoning laws and Dynamite Hill are discussed in chapter 1.

44   Earlier known as Industrial High: A. H. Parker High School, accessed May 6, 2020, Birmingham City Schools, https://www.bhamcityschools.org.

44   Records from the Home Owners Loan Corporation: Robert K. Nelson and the University of Richmond Digital Scholarship Lab, *Mapping Inequality: Redlining in New Deal America*, accessed May 6, 2020, https://dsl.richmond.edu.

44   Tax records from the 1960s: Jefferson County Board of Equalization Appraisal Files, 1939–1977, Archives and Manuscripts Department, Birmingham Public Library.

45   The ACMHR helped to coordinate: A *New York Times* obituary of Woods places him as pastor of St. Joseph's at the time of the 1963 Sixteenth Street Baptist Church bombing, but a 2005 St. Joseph's directory states that his tenure there began in 1967. He remained pastor until his 2008 death. See Dennis Hevisi, "Abraham Woods, Civil Rights Pioneer, Dies at 80," *New York Times*, November 12, 2008, accessed October

8, 2020, https://www.nytimes.com; and St. Joseph's Baptist Church, Pictorial Directory, 2005.

45   Many working people: Horace Huntley and John W. McKerley, *Foot Soldiers for Democracy: The Men, Women, and Children of the Birmingham Civil Rights Movement* (Urbana: University of Illinois Press, 2009), ix.

45   As historian Robin D. G. Kelley explains: Robin D. G. Kelley, *Race Rebels: Culture, Politics, and the Black Working Class* (New York: Free Press, 1994), 55–75.

46   Mary Rutledge, an East Lake domestic worker: Rutledge, Birmingham Civil Rights Institute oral history interview.

46   Maybe insisting on her soap opera "stories": Fannie Lou Hamer, quoted in Jerry Demuth, "Fannie Lou Hamer: Tired of Being Sick and Tired," *The Nation*, June 1, 1964, accessed May 18, 2020, https://www.thenation.com.

Chapter Three

50   On December 5, 1957: Myrna Ann Cumby, "Teen of the Week: Fairfield Senior Eyes Career as Painter," *Birmingham Post-Herald*, December 5, 1957, Vertical File: Artists—Birmingham, Southern History Department, Birmingham Public Library.

54   Those paintings now hang: In conversations with relatives, I employ first and family names. Conversations with David Armstrong's acquaintances refer to them using first-name pseudonyms, at their request.

55   The Actors Theatre produced: Emmett Weaver, "'Can-Can' Has Bright Moments," *Birmingham Post-Herald*, September 30, 1965, Vertical File: Birmingham Theatres—Actors, Southern History Department, Birmingham Public Library; Lily May Caldwell, "'Can-Can' Opens Run Here, More Comedy than Musical," *Birmingham News*, September 30, 1965, Vertical File: Birmingham Theatres—Actors, Southern History Department, Birmingham Public Library.

57   After talking to Hugh and John: Howard Cruse, telephone interview, December 13, 2014.

57   When I moved to New York: The acronym continues to shift. A brief history can be found in Michael Gold, "The ABCs of L.G.B.T.Q.I.A.+," *New York Times*, June 21, 2018, updated June 7, 2019, accessed May 19, 2022, http://newyorktimes.com; in order to be as inclusive as possible, I follow in this book (unless quoting a source) the lead of the LGBTQ+ advocacy organization, the Human Rights Campaign, https://www.hrc.org/; as Gold explains at the end of his article, the "plus" sign is "not just a mathematical symbol anymore, but a denotation of everything on the gender and sexuality spectrum that letters and words can't yet describe."

57   Vulcan was built to advertise: Philip A. Morris, *Vulcan and His Times* (Birmingham: Birmingham Historical Society, 1995).

58   When I was in college: A 1982 recording of "Moon over Homewood" by WYDE disc jockeys Jack Voorhies and Steven Christie (performing as Chick Churn and the Chillydippers) can be found on YouTube.

60   Just three months after Connor penned the letter: Tom Lankford, "Crackdown on Sex Perverts Ordered for the City by Connor," *Birmingham News*, August 8, 1962, Vertical File: Sex Crimes, Southern History Department, Birmingham Public Library.

61   To get my PhD: Toni Morrison, *Song of Solomon* (New York: Vintage, 1977), 329.

Chapter Four

63 Rather than creating a desegregation plan: *Brown v. Board of Education of Topeka, Kansas*, 347 U.S. 483 (1954), accessed October 13, 2020; and *Brown v. Board of Education of Topeka, Kansas* (implementation decree), 349 U.S. 294 (1955), accessed October 13, 2020, https://www.loc.gov.

63 Second was a 1956 "freedom of choice" law: Eskew, *But for Birmingham*, 189.

64 Freedom of choice laws: "Massive resistance" is a term coined in 1956 by Virginia senator Harry F. Byrd to describe the laws, policies, and tactics that white people could employ to combat school desegregation in the wake of the *Brown* decision. See George Lewis, *Massive Resistance: The White Response to the Civil Rights Movement* (London: Hodder Arnold 2006); and, for women's participation, Rebecca Brückmann, *Massive Resistance and Southern Womanhood: White Women, Class, and Segregation* (Athens: University of Georgia Press, 2021).

64 Birmingham had its own riots: Armstrong's experiences are described in an Oscar-nominated short film, *The Barber of Birmingham: Foot Soldier of the Civil Rights Movement*, directed by Gail Dolgin and Robin Fryday (The Video Project, 2012).

64 The commanding officer: James Armstrong, Oral History, in Horace Huntley and John W. McKerley, eds., *Foot Soldiers for Democracy: The Men, Women, and Children of the Birmingham Civil Rights Movement* (Urbana: University of Illinois Press, 2009), 42–43; and Jeremy Gray, "Amid Protests, Riots, 5 Black Students Changed Birmingham Schools Forever 50 Years Ago This Week," Al.com, September 8, 2013, accessed May 20, 2020, https://www.al.com.

64 Lingo's actions resembled: Debbie Elliott, "Wallace in the Schoolhouse Door: Marking the 40th Anniversary of Alabama's Civil Rights Standoff," *Morning Edition*, National Public Radio, June 11, 2003.

64 Wallace told those present: George C. Wallace, Statement and Proclamation, June 11, 1963, Alabama Department of Archives and History, accessed June 18, 2020, http://digital.archives.alabama.gov.

65 His 1963 inaugural address: George C. Wallace, Inaugural Address, January 14, 1963, Alabama Department of Archives and History, accessed June 18, 2020, http://digital.archives.alabama.gov.

65 Birmingham grudgingly complied: Edmund W. Gordon, et al., *Desegregation in Birmingham, Alabama: A Case Study* (Washington, DC: US Department of Health, Education, and Welfare, 1974), 8–14.

68 They began trickling: George C. Wallace, "Suggested Busing Letter," September 21, 1971; Letter to William McCullough, August 31, 1971; and Letter to Eva M. Jackson, June 10, 1971; Alabama Governor Administration Files, Folders 9 and 10, Alabama Department of Archives and History.

70 In 1967, my first-grade year: Gordon, *Desegregation in Birmingham*, 11.

71 Along the way, child readers learn: Frank L. Owsley, John Craig Steward, and Gordon T. Chappell, eds., *Know Alabama: An Elementary History* (Birmingham: Colonial Press, 1957), 71, 146, 247.

72 This chapter's "you" especially enjoys: Owsley et al., *Know Alabama*, 97–98.

74 As writer Lillian Smith explains: Lillian Smith, *Killers of the Dream* (New York: W. W. Norton, 1949), 39.

76 That year, state champion Banks met its rival Woodlawn: Bob Carlton, "Woodlawn

vs. Banks 1974: Remembering the Biggest Game in Alabama High School Football History," Al.com, March 6, 2019, accessed September 1, 2021, https://www.al.com. Nathan has also written about the game in his memoir, *Touchdown Tony: Running with a Purpose: The Making of a Man and the Healing of a City* (New York: Howard Books, 2015). The book was made into an inspirational Christian film, *Woodlawn* (Scottsdale, AZ: Pure Flix Entertainment, 2015). Rutledge and Nathan would go on to play football for the University of Alabama, under Coach Paul "Bear" Bryant, and later to successful NFL careers. Nathan's brother Vincent attended elementary school with me during grades four through eight at Robinson, but I was unable to find him to discuss our shared experiences.

76   The Facebook page's moderator: Sonya Gravlee, Facebook post, January 12, 2014, Banks High School Alums, accessed June 24, 2020, https://www.facebook.com.

77   Some of my classmates have mixed feelings: Laurette Orum Hall, telephone interview, April 14, 2016.

77   A former neighbor: Connie Norton Scott, telephone interview, April 14, 2016.

77   The sister of a high school friend: Mabel Dickerson MacMillan, Facebook Messenger, June 25, 2020.

Chapter Five

78   By the year's end: Thomas Spencer, "An Old Cloud of Polluted Air Lifts from Birmingham's Shoulders," *Birmingham News*, November 13, 2011, updated January 14, 2019, accessed May 27, 2020, https://www.al.com.

79   Soon Kelly was coming over: The names "Kelly" and "Jimmy" are pseudonyms.

83   During the 1970s: For more information on Campus Crusade for Christ, see John G. Turner, *Bill Bright and Campus Crusade for Christ: The Renewal of Evangelicalism in Post-War America* (Chapel Hill: University of North Carolina Press, 2008), and the organization's (renamed Cru in 2011) website, accessed March 2, 2020, https://www.cru.org.

83   Such bedfellows were hardly strange in 1976: Turner, *Bill Bright*, 147–48; and Kenneth L. Woodward, "Born Again! The Year of the Evangelicals," *Newsweek*, October 25, 1976, 68–78.

83   In Training Union: Teaching yoga to K–12 students has been illegal in Alabama since 1993. See Meryl Kornfield, "Alabama Might Overturn Its 28-Year-Ban on Yoga in Schools. Just Don't Say 'Namaste,'" *Washington Post*, March 13, 2021, accessed April 6, 2021, https://www.washingtonpost.com.

84   It only takes a spark: For a history of "Pass It On," the popular hymn by Christian composer Kurt Kaiser, see C. Michael Hawn, "History of Hymns: 'Pass It On,'" The United Methodist Church: Discipleship Ministries, July 2, 2014, accessed April 6, 2021, https://www.umcdiscipleship.org.

85   The letters spelled out "ichthys": Elesha Coffman, "What Is the Origin of the Christian Fish Symbol?" *Christianity Today*, August 8, 2008, accessed March 2, 2020, https://www.christianitytoday.com.

85   Bill assigned us Hal Lindsey: Hal Lindsey, *Late Great Planet Earth* (Grand Rapids, MI: Zondervan, 1970).

88   Looking back, I can see: "Warning Signs for Young Children," Rape, Abuse, and Incest National Network (RAINN), accessed October 12, 2020, https://www.rainn.org.

88   Consider the 1968 hit: Gary Puckett and the Union Gap, *Young Girl*, CBS 78–549, 1968.

89   "Fifteen may get you twenty": Jimmy Buffett, "Livingston Saturday Night," on *Son of a Son of a Sailor*, ABC Dunhill, AA-1046, 1978.

89   One out of every six women: US Bureau of Justice Statistics, *Sexual Assault of Young Children as Reported to Law Enforcement, July 1, 2000*, accessed October 12, 2020, https://www.bjs.gov.

89   According to Alabama laws: Alabama Criminal Code, § 12-13-5, "Sexual Offenses: Rape and Related Offenses"; § 13-1-13, "Carnal Knowledge—Girl Under 12 Years of Age" (1975), accessed October 12, 2020, http://alisondb.legislature.state.al.us.

Chapter Six

93   A former client named: Michael [last name redacted by request], email to the author, November 21, 2011.

93   Another Birmingham resident: Jim [last name redacted by request], interview, June 26, 2012.

94   One former customer: Anonymous Comment, "A Blast from the Past," *Just Jennifer* (blog), September 15, 2013, accessed July 7, 2020, http://justjenniferblog.blogspot .com.

94   Activist Leslie Feinberg: Leslie Feinberg, *Transgender Warriors: Making History from Joan of Arc to Dennis Rodman* (Boston: Beacon Press, 1997).

95   An August 1973 newspaper profile: Kay Kent, "Ready for Sex Change, Sid Looks for Medical Center," *Birmingham Post-Herald*, August 15, 1973, E:1.

95   Paralleling Sid's life: See, for example, the oral histories gathered by James T. Sears in *Rebels, Rubyfruit, and Rhinestones* and *Lonely Hunters: An Oral History of Lesbian and Gay Southern Life, 1948–1968* (Boulder, CO: Westview Press, 1997); and by E. Patrick Johnson in *Sweet Tea: Black Gay Men of the South, An Oral History* (Chapel Hill: University of North Carolina Press, 2011), and *Black. Queer. Southern. Women. An Oral History* (Chapel Hill: University of North Carolina Press, 2018).

95   Although "sex change" became a household term: Deirdre N. McCloskey, *Crossing: A Memoir* (University of Chicago Press, 1999).

96   Crackdowns on Birmingham's LGBTQ+ residents: Tom Lankford, "Crackdown on Sex Perverts Ordered for City by Connor," *Birmingham News*, August 8, 1962, Vertical File: Sex Crimes, Southern History Department, Birmingham Public Library; Tom Gibson, "Panel Asks 5 Laws against Sex Crimes," *Birmingham News*, August 13, 1967, Vertical File: Sex Crimes, Southern History Department, Birmingham Public Library; and Anita Smith, "Treatment for Sex Criminal Not Easy," *Birmingham News*, May 17, 1967, Vertical File: Sex Crimes, Southern History Department, Birmingham Public Library.

96   Ford had hers at UCLA Medical Center: Kent, *Birmingham Post-Herald*, E:1.

96   That journey did not end: This list is compiled using different passages in McCloskey and selections from Ford's legal papers, shared with me by Chervis Isom, one of Ford's attorneys at Berkowitz, Lefkovits, Isom & Kushner (now Baker Donelson).

98   On Monday, April 4, 1977: "20 Killed as Tornado Rips County," *Birmingham News*, April 5, 1977, A:1.

98   Jody and Wanda, still together: Harold Kennedy, "Sex-Change Beautician Killed," *Birmingham News*, April 5, 1977, A:1.

98   In the September 1977 trial: Andrew Kilpatrick, "Larry Maddox Found Innocent in Shooting Death of Ms. Sid," *Birmingham News*, September 17, 1977, A:2.

99   Today, Ford's name appears regularly: Invisible Histories Project, accessed July 7, 2020, https://invisiblehistory.org.

99   To better understand: Howard Cruse, The Long and Winding Stuck Rubber Road, accessed July 3, 2020, http://www.howardcruse.com.

100   As Cruse explained: Howard Cruse, telephone interview, December 13, 2014.

100   LGBTQ+ oral histories: Sears, Lonely Hunters, 148–49; Johnson, Black. Queer. Southern. Women, 380; and Johnson, Sweet Tea, 386.

101   In an article titled: Koritha Mitchell, "Love in Action: Noting Similarities between Lynching Then and Anti-LGBT Violence Today," Callaloo 36, no. 3 (2013): 690.

102   The latter term was frequently employed: The "Black Brute" stereotype has a long history. A good starting point is Brent Staples, "The Racist Trope That Won't Die," New York Times, June 17, 2018, accessed July 30, 2020, https://www.nytimes.com; and "The Brute Caricature," Jim Crow Museum of Racist Memorabilia, Ferris State University, accessed July 30, 2020, https://www.ferris.edu.

102   McDonald argued as well: American Bar Association, National Task Force on Stand Your Ground Laws, Report and Recommendations, September 2015, accessed July 30, 2020, https://www.americanbar.org.

102   Such is also true for today's hate crimes: Human Rights Campaign, "New FBI Statistics Show Alarming Increase in Number of Reported Hate Crimes," November 13, 2018, accessed July 30, 2020, https://www.hrc.org.

102   "Know-your-place-aggression": Mitchell, "Love in Action," 701.

103   At the time of this writing: Rebecca Griesbach, "Groups Say They'll Sue to Dismantle Alabama's New Transgender Laws," AL.com, April 8, 2022, accessed May 25, 2022, https://al.com; Bryan Lyman, "Gov. Ivey Signs Bills Targeting Transgender Youth in Alabama," Montgomery Advertiser, April 8, 2022; accessed May 25, 2022, https://montgomeryadvertiser.com.

103   Positions like Ivey's: Kirby Wilson and Jeffrey S. Solochek, "DeSantis Signs So-Called 'Don't Say Gay' Bill," Tampa Bay Times, March 28, 2022, accessed May 25, 2022, https://tampabay.com; "Unprecedented Onslaught of State Legislation Targeting Transgender Americans," Human Rights Campaign, accessed May 25, 2022, https://www.hrc.org.

Chapter Seven

105   On the morning of September 15, 1963: Details involving the church bombing, discussed here and below, can be found in Diane McWhorter, Carry Me Home: Birmingham, Alabama: The Climactic Battle of the Civil Rights Revolution (New York: Simon and Shuster, 2001); Frank Sikora, Until Justice Rolls Down: The Birmingham Church Bombing Case (Tuscaloosa: University of Alabama Press, 1991); and the Robert E. Chambliss Papers, 1972–1987, Birmingham Public Library Department of Archives and Manuscripts. The trial transcript for the State of Alabama vs. Robert E. Chambliss, 1977, is available online at https://bplonline.contentdm.oclc.org.

106   Gov. George Wallace did nothing to help: The Inaugural Address of Governor George C. Wallace, January 14, 1963, Alabama Department of History and Archives (digital copy), accessed September 3, 2019, http://digital.archives.alabama.gov.

108   White complicity was a major theme: Martin Luther King Jr., "Letter from Birmingham Jail," Why We Can't Wait (New York: Penguin Random House, 1964), 97.

108   On September 16, 1963: The Charles Morgan Project, an antiracism advocacy group

in Birmingham, re-creates the speech on its website, accessed June 15, 2021, https://www.morganproject.org.

109 Eugene Patterson, editor of the *Atlanta Constitution*: Eugene Patterson, "A Flower for the Graves," *Atlanta Constitution*, September 16, 1963, available from the Poynter Institute, accessed September 3, 2019, https://www.poynter.org.

110 Morgan's speech received polite applause: See the Morgan Project and Roy Peter Clark, "One Small Shoe: A Legacy of the Birmingham Church Bombing," CNN, September 12, 2013, accessed June 15, 2021, https://www.cnn.com.

112 *Four Spirits*, by locally born artist Elizabeth MacQueen. The man who died after falling into a Sloss Furnaces cauldron, according to the unfounded local legend, was MacQueen's great-grandfather James McQueen, president of Sloss-Sheffield Steel and Iron Company from 1918 to 1925. https://www.macqueenfineart.com.

113 I interviewed both: William Joseph Baxley II, telephone interview, April 1, 2013; and Arthur J. Hanes Jr., personal interview, May 8, 2013.

115 Such "atonement trials": Jack Davis, quoted in Rick Bragg, "Alabama Faces Old Wound in One Last Trial," *New York Times*, May 12, 2002, accessed September 3, 2019, https://www.nytimes.com.

115 After Cherry's conviction: For example, see Rick Bragg, "38 Years Later, Last of Suspects Is Convicted in Church Bombing, *New York Times*, May 23, 2002, accessed September 3, 2019, https://www.nytimes.com.

116 His words remind me that history is never tidy: Complicating the progress narrative is field standard for Civil Rights Movement historiography. Good starting points include Renee C. Romano and Leigh Raiford, eds., *The Civil Rights Movement in American Memory* (Athens: University of Georgia Press, 2006); and Jeanne Theoharis, *A More Beautiful and Terrible History: The Uses and Misuses of the Civil Rights History* (Boston: Beacon Press, 2008).

116 A month after our 2013 interview: US Supreme Court, *Shelby County v. Holder*, accessed October 14, 2020, https://www.supremecourt.gov.

116 Two months after I interviewed Hanes: "About," Black Lives Matter, accessed October 14, 2020, https://blacklivesmatter.com.

116 Five months after my Hanes interview: Vanessa Romo, "Alabama Governor Apologizes to Surviving '5th Girl' of 1963 KKK Bombing," NPR, accessed October 14, 2020, https://www.npr.org.

Chapter Eight

119 Then again, neither did Montgomery: The scholarly literature on Parks and Montgomery is extensive. A good starting point can be found in Danielle McGuire, *At the Dark End of the Street: Black Women, Rape, and Resistance—A New History of the Civil Rights Movement from Rosa Parks to the Rise of Black Power* (New York: Knopf, 2010).

120 In an oral history: Bernard Johnson, Oral History Interview with Horace Huntley, Birmingham Civil Rights Institute Oral History Project, July 3, 1997.

120 In an article on bus desegregation: Sarah Frohardt-Lane, "Desegregating Birmingham's Buses: African Americans' Protracted Struggle and White 'Civil' Resistance," *Journal of Southern History* 86, no. 2 (May 2020): 312, 286.

120 Eastwood opened in 1960: The website Birmingham Rewound maintains a section on the mall, with a history, photographs, patrons' memories, accessed 25 June 2020, http://www.birminghamrewound.com.

121 I wound up waiting tables: Like many restaurants then and now, Great American paid servers below the minimum wage, which tips were supposed to round out. If servers didn't make their tips, the restaurant would up their pay to equal the going rate, then $2.30 an hour. See US Department of Labor, "History of Federal Minimum Wage Rates under the Fair Labor Standards Act, 1938–2009," accessed June 25, 2020, https://www.dol.gov.

125 Sometimes they waited for me: A T. P. Crockmier's still exists in Mobile, Alabama. See https://tpcrockmiers.com, accessed June 25, 2020.

126 Not long after: Shauna Stuart, "'We are all part of her legacy': Bonita Carter Honored with a New Memorial Sign in Birmingham," AL.com, October 26, 2019, accessed June 25, 2020, https://www.al.com.

126 Birmingham was well on its way: US Census Bureau, Quick Facts: Birmingham, Alabama, accessed June 25, 2020, https://www.census.gov.

127 Mark, whom I found: Mark Maisel, telephone interview, June 4, 2021.

128 Both malls gave way: J. Mills Thornton, *Dividing Lines: Municipal Politics and the Struggle for Civil Rights in Montgomery, Birmingham, and Selma* (Tuscaloosa: University of Alabama Press, 2002), 190.

128 After the city of Hoover: US Census Bureau, Quick Facts: Hoover, Alabama, accessed June 25, 2020, https://www.census.gov.

128 The ruling: Vann R. Newkirk II, "How *Shelby County v. Holder* Broke America," *The Atlantic*, July 10, 2018, accessed July 25, 2020, https://www.theatlantic.com.

Chapter Nine

135 The bottom line is that: Writer Linda Carroll distills for general audiences the research of Dr. Renee Hsia, a professor of emergency medicine and health policy, in "Ambulances Show Up Faster in Wealthier Neighborhoods than in Poor Ones, Study Finds," *Business Insider*, December 4, 2018, accessed June 21, 2021; https://www.businessinsider.com; Chanelle N. Jones writes on 911 and racial profiling in "#LivingWhileBlack: Racially Motivated 911 Calls as a Form of Private Racial Profiling," *Temple Law Review Online* 92 (2020): 55–93; and Megan Armstrong describes white women's roles in "From Lynching to Central Park Karen: How White Women Weaponize White Womanhood," *Hastings Women's Law Journal* 32, no. 1 (Winter 2021): 27–52. See also the history of race within the development of the 911 system, in Katrina Feldkamp and S. Rebecca Neusteter, "The Little-Known, Racist History of the 911 Emergency Call System," *In These Times*, January 26, 2021, accessed June 21, 2021, https://inthesetimes.com.

136 I also learned later that schizophrenic symptoms: T. M. Luhrmann and Jocelyn Marrow, eds., *Our Most Troubling Madness: Case Studies in Schizophrenia across Cultures* (Berkeley: University of California Press, 2016).

136 As southern white women: Equal Justice Initiative, Lynching in America: Confronting the Legacy of Racial Terror, accessed July 2, 2020, https://eji.org; Ida B. Wells, *Southern Horrors and Other Writings: The Anti-Lynching Campaign of Ida B. Wells, 1892–1900*, ed. Jacqueline Jones Royster (Boston: Bedford Books, 1997), 58; Stewart E. Tolnay and E. M. Beck, *A Festival of Violence: An Analysis of Southern Lynchings, 1882–1930* (Urbana: University of Illinois Press, 1995).

138 The news report was covering: The incident received extensive coverage in state and national media. An entry point into the story can be found at "Trayvon Martin

Shooting Fast Facts," CNN, updated February 16, 2020, accessed February 29, 2020, https://www.cnn.com. Although attorneys did not invoke a "Stand Your Ground" defense for Zimmerman, the case acted as a referendum on the infamous Florida law. On this point, see Ta-Nehisi Coates, "How Stand Your Ground Relates to George Zimmerman, *The Atlantic*, July 16, 2013, accessed February 29, 2020, https://www .theatlantic.com. Martin's death helped to ignite the political movement Black Lives Matter. See "Six Years Strong," Black Lives Matter, accessed February 29, 2020, https://blacklivesmatter.com.

Chapter Ten

140   Most link the idea to a social media hashtag: Aja Romano, "A History of 'Wokeness,'" *Vox*, October 9, 2020, accessed July 24, 2021, https://www.vox.com; William Melvin Kelley, "If You're Woke You Dig It," *New York Times*, May 20, 1962, accessed July 24, 2021, www.newyorktimes.com.

141   During the later years: Ishaan Tharoor, "The U.S. and British Right Ramp Up the War on 'Wokeness,'" *Washington Post*, April 9, 2021, accessed July 24, 2021, https://www .washingtonpost.com.

141   Perhaps someone should tell those "antiwoke" conservatives: Fred C. Hobson, *But Now I See: The White Southern Racial Conversion Narrative* (Baton Rouge: Louisiana State University Press, 1999), 1–7.

144   To begin, today's public K–12 classrooms: A good overview of these assessments on the state and national levels can be found in Thomas Hallock, "A Is for Acronym," in *A Road Course in Early American Literature: Teaching and Travel from Aztlán to Amherst* (Tuscaloosa: University of Alabama Press, 2021), 123–29.

144   Brazilian educator Paulo Freire describes such a practice: Paulo Freire, *Pedagogy of the Oppressed* (London: Bloomsbury, 2000, first published 1970), 71–86.

144   They likely were exposed to the topic: See CPALMS, Standards: Information and Resources, accessed July 13, 2020, https://www.cpalms.org.

144   Although Florida's legislature mandates: Title XLVIII, Chapter 1003.42 (f), "Required Instruction," 2019 Florida Statutes, accessed July 13, 2020, http://www.leg .state.fl.us.

145   The organization Learning for Justice: Learning for Justice, Executive Summary, *Teaching the Movement: 2014*, accessed July 13, 2020, https://www.tolerance.org.

145   Second, focusing on the familiar: Jacquelyn Dowd Hall, "The Long Civil Rights Movement and the Political Uses of the Past," *Journal of American History* 91, no. 4 (March 2005): 1233. Scholars have been advocating for more-complex ways of teaching the movement for more than twenty years. See, for example, Julie Buckner Armstrong, Susan Hult Edwards, Houston Bryan Roberson, and Rhonda Y. Williams, eds., *Teaching the American Civil Rights Movement: Freedom's Bittersweet Song* (New York: Routledge, 2002); and, more recently, Hasan Kwame Jeffries, ed., *Understanding and Teaching the Civil Rights Movement* (Madison: University of Wisconsin Press, 2020).

145   Consider the controversy that emerged in 2021: Jeffrey Solochek, "Florida Education Board Votes to Keep Critical Race Theory out of Schools," *Tampa Bay Times*, June 10, 2021, accessed June 22, 2021, https://www.tampabay.com. A very good, accessible overview of critical race theory can be found in Richard Delgado and Jean Stefancic, *Critical Race Theory: An Introduction*, 3rd ed. (New York: New York University Press, 2017).

147 A Barrett-to-Banks student named Jerri: Jerri Haslam, telephone interview, June 19, 2020.
147 A Harvard University research team: Opportunity Atlas, accessed August 10, 2020, https://www.opportunityatlas.org.
148 *Birmingham News* columnist: John Archibald, *Shaking the Gates of Hell: A Search for Family and Truth in the Wake of the Civil Rights Revolution* (New York: Knopf, 2021).
149 Statistics from the American Academy of Arts and Sciences: American Academy of Arts and Sciences, "Racial, Ethnic Distribution of Advanced Degrees in the Humanities," accessed July 14, 2020, https://www.amacad.org.
150 Consider, for example, textbooks in my field of study, American literature: Ronald Gottesman et al., *The Norton Anthology of American Literature*, 1st ed. (New York: Norton, 1979). See also English Department, University of Texas at Arlington, Covers, Titles, and Tables: The Formations of American Literary Canons in Anthologies, accessed July 14, 2020, https://library.uta.edu; and Paul Lauter, "Reconstructing American Literature: A Synopsis of the Educational Project of the Feminist Press," *MELUS* 11, no. 1 (Spring 1984): 33.
150 Part of the problem for all of us is laziness: Frances E. Jensen and Amy Ellis Nutt, *The Teenage Brain: A Neuroscientist's Guide to Raising Adolescents and Young Adults* (New York: Harper, 2015).
151 On the other hand, just before graduating: The term "matrix of domination" comes from Patricia Hill Collins, *Black Feminist Thought: Knowledge, Consciousness, and the Politics of Empowerment* (1990; rpt., New York: Routledge, 2000); more broadly, we examined the concept of "intersectionality," a term coined by Kimberlé Crenshaw that now describes field-standard analytical frameworks of feminist thought; see "Demarginalizing the Intersection of Race and Sex: A Black Feminist Critique of Antidiscrimination Doctrine, Feminist Theory, and Antiracist Politics," *University of Chicago Legal Forum* 1989, no. 1 (1989): 139–67; the Audre Lorde reference is from the book *Sister Outsider: Essays and Speeches* (1984; rpt. Berkeley: Crossing Press, 2007), 110-13.

Chapter Eleven

153 The prestigious "Screaming Eagles": United States Army, "Welcome to the 101st Airborne Division (Air Assault)," acccessed August 14, 2020, https://www.army.mil.
153 Known as the "Little Rock Nine": A good overview of the incident can be found in Karen Anderson, *Little Rock: Race and Resistance at Central High School* (Princeton: Princeton University Press, 2013).
154 One of the most frequently reproduced photographs: An example can be found at the online *Encyclopedia of Arkansas*: "Elizabeth Eckford Denied Entrance to Central High," accessed October 29, 2020, https://encyclopediaofarkansas.net.
154 Eckford had missed a communication: Anderson, *Little Rock*, 99; Daisy Bates, *The Long Shadow of Little Rock* (Fayetteville: University of Arkansas Press, 1986), 69–76.
154 The violence that the students faced: Melba Patillo Beals, *Warriors Don't Cry* (Simon and Schuster, 1994), 119, 121–22; Anderson, *Little Rock*, 99–101.
155 Beals, in her memoir: Beals, *Warriors Don't Cry*, 109.
156 Uncle Bobby's words recall the lines: Cyrus Cassells, "Soul Make a Path through Shouting," in *Soul Make a Path through Shouting* (Port Townsend, WA: Copper Canyon Press, 1994), 17–20.

156 "This here is a battle": Beals, *Warriors Don't Cry*, 113.

156 As Zora Neale Hurston's character: Zora Neale Hurston, *Their Eyes Were Watching God* (1937; rpt. Urbana: University of Illinois Press, 1978), 285.

159 For Shuttlesworth, education was a major front: Andrew M. Manis, *A Fire You Can't Put Out: The Civil Rights Life of Birmingham's Reverend Fred Shuttlesworth* (Tuscaloosa: University of Alabama Press, 1999), 145–58.

159 Birmingham's demographics shifted: United States Census Bureau, *2010 Census of Population and Housing*, accessed August 17, 2020, https://www.census.gov.

160 Police violence and mass incarceration: Michelle Alexander, *The New Jim Crow: Mass Incarceration in the Age of Color Blindness* (New York: New Press, 2010), 6.

161 One example can be found in Gardendale: Nikole Hannah-Jones, "The Resegregation of Jefferson County," *New York Times*, September 6, 2017, accessed August 17, 2020, https://www.nytimes.com.

161 As civil rights attorney and author: Alexander, *New Jim Crow*, 2.

161 In 2007 Pinellas County stopped busing students: Cara Fitzpatrick, Lisa Gartner, Michael LaForgia, and Dirk Shadd, "Failure Factories," *Tampa Bay Times*, August 12–October 17, 2015, accessed August 17, 2020, https://projects.tampabay.com. Since the *Times* article came out, one of those schools, Lakewood Elementary, has made a dramatic turnaround, from an "F"-rated to an "A" school. See Marlene Sokol and Romy Ellenbogen, "St. Petersburg's Lakewood Elementary, Once an 'F' School, Now Has an 'A,'" *Tampa Bay Times*, August 11, 2021, accessed September 8, 2021, https://www.tampabay.com.

162 The demographics are revealing: Lakewood High School, *School Improvement Plan 2019–2020*, Florida Continuous Improvement Management System (Pinellas County), accessed August 17, 2020, https://www.floridacims.org.

163 That system, according to the American Civil Liberties Union: American Civil Liberties Union, "School to Prison Pipeline," accessed August 17, 2020, https://www.aclu.org.

164 Eckford wound up taking correspondence courses: "Elizabeth Ann Eckford," *Encyclopedia of Arkansas*, accessed August 17, 2020, https://encyclopediaofarkansas.net.

165 In it was a commendation letter: William A. Kuhn, Colonel, to Private First Class Bobby D. Hughes, November 20, 1957.

Chapter Twelve

168 Prior to the 1810s: This capsule history of Village Creek that follows derives from the US Army Corps of Engineers, *Village Creek: An Architectural and Historical Resources Survey* (Birmingham: Birmingham Historical Society, 1985), 1–14; my gratitude to Kathryn Holland Braund, historian of early Alabama and its Native histories, for clarification about the Muscogee/Creeks in Jefferson County.

169 But relocation does not solve all the environmental problems: On the Dursban spill, see Alabama Department of Environmental Management, *Alabama Hazardous Substance Cleanup Fund* (Annual Legislative Report, 1998), 14–16. On the watercress darter, see Katie R. Shaddix, "Over a Thousand Endangered Fish Killed at Roebuck Springs," *Birmingham News*, September 25, 2008, accessed September 7, 2020, https://www.al.com; Freshwater Land Trust, "Roebuck Springs Restoration Complete," accessed September 7, 2020, http://freshwaterlandtrust.org; and "Alabama: Birmingham Subject to Fine for Fish Kill," *New York Times*, June 24, 2010, accessed

September 7, 2020, https://www.nytimes.com. On the Superfund site, see Dennis Pillion, "North Birmingham's 35th Avenue EPA Superfund Site Explained," AL.com, May 11, 2017, accessed September 8, 2020, https://www.al.com.

170 Three organizations: These members from each were very helpful to my understanding of the creek and its history: Carolyn Buck, Freshwater Land Trust, telephone interview, April 14, 2021, https://freshwaterlandtrust.org; Yohance Owens, Village Creek Society, telephone interview, April 19, 2021, https://villagecreeksociety.org; and Nelson Brook, Black Warrior Riverkeeper, telephone interview, May 5, 2021, https://blackwarriorriver.org.

171 I also couldn't shake the words: Black Warrior Riverkeeper, *44 Miles down Village Creek*, 2006, available on YouTube, accessed August 10, 2021, https://www.youtube.com.

171 My spouse, Thomas Hallock: Tom writes a column on urban nature, called "City Wilds," for Tampa Bay's alternative weekly *Creative Loafing*; see https://www.cltampa.com. He has also supervised student publications on waterways local to St. Petersburg, Florida. See Anna Maria Lineberger, Dylann Furness, and Kelly Kennedy, eds., *Voices of Booker Creek* (St. Petersburg: Tampa Bay Writers Network, 2020); and Hannah Gorski, Alison Hardage, and Michelle Sonnenberg, eds., *Salt Creek Journal: Nature, Community, and Place in South St. Petersburg* (St. Petersburg: Tampa Bay Writers Network, 2016).

173 The area is closed off for two reasons: See Alabama Department of Youth Services, Vacca Campus, accessed August 10, 2021, https://dys.alabama.gov; the biography of Industrial School founder Elizabeth Johnston, Mary Johnston Avery, *She Heard with Her Heart* (Birmingham: Birmingham Publishing Company, 1944); and Virginia Pounds Brown, *Grand Old Days of Birmingham Golf: 1898 – 1930* (Birmingham: Beechwood Books, 1984).

176 How to write about urban nature in 3 easy steps: Thomas Hallock, via Twitter @ tbhallock, April 11, 2021, accessed August 10, 2021, https://twitter.com.

178 The final segment of Village Creek: Thomas Spencer, "Village Creek Canyon Trip," AL.com, April 19, 2010, updated January 14, 2019, accessed August 10, 2021, https://www.al.com.

179 Take, for example, an old coal mine: W. David Lewis, *Sloss Furnaces and the Rise of the Birmingham District: An Industrial Epic* (Tuscaloosa: University of Alabama Press, 1994), 286; Shorpy's name is used for an online collection of vintage photographs, which also records his history, accessed August 10, 2021, https://www.shorpy.com; the Birmingham Public Library maintains an online database of news articles devoted to mining disasters from 1898 to 1938, accessed August 10, 2021, http://bpldb.bplonline.org.

180 Also hard to reconcile: William Thornton, "Alabama Coal Plant Again Listed as Top Greenhouse Gas Emitter in the Country," AL.com, February 26, 2021, accessed August 10, 2021, https://www.al.com.

Chapter Thirteen

182 Among the residents displaced: Nancy Raabe, "'Sandman' Fights for Art: Sculptor Wrestles Airport Relocation, Theft," *Birmingham News*, November 29, 1996, F:1; and "Artist, Airport Reach Agreement on Moving Works," *Birmingham News*, October 31, 1997, B:1; see also Souls Grown Deep, accessed September 24, 2020, https://www.soulsgrowndeep.org.

182   During one of my first research trips: Alice Walker, Oral History Interview, August 19, 2010, Birmingham Civil Rights Institute Archives, Vol. 59, Section 5.

183   The irony here is that Birmingham: Wayne Flynt, "Birmingham and Atlanta: A Tale of Two Cities," AL.com, July 10, 2019, accessed September 24, 2020, https://www .al.com.

183   It was Walker herself: Alice Walker, "In Search of Our Mothers' Gardens," *In Search of Our Mothers' Gardens: Womanist Prose* (New York: Harcourt, 1983), 406.

184   Their art yards bring Africa to an epicenter of Jim Crow: bell hooks, "Choosing the Margin as a Space of Racial Openness," *Framework: The Journal of Cinema and Media* 36 (1989): 15–23.

184   Minter lives with his wife, Hilda: "Joe Minter: Biography," Souls Grown Deep Foundation, accessed September 25, 2020, https://www.soulsgrowndeep.org.

186   Holley's story begins similarly: Michael Tortorello, "Scrap-Iron Elegy," *New York Times*, April 24, 2013, accessed September 25, 2020, https://www.nytimes.com; "Lonnie Bradley Holley," in *Revelations: Alabama's Visionary Folk Artists*, ed. Kathy Kemp, 86–95 (Birmingham, AL: Crane Hill, 1994); Jim Auchmutey, "Sandman's Blues: Southern Folk Artist Lonnie Holley Is at a Crossroads," *Atlanta Journal-Constitution*, March 14, 1999: A:1; and Mark Binelli, "Lonnie Holley: The Insider's Outsider," *New York Times Magazine*, January 23, 2014.

187   A telling story about Holley: Matt Arnett, "From Many, One: The Music of Lonnie Holley," *Mith*, Jagjaguwar, 2018.

188   A catalog from a Birmingham Museum of Art exhibit: Thomas W. Southall, "Photographic Traces," *Do We Think Too Much? I Don't Think We Can Ever Stop* (Ikon Gallery/ Birmingham Museum of Art, 2004), 17; David Moos, "Eloquence as Action: The Art of Lonnie Holley," *Do We Think Too Much? I Don't Think We Can Ever Stop*, 23.

188   Is he the visionary maker: Emily Hanna, Curator of Arts for Africa and the Americas, Birmingham Museum of Art, quoted in Tortorello.

188   Poet and cultural critic Amiri Baraka: Amiri Baraka, "Revolutionary Democratic Art from the Cultural Commonwealth of Afro America," *Souls Grown Deep: African American Vernacular Art of the South*, vol. 1, ed. Paul and William Arnett (Atlanta: Tinwood Books, 2000), 505.

189   Two studies in particular: Brian Norman and Piper Kendrix Williams, eds. *Representing Segregation: Toward an Aesthetics of Living Jim Crow and Other Forms of Racial Division* (Albany: SUNY Press, 2010), 4–7; see also Brian Norman, "The Dilemma of Narrating Jim Crow," *The Cambridge Companion to American Civil Rights Literature* (New York: Cambridge University Press, 2015), 42–44; and Grey Gundaker and Judith McWillie, *No Space Hidden: The Spirit of African American Yard Work* (Knoxville: University of Tennessee Press, 2005), 145.

189   Wildness: Gundaker and McWillie, *No Space Hidden*, 86, 28–41.

190   Both Norman/Williams and Gundaker/McWillie blur: Norman and Williams, *Representing Segregation*, 5–6; Gundaker and McWillie, *No Space Hidden*, 88–89.

191   After Holley's move: Qtd. in Auchmutey, "Sandman's Blues."

191   Holley, who led a chaotic childhood: Holley, qtd. in Gundaker and Willie, *No Space Hidden*, 75–76.

191   Minter's adult life, like Holley's childhood: Joe Minter, *To You through Me: The Beginning of a Link of a Journey of 400 Years* (self-published, n.d.), 38–39.

192   Minter, speaking to the process: Minter, *To You through Me*, 38.

192   Encountering a Minter or Holley work: Gundaker and McWillie, *No Space Hidden*, 154–57; Norman and Williams, *Representing Segregation*, 2.

192   Elsewhere: Norman, 42; and Kevin Young, *The Grey Album: On the Blackness of Blackness* (Minneapolis: Graywolf Press, 2012), 53.

193   Gundaker and McWillie point out: Gundaker and McWillie, *No Space Hidden*, 24–25.

Chapter Fourteen

197   I couldn't help but think: Sena Jeter Naslund, *Four Spirits* (New York: Harper Perennial, 2003), 384.

199   It ran on the *New York Times*' front page: Claude Sitton, "Violence Explodes at Racial Protests in Alabama," *New York Times*, May 4, 1963, accessed October 22, 2020, https://www.nytimes.com.

199   As King noted: Martin Luther King Jr., "Letter from Birmingham Jail," in *Why We Can't Wait* (New York: Signet Classics, 1963), 90.

199   Men like Moore and Hudson risked their lives: Diane McWhorter discusses the photograph's background in *Carry Me Home: Birmingham, Alabama: The Climactic Battle of the Civil Rights Revolution* (New York: Simon and Schuster, 2001), 372–76.

201   Even the people in the photograph: McWhorter, *Carry Me Home*, 375; Diane McWhorter, "The Moment That Made a Movement," *Washington Post*, May 2, 1993, accessed October 22, 2020, https://www.washingtonpost.com; Wallace E. Chilcoat, interviewed by Betty Hanson, September 20, 1996, Birmingham Civil Rights Institute Oral Histories; and Walter Lee Gadsden, interviewed by Lola Hendricks, May 25, 1996, Birmingham Civil Rights Institute Oral Histories

202   In 2017 Malcolm Gladwell: Malcolm Gladwell, *The Foot Soldier of Birmingham*, accessed October 22, 2020, http://revisionisthistory.com. Gladwell also discusses the image in *David and Goliath: Underdogs, Misfits, and the Art of Battling Giants* (New York: Little, Brown, 2013).

202   Just before I finished this book: Thomas Hallock, *A Road Course in Early American Literature: Travel and Teaching from Aztlán to Amherst* (Tuscaloosa: University of Alabama Press, 2021), 148.

205   The memorial complex, especially the Birmingham Civil Rights Institute: See, for example, Victoria J. Gallagher, "Memory and Reconciliation in the Birmingham Civil Rights Institute," *Rhetoric and Public Affairs* 2, no. 2 (1999): 303–20, which looks at how the institute's displays create a narrative of progress; Glenn T. Eskew, "From Civil War to Civil Rights," *International Journal of Hospitality & Tourism Administration* 2, no. 3–4 (2001): 201–14, which looks at the ways civil rights tourism gets packaged to exist easily alongside that of Confederate tourism, under the rubric of "heritage"; Kristin Poirot, "Gendered Geographies of Memory: Place, Violence and Exigency at the Birmingham Civil Rights Institute," *Rhetoric and Public Affairs* 18, no. 4 (2015): 621–47, which examines how women's participation gets marginalized in the institute's displays; and Owen J. Dwyer and Derek H. Alderman, *Civil Rights Memorials and the Geography of Memory* (Chicago: Center for American Places at Columbia College Chicago, 2008), which argues that "commemorating the Movement is but the latest battle in the ongoing campaign for civil rights" (23).

FURTHER READING AND VIEWING ON BIRMINGHAM

Archibald, John. *Shaking the Gates of Hell: A Search for Family and Truth in the Wake of the Civil Rights Revolution*. New York: Knopf, 2021.

Arrington, Richard Jr. *There's Hope for the World: The Memoir of Birmingham, Alabama's First African American Mayor*. Tuscaloosa: University of Alabama Press, 2008.

Avnet, Jon, dir. *Fried Green Tomatoes*. Universal, 1991.

Cobbs, Elizabeth H. (Petric J. Smith). *Long Time Coming: An Insider's Story of the Birmingham Church Bombing That Rocked the World*. Birmingham: Crane Hill, 1994.

Connerly, Charles E. *"The Most Segregated City in America": City Planning and Civil Rights in Birmingham, 1920–1980*. Charlottesville: University of Virginia Press, 2005.

Covington, Vicki. *The Last Hotel for Women*. Tuscaloosa: University of Alabama Press, 1999.

Cruse, Howard. *Stuck Rubber Baby*. 1995. Reprint. New York: DC Comics, 2010.

Curtis, Christopher Paul. *The Watsons Go to Birmingham—1963*. New York: Laurel Leaf Books, 1995.

Davies, Sharon. *Rising Road: A True Tale of Love, Race, and Religion in America*. New York: Oxford University Press, 2010.

Davis, Angela. *Angela Davis: An Autobiography*. New York: International, 1974.

Erwin, Jon, and Andrew Erwin, dir. *Woodlawn*. Universal, 2015.

Durr, Virginia Foster. *Outside the Magic Circle: The Autobiography of Virginia Foster Durr*. Tuscaloosa: University of Alabama Press, 1990.

Eskew, Glenn T. *But for Birmingham: The Local and National Movements in the Civil Rights Struggle*. Chapel Hill: University of North Carolina Press, 1997.

Feldman, Lynne B. *A Sense of Place: Birmingham's Black Middle-Class Community, 1890–1930*. Tuscaloosa: University of Alabama Press, 1999.

Flagg, Fannie. *Fried Green Tomatoes at the Whistle Stop Cafe*. New York: Ballantine Books, 1987.

Flynt, Wayne. *Poor but Proud: Alabama's Poor Whites*. Tuscaloosa: University of Alabama Press, 1989.

Franklin, Jimmie Lewis. *Back to Birmingham: Richard Arrington, Jr., and His Times*. Tuscaloosa: University of Alabama Press, 1989.

Grooms, Anthony. *Bombingham*. New York: Free Press, 2001.

Hemphill, Paul. *Leaving Birmingham: Notes of a Native Son*. Tuscaloosa: University of Alabama Press, 1993.

Horton, Randall. *Dead Weight: A Memoir in Essays*. Chicago: Northwestern University Press, 2022.

Hrabowski, Freeman III. *Holding Fast to Dreams: Empowering Youth from the Civil Rights Crusade to STEM Achievement*. Boston: Beacon Press, 2016.

Huntley, Horace, and John W. McKerley, eds. *Foot Soldiers for Democracy: The Men, Women,* and Children of the Birmingham Civil Rights Movement. Chicago: University of Illinois Press, 2009.

Huntley, Horace, and David Montgomery, eds. Black Workers' Struggle for Equality in Birmingham. Chicago: University of Illinois Press, 2004.

Isom, Chervis. The Newspaper Boy: Coming of Age in Birmingham, Alabama, during the Civil Rights Era. Working Writer's Discovery Group, 2013.

Kelley, Robin D. G. Culture, Politics, and the Black Working Class. New York: Free Press, 1994.

———. Hammer and Hoe: Alabama Communists during the Great Depression. Chapel Hill: University of North Carolina Press, 1990.

King, Martin Luther Jr. Why We Can't Wait. Boston: Beacon Press, 2011.

LaMonte, Edward Shannon. Politics and Welfare in Birmingham, 1900–1975. Tuscaloosa: University of Alabama Press, 1995.

Lee, Spike, dir. 4 Little Girls. HBO, 1997.

Lewis, John, et al. March. 3 vols. New York: Penguin/Random House, 2013–16.

Loder-Jackson, Tondra L. Schoolhouse Activists: African American Educators and the Long Birmingham Civil Rights Movement. Albany: State University of New York Press, 2015.

Manis, Andrew M. A Fire You Can't Put Out: The Civil Rights Life of Birmingham's Reverend Fred Shuttlesworth. Tuscaloosa: University of Alabama Press, 1999.

McDowell, Deborah. Leaving Pipe Shop: Memories of Kin. New York: W. W. Norton, 1998.

McKinstrey, Carolyn Maull. While the World Watched: A Birmingham Bombing Survivor Comes of Age during the Civil Rights Movement. Tyndale House, 2011.

McKiven, Henry Jr. Iron and Steel: Class, Race, and Community in Birmingham, 1873–1920. Chapel Hill: University of North Carolina Press, 1995.

McWhorter, Diane. Carry Me Home: Birmingham, Alabama: The Climactic Battle of the Civil Rights Revolution. New York: Simon and Schuster, 2001.

Naslund, Sena Jeter. Four Spirits. New York: Harper Perennial, 2003.

Nathan, Tony. Touchdown Tony: Running with a Purpose: The Making of a Man and the Healing of a City. New York: Howard Books, 2015.

Patterson, Nick. Birmingham Foot Soldiers: Voices from the Civil Rights Movement. Charleston, SC: History Press, 2014.

Percy, Walker. The Last Gentleman. New York: Farrar, Straus and Giroux, 1966.

Raines, Howell. My Soul Is Rested: The Story of the Deep South in the Civil Rights Movement. New York: Penguin Books, 1983.

Sikora, Frank. Until Justice Rolls Down: The Birmingham Church Bombing Case. Tuscaloosa: University of Alabama Press, 1991.

White, Marjorie L. A Walk to Freedom: The Reverend Fred Shuttlesworth and the Alabama Christian Movement for Human Rights, 1956–1964. Birmingham: Birmingham Historical Society, 1998.

White, Marjorie L., and Andrew M. Manis, eds. Birmingham Revolutionaries: The Reverend Fred Shuttlesworth and the Alabama Christian Movement for Human Rights. Macon, GA: Mercer University Press, 2000.

Widell, Robert W. Jr. Birmingham and the Long Black Freedom Struggle. New York: Palgrave Macmillan, 2013.

INDEX

Page numbers in italics refer to figures.